GOLD

B1 Preliminary

NEW EDITION

CONTENTS

Introduction p. 4

Unit		Grammar	Vocabulary
1	Identity p. 6	Question forms p. 6 Present simple with adverbs of frequency p. 10	Deducing words in context p. 8 Describing people p. 9
2	The business of food p. 12	Present simple and present continuous p.12 Modals of possibility p. 15	Food collocations p. 12 Suffixes p. 15
3	Mind your manners p. 18	-ing forms and infinitives p. 19 Modals of obligation p. 21	Describing feelings p. 18 Phrasal verbs p. 21, p. 22
4	Then and now p. 24	used to p. 26 Past simple and present perfect p. 28	Linkers of addition and contrast p. 27 Town and city p. 28
5	Share and share alike p. 30	Comparatives and superlatives p. 32 too and enough, so and such p. 35	Sharing p. 30 Clothes p.30 Verbs related to clothes p. 31 Order of adjectives p. 31 House and home p. 34
6	You live and learn p. 36	Past simple and past continuous p. 39 Past perfect p. 40	Prepositional phrases p. 38 Education p. 39 Adverbs p. 39
7	Water p. 42	Countable and uncountable nouns p. 43 Articles p. 45	Weather p. 42 Adjectives and prepositions p. 45
8	Nearly famous p. 48	Reported speech p. 49 Reported questions p. 52	Entertainment p. 49 -ed and –ing adjectives p. 53
9	Creativity p. 54	Modals of ability p. 54 Relative clauses p. 57	Formal language p. 56 Job skills p. 57 Prefixes p. 57
10	What's it worth? p. 60	Passive voice p. 60 get/have something done p. 63	Verbs and prepositions p. 62 Shops and services p. 62
11	A small world p. 66	Future forms p. 68 will and be going to p. 71	Travel and transport p. 66 Phrasal verbs of travel p. 66 Compound adjectives p. 68
12	Extreme p. 72	Zero and first conditionals p. 72 Second conditional p. 74	Sport and leisure p. 73 do, go, play p. 74 Confusing words p. 77

Vocabulary bank p. 78   **Common errors: B1 Preliminary** p. 86   **Exam strategies** p. 90   **Practice test** p. 98

CONTENTS

Reading	Listening	Speaking	Writing
Gapped text (Part 4) p. 7	Multiple choice, pictures (Part 1) p. 8	General questions (Part 1) p. 10	Article (Part 2) p. 11
Multiple choice, long text (Part 3) p. 14	Multiple choice, long text (Part 4) p. 16	Individual long turn (Part 2) p. 13	Story (Part 2) p. 17
Open cloze (Part 6) p. 21	Multiple choice, short texts (Part 2) p. 18	Individual long turn (Part 2) p. 20	Email (Part 1) p. 23
Multiple-choice cloze (Part 5) p. 26	Multiple choice, pictures (Part 1) p. 25	Collaborative task (Part 3) p. 24	Article (Part 2) p. 29
Multiple matching (Part 2) p. 32	Gap-fill (Part 3) p. 31	Individual long turn (Part 2) p. 34	Email (Part 1) p. 35
Multiple choice, short texts (Part 1) p. 37	Multiple choice, short texts (Part 2) p. 40	General questions (Part 1) p. 36 Discussion (Part 4) p. 36	Story (Part 2) p. 41
Gapped text (Part 4) p. 44	Multiple choice, long text (Part 4) p. 43	Collaborative task (Part 3) p. 46 Discussion (Part 4) p. 47	Email (Part 1) p. 47
Multiple-choice cloze (Part 5) p. 52	Gap-fill (Part 3) p. 48	General questions (Part 1) p. 50 Individual long turn (Part 2) p. 51	Article (Part 2) p. 53
Multiple matching (Part 2) p. 55	Multiple choice, long text (Part 4) p. 56	Collaborative task (Part 3) p. 58	Story (Part 2) p. 59
Open cloze (Part 6) p. 61	Gap-fill (Part 3) p. 63	Collaborative task (Part 3) p. 64 Discussion (Part 4) p. 64	Article (Part 2) p. 65
Multiple choice, long text (Part 3) p. 67	Multiple choice, pictures (Part 1) p. 70	General questions (Part 1) p. 69 Individual long turn (Part 2) p. 69	Email (Part 1) p. 71
Multiple choice, short texts (Part 1) p. 76	Multiple choice, short texts (Part 2) p. 72	Collaborative task (Part 3) p. 74 Discussion (Part 4) p. 75	Story (Part 2) p. 77

Answer key p. 115   **Audio scripts** p. 130

Introduction to the Gold B1 Preliminary Exam Maximiser

The **Gold B1 Preliminary Exam Maximiser** is specially designed to maximise your chances of success in the Cambridge English Qualifications: B1 Preliminary exam, which is at **B1** level on the Common European Framework of Reference.

The **Exam Maximiser** will help you prepare for the Cambridge English Qualifications: B1 Preliminary exam. It provides:

- **practice and revision** of the important vocabulary, grammar and skills (reading, writing, listening and speaking) that you study in the Gold B1 Preliminary Coursebook
- more **information about the kinds of questions** you will have to answer in the exam
- help with techniques you need for **exam tasks** and **exam-style activities** for you to practise these
- a section on **common language errors at B1 level** and practice activities to help you avoid these errors
- a complete **Practice test** to use before you take the Cambridge English Qualifications: B1 Preliminary exam.

How can I use the Gold B1 Preliminary Exam Maximiser?

The **Exam Maximiser** is very flexible and can be used by students in different situations and in a variety of ways. Here are some typical situations:

You are doing a Cambridge English Qualifications: B1 Preliminary course with other students. You are all planning to take the exam at the same time.

You use the **Gold B1 Preliminary Coursebook** in class. Sometimes you do related activities from the **Exam Maximiser** in class, but your teacher may ask you to do some activities at home. You may use everything in the **Exam Maximiser** or just parts of it, depending on your needs and the time you have available.

You have already done a Cambridge English Qualifications: B1 Preliminary course and are now studying intensively for the exam.

As you have already worked through the **Gold B1 Preliminary Coursebook** or other B1 Preliminary coursebook, you use the **Exam Maximiser** in class.

You have a very short time before you take the Cambridge English Qualifications: B1 Preliminary exam.

Your level of English is already nearing Cambridge English Qualifications: B1 Preliminary exam level, though you have not followed an exam coursebook. You use the **Exam Maximiser** without a coursebook because you need practice in the exam tasks and how to approach them.

You are preparing for the exam on your own.

You can use the **Exam Maximiser** by yourself to practise exam tasks. The **Gold B1 Preliminary Exam Maximiser** gives clear guidance on exam techniques and has answers and audio scripts at the back of the book.

What is in each unit?

The **Gold B1 Preliminary Exam Maximiser** follows the structure of the **Gold B1 Preliminary Coursebook**. Each unit provides more work on the language, skills and exam techniques you studied in the Coursebook unit.

There are **Vocabulary** sections which practise the words and expressions you studied in the Coursebook and also introduce some new words and expressions. There are activities including exam-style tasks and also crosswords and wordsearch grids for fun.

The **Grammar** sections have activities that practise and revise the grammar points you studied in the Coursebook.

Speaking sections provide activities in language and strategies to help you with the Speaking test. You listen to or read examples of students doing tasks and complete activities to help your own speaking skills.

Every unit has a **Listening** section and a **Reading** section, which give you information about the exam and techniques to use. Many sections have activities for you to practise unfamiliar words and phrases.

There are **Writing** sections, which develop the skills required to complete the exam tasks, and tasks for you to write your own answers. You can check your written work against sample answers.

At the back of the book, there is a **Vocabulary bank** and examples of **common language errors at B1 level** with short activities to help you avoid them.

After you have worked through all the units, you can try the **Practice test** at the back of the book. If you do this under timed exam conditions it will give you a good idea of what to expect in the exam itself.

About the exam

The Cambridge English Qualifications: B1 Preliminary exam is made up of four papers, each testing a different area of ability in English – Reading, Writing, Listening and Speaking. Each paper is worth 25 percent of the total mark.

Reading (45 minutes)

The Reading paper has six parts with a total of 32 questions.

Reading	
Part 1 Multiple choice, short texts	You choose the correct answer from three possible options for each of five very short texts (e.g. signs, messages, postcards, notes, emails, labels).
Part 2 Multiple matching	You read descriptions of five people, then match each person's requirements to one of eight short texts.
Part 3 Multiple choice, long text	You read one long text and answer five multiple-choice questions about it. Each question has four options.
Part 4 Gapped text	You read one text which has five gaps in it. You choose the sentence which fits each gap from a choice of eight.
Part 5 Multiple choice cloze	You complete a short text with six gaps by choosing the correct word from four possible answers for each gap.
Part 6 Open cloze	You read a text with six gaps. You write the word which fits each gap.

Writing (45 minutes)

The Writing paper has two tasks.

Writing	
Part 1 Email	You write an email in reply to an email which has notes on it. You write around 100 words.
Part 2 Article or story	You choose one of two tasks and write around 100 words. You can either write an article or write a story using the first line you are given.

Listening (approximately 30 minutes)

The Listening paper has four parts with a total of 25 questions. You have time to read the questions at the start of each part. You hear each recording twice.

Listening	
Part 1 Multiple choice, pictures	You listen to seven short recordings and, for each one, choose the correct picture out of three options.
Part 2 Multiple choice, short texts	You listen to six short conversations on different topics and choose the correct answer from three options.
Part 3 Gap-fill	You listen to someone giving information and complete six gaps in a page of notes or sentences.
Part 4 Multiple choice, long text	You listen to an interview and then choose the correct answers to six questions from three options.

Speaking (10–12 minutes)

There are four parts to the Speaking test. You take the Speaking test with another candidate, and there will be two examiners. One examiner asks the questions and the other examiner just listens.

Speaking	
Part 1 General questions (2–3 minutes)	You answer the examiner's questions about your present situation, past experiences and future plans.
Part 2 Individual long turn (2–3 minutes)	You talk about a photograph for about one minute. Your partner describes a different photograph. The photographs do not have a matching theme.
Part 3 Collaborative task (2–3 minutes)	You look at a set of pictures and discuss a situation that the examiner gives you with your partner.
Part 4 Discussion (3 minutes)	You answer the examiner's questions, which are related to the situation you discussed in Part 3. You may also be asked to comment on your partner's answers, so you need to listen to what they say.

1 Identity

Grammar
question forms ▶ CB page 7

1 Put the words in the correct order to form questions.

1 your / is / name / what / ?
2 like / you / name / do / your / ?
3 get / how / you / name / your / did / ?
4 what / your / interests / are / ?
5 kind / personality / you / what / have / do / of / ?
6 your / is / job / what / ideal / ?

2 Answer the questions in Activity 1.

3 You are going to read an article called *What problems can your name cause?* What do you think the answer to the question is?

4 Read the article. Was your answer to Activity 3 correct?

WHAT PROBLEMS CAN YOUR NAME CAUSE?

Many parents find it difficult to choose a name for their new baby but their decision can be very important.

Research shows that the name you give a child can have a long-lasting effect on them because their name can influence the way they think about themselves or even affect their personality. For example, if parents give their baby an unusual name or one with a difficult spelling, it means the child always has to explain their name to others. It can also change the expectations people have of them.

It is said that 20 percent of parents regret the name they chose for their child. Others later discovered names they liked better than the one they'd chosen for their baby. Maybe the solution is for us to choose our own names!

5 Complete the questions. Use one word in each gap. Then match the questions to the answers A–E.

1 Why is .... important to choose the right name for a child?
2 .... you think a name can influence a child's behaviour?
3 .... is the problem for a child who has an unusual name?
4 .... many parents wish they had chosen a different name?
5 .... is the answer to the problem of having a name you don't like?

A Yes, because it can change the way a child thinks about themself.
B An unusual name can sometimes cause a child problems.
C We should choose our own names.
D The child has to explain it to other people.
E 20 percent of parents regret their choice of name for their child.

6 Find and correct seven mistakes in the conversation.

Steve: Hi, I'm Steve.
Bailey: I'm Bailey. Nice to meet you.
Steve: Sorry, I didn't catch that – what your name?
Bailey: Bailey. Are you think it's an unusual name?
Steve: Yes! Where it does come from?
Bailey: I think it's popular in Australia.
Steve: Did you been there?
Bailey: No, I haven't – it's a long way away!
Steve: So who did gave you that name?
Bailey: Actually, it was my dad – he just liked it. So am I!
Steve: Are you ever have any problems with the name?
Bailey: Well, it can be a name for both boys and girls.
Steve: Have people find that confusing?
Bailey: Definitely! Before they meet me, they often think I'm a boy!

7 ▶ 01 Listen and check your answers to Activity 6.

8 There is one word missing in each question. Add the missing word in the correct place in each question.

1 Where you go on holiday last year?
2 What your favourite animal?
3 What you enjoy doing at the weekends?
4 What your best friend like?
5 Did you anything special last week?
6 What you think you are going to do this evening?
7 How do you get school every morning?
8 When your last birthday?

Reading
Gapped text (Part 4) ▶ CB page 8

About the exam:
In this part of the exam you read a text from which five sentences have been removed. These are given after the text. They are in a different order and are mixed up with three other sentences that don't belong in the text. You decide which sentences belong in the text and where they go.

Strategy:
- Read the text quickly without paying attention to the gaps. Think about where you might see it and what it is about.
- Read the sentences below the text.
- Read the parts of the text before and after each gap.
- Find a sentence where tenses, vocabulary, pronouns (e.g. *they*, *them*) and reference words (e.g. *this*, *these*, *it*, *one*) connect with the information before and after the gap.
- When you have completed the text, read it again to make sure it makes sense.

1 Five sentences have been removed from the text below. For each question, choose the correct answer. There are three extra sentences which you do not need to use.

A new me in thirty days?

A few weeks ago, I read an article about our habits and how they influence the way we see ourselves. The idea was that if you change a negative habit or create a positive habit, you can actually begin to feel better about yourself. **(1)** ……….. This isn't as easy as it sounds, which is why the article was called 'The Thirty-Day Challenge'.

There were lots of useful suggestions for creative habits to take up. **(2)** ……….. Naturally, there were also some great suggestions of bad habits to give up, like eating sweets or watching TV.

I decided to try the thirty-day challenge. I need to get fit, so my first plan was to go for a fifteen-minute run every day. The only problem I had was the weather – it was the middle of winter! **(3)** ……….. So I needed to think again.

My next idea was to try not to switch on my phone until lunchtime. I knew it would be difficult but I didn't realise how badly my friends would react. **(4)** ……….. So instead, I decided to try learning something. I'm studying Korean and we have a test soon. **(5)** ……….. If I can keep up this study habit, I'm sure I'll do well in class.

But can I really carry on with this routine for thirty days? I'm not so sure about that!

A Some of the ideas were pretty stupid really.
B They all started to complain that I hadn't answered their messages.
C Thirty days doesn't seem like such a long time.
D The writer says that all you have to do is to keep up the good one or avoid the bad one for thirty days.
E I kept forgetting to charge it.
F I knew that on some days I wouldn't want to go outside.
G I'm trying to memorise five new words every day.
H These were things like drawing a picture or learning something new every day.

1

Vocabulary
deducing words in context
▶ CB page 9

1 Match the underlined words and phrases in the text on the previous page to the definitions.

1 stop doing something
2 have an effect on
3 continue doing something difficult
4 start something electrical
5 become interested in a new activity and start doing it
6 become strong and healthy through exercise
7 suddenly understand something
8 keep going with something

2 Complete the sentences with the underlined words and phrases from the text on the previous page.

1 I hate doing exercise, but my friend persuaded me to .... golf and now I love it.
2 I get very enthusiastic about trying new things, but I find it hard to .... any kind of regular practice.
3 Most people .... their mobile phones the moment they wake up in the morning.
4 My friends often try to .... my decisions, but I try to ignore them and do what I want.
5 My cousin is trying to .... so he jogs two kilometres every morning before work.
6 I didn't .... how hard it would be to change my habits!
7 When I started doing yoga I didn't really like it, but I've managed to .... it for almost three years now.
8 I know they're not good for me but I don't think I could .... eating donuts – I love them too much!

Listening

Multiple choice, pictures (Part 1)
▶ CB page 10

About the exam:
In this part of the exam you hear recordings of seven separate monologues or dialogues. There are three pictures for each recording. You choose the correct picture for each one. You hear each recording twice.

Strategy:
- Read the question and check each picture to see how they are different from each other.
- The first time, listen for key words and think about the correct answer.
- The second time, listen to confirm your answer.

1 ▶ 02 For each question, choose the correct answer.

1 Which picture shows the woman's brother?

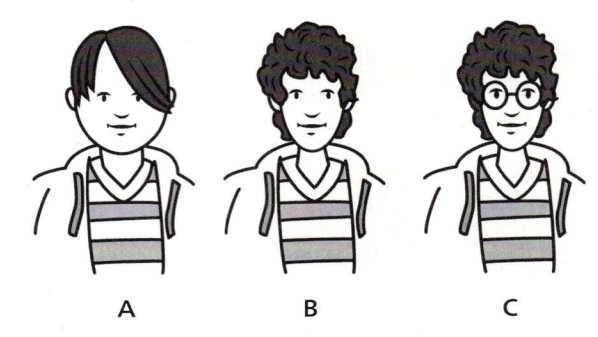

A   B   C

2 How did the man find out about the football result?

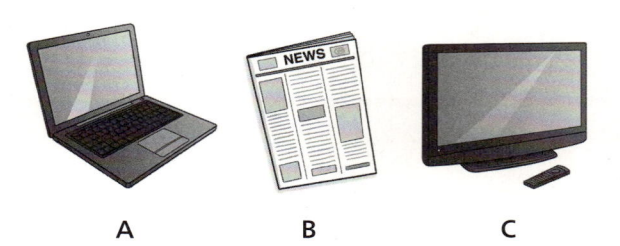

A   B   C

3 What will the weather be like at the weekend?

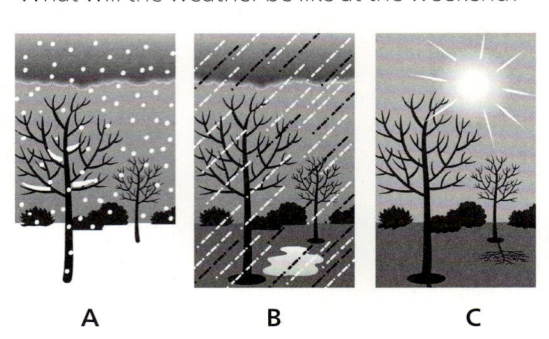

A   B   C

4 Where will the man go first?

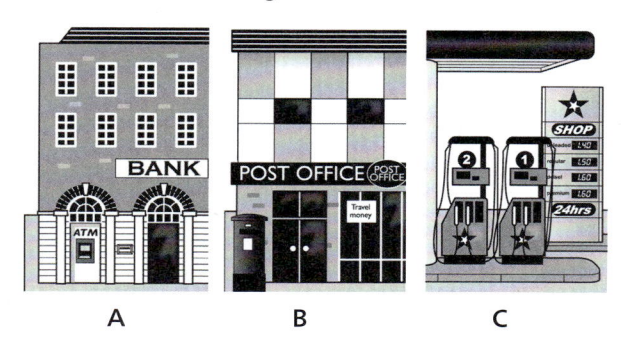

A B C

5 What did the woman buy for Julia's birthday?

A B C

6 Which television programme does the man want to watch?

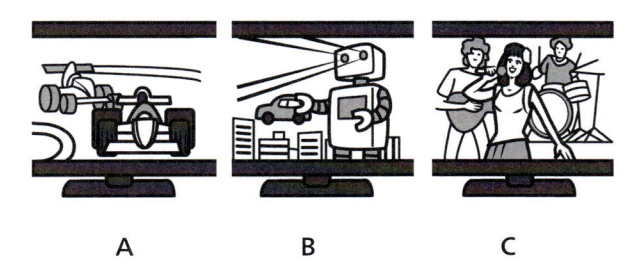

A B C

7 What will the woman wear to the theatre?

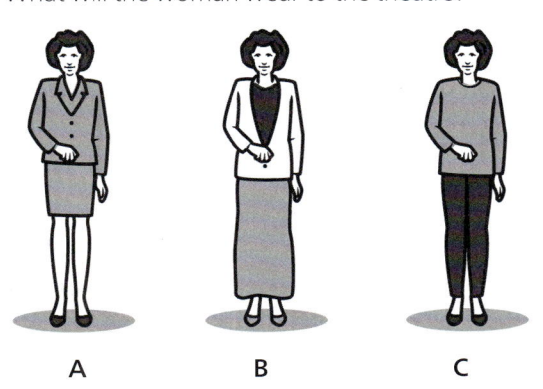

A B C

Vocabulary
describing people ▶ CB page 11

1 Do the crossword.

Across

1 I am quite .... when I meet new people – I can never think of anything to say and my face goes red.
4 I'm an extrovert and I'm always very .... and happy.
6 My friend is often late – he's not very .... and never knows what the time is.
8 My sister is very .... and she loves spending her money buying presents for other people.
10 Sam is a very .... person who finds it very difficult to relax, especially before exams.

Down

2 My friend always tells the truth. She's very ....
3 Sue is a very .... person who always does what she says she will do.
5 I'm very interested in finding out about anything new – my mother says I've always been a .... person.
7 I really want to do well in my career – I'm very ....
9 My sister is quite .... Even quite unimportant things can upset her.
11 I make lists of the things I need to do every day. I suppose you could say that I'm quite ....

2 ▶ 03 You will hear three people talking about their friends. Listen and match descriptions 1–3 to pictures A–C.

A   B   C

3 Complete the descriptions from Activity 2 with words to describe people's appearance. Use one word in each gap.

1 My friend Janet is .... She's got very pretty .... hair. She's a bit .... so she's always careful about what she eats.

2 Nick is very ...., in my opinion. He's almost completely .... but that lack of hair makes him even more handsome. He's quite .... , I suppose, but he does a lot of training so that's why.

3 Tim is quite .... He's in his early twenties but he's always very .... because he works in an office. Over the last couple of months he's grown a .... I think it really suits him.

4 Listen again and check your answers to Activity 3.

Grammar

present simple with adverbs of frequency ▶ CB page 12

1 Put the words in brackets into the correct place in the sentences.

1 I watch a film on television in the evening. (normally)
2 I'm happy to go to the cinema with friends. (always)
3 I don't watch films on my tablet because the screen is too small. (often)
4 I'm surprised when people say they don't enjoy sport. (frequently)
5 I don't go out to restaurants with friends during the week. (usually)
6 I go for a run. (once a day)

2 Find and correct the mistakes with the position of adverbs in three of the sentences. Tick (✔) the sentences that are correct.

1 How often do you see your close friends?
2 How do you meet normally new people?
3 Do you use any social networking sites regularly?
4 It's nice to always make new friends.
5 I chat all the time to my friends.
6 I meet up with my cousins a few times a year.

Speaking

General questions (Part 1)
▶ CB page 13

About the exam:
In this part of the exam you have to answer questions about yourself. First the examiner asks you and your partner four standard questions about your name, where you come from and what you do. (Phase 1). After this the examiner asks you and your partner different questions on topics like your family, your interests and your future plans (Phase 2).

Strategy:
• In the first phase, give short answers.
• In the second phase, give longer answers. Try to say interesting things about yourself, but don't prepare speeches.

1 Complete the examiner's questions with the words in brackets in the correct order.

Phase 1

1 What ....?
(your / is / name)
2 Where ....?
(you / do / live)
3 Do ....?
(work / you / a / student / or / are / you)
4 What ....?
(do / do / you)

Phase 2

5 How ....?
(you / do / travel / work / to / or / college / every day)
6 Do ....?
(like / town / you / live / the / in / you)
7 Who ....?
(live / you / do / with)
8 Tell us ....
(your / about / family)
9 What ....?
(like / do/ weekends / you / doing / at)
10 What ....?
(your / is / time / favourite / day / of)

2 Match answers A–D to four of the Phase 2 questions (5–10) from Activity 1.

A My mother, father and two brothers, who are older than me. My grandmother lives very near us, too, and we see her every day.

B It's a great place – there are lots of things to do in the evenings, and places to meet friends. I love living there.

C I usually go by bus, or I cycle. I like meeting my friends on the bus, but it's also nice to cycle.

D I love the morning when it's sunny and the birds are singing. I often get up early and it's so quiet and peaceful then.

3 ▶ 04 Listen and check your answers to Activity 2.

4 Write your own answers to the questions in Activity 1. Try to give some interesting details about yourself.

5 Some words sound almost the same as other words but are spelt differently. Choose the correct alternative in each question.

1 *Where/Wear* do you come from?
2 Have you lived *there/their* for a long time?
3 Do you know *weather/whether* Steve wants to come to the cinema?
4 Is Susan *hear/here* yet?

Writing
Article (Part 2) ▶ CB page 14

About the exam:
In Part 2 of the Writing paper you choose to write one task from two options, an article or a story. For the article, you are given questions to answer, and you should try to be interesting in your writing. You don't have to write exactly 100 words but you should try to write at least 80 and not more than 110.

Strategy:
- Read the question carefully, and decide what you must write about.
- Plan your article. Think about what information you should include and what language to use.
- Think of ways to make your article interesting for the reader, for example by using questions and a variety of adjectives.
- Think of an interesting introduction and a conclusion.
- Write your article using about 100 words. Organise it into paragraphs.
- Check what you have written, especially spelling, punctuation and grammar.

1 Look at the exam task and the article a student has written. Put the paragraphs in the correct order.

> You see this notice on an English-language website.
>
> **Articles wanted!**
>
> We want to know about a musician you are really keen on. What are they like? What kind of music do they play? Why do you like them so much?
>
> Write an article answering these questions and we will put it on our website.
>
> Write your **article** in about **100 words**.

A Firstly, he's good-looking, and is kind and generous. He always talks to fans after a concert, and usually signs autographs. He is sociable and makes you feel as though you really know him well.

B My favourite musician is Mick Evans, a guitarist. He's not well-known, and at the moment he only plays locally. So why do I like him so much?

C I suppose I like him because I think he might become very famous. Then I'll have been the first to discover him!

D He normally plays rock music, but he can also sing ballads. He is sensitive and has a great voice, and he generally writes his own songs.

2 Now write your own answer to the exam task in Activity 1.

2 The business of food

Vocabulary

food collocations CB page 17

1 Choose the correct words to complete the sentences.

1. I know that *fried/boiled* potatoes contain a lot of fat, but they're very tasty!
2. I often have *takeaway/spicy* food when I don't want to cook for myself.
3. I'd like to stop eating meat and follow a *fresh/vegetarian* diet but it would be difficult.
4. I hate drinking *soft/fizzy* water – the bubbles go up my nose!
5. I prefer *sweet/sour* food so I always have a big dessert!
6. Some people like *mild/hot* food, so they don't use lots of pepper and other spices in their cooking.
7. Fish and *chips/potatoes* is a popular English meal.
8. In some countries *raw/local* fish is a delicacy, although I prefer it cooked!

Grammar

present simple and present continuous
▶ CB page 18

1 Find and correct the mistakes with verb forms in five of the sentences. Tick (✔) the sentence that is correct.

1. I'm not really enjoying watching cooking programmes on TV. I think they're boring.
2. Can you answer the phone? I cook and my hands are covered in oil.
3. First you fry the onions. Then you add the spices.
4. This pineapple is weighing almost a kilo. It's enormous!
5. I try to find a recipe for tiramisu on the internet but there are so many I don't know where to start.
6. I'm not knowing how to make a Spanish omelette.

2 Read the email to decide if this sentence is true or false.

Sara always has a really big breakfast.

Hi Nick,

How are you? It's the Easter holidays here and I **(1)** _____ (enjoy) just staying at home. It's always the same in the holidays – I never **(2)** _____ (get up) early and I always **(3)** _____ (spend) ages having breakfast. Normally, I **(4)** _____ (not have) time for more than a bowl of cereal and a cup of tea so it's a real treat. Of course, at the weekends Josh sometimes **(5)** _____ (cook) a traditional English breakfast. **(6)** _____ (you / know) how to do that? You **(7)** _____ (fry) eggs, bacon, sausages, mushrooms and tomatoes and **(8)** _____ (make) loads of toast to go with it.

Josh and I **(9)** _____ (try) to lose weight at the moment but it's very hard at Easter. We **(10)** _____ (only / have) fruit and yoghurt this week to prepare for the proper diet. Every year I **(11)** _____ (promise) myself I won't eat too many Easter eggs but I'm a chocoholic, as you **(12)** _____ (know), and they are so delicious!

Anyway, I have to go now. Write soon and tell me about your Easter holidays.

Sara

3 Complete the email in Activity 2 with the present simple or present continuous form of the verbs in brackets.

Speaking
Individual long turn (Part 2)
▶ CB page 19

About the exam:
In this part of the exam you are given a photograph to talk about by yourself for about a minute. Your partner is given a different photograph to talk about on another topic.

Strategy:
- The examiner will tell you the topic of your photograph.
- You describe what you can see in the photograph. You could start with a summary of the photograph, then describe the place, what the people look like, what they're wearing, what they're doing, and the things you can see.
- It doesn't matter if you don't know the word for something. You can't ask the examiner but you can describe the object instead.

1 Look at the photographs. Which of the things in the box can you find in each photograph? Which three things can you find in both photographs? Which two things are not in either photograph?

apron	bag	basket	bottle of water	
bowl	bread	cardigan	curtain	eggs
fruit	grass	kitchen	knife	lake
milk	picnic	salad	table	tablecloth

2 ▶05 Look at photograph A. It shows people eating outside. Read what a student said about the photograph. Find and correct three mistakes with vocabulary. Then listen to check your answers.

In the photograph I can see a family having a picnic. There is a mother, a father and two children. They are sitting around a long table which has a curtain on it. The table is outside near a sea and it is on some grass. There are some trees and mountains in the background. The weather is quite good but they are all wearing warm clothes. On the table there is some fruit and a bowl of something – I think it's cakes – and some bread. On the left the father is pouring his daughter a drink of water and on the other side of the table the mother and her daughter are smiling. They all look happy.

3 ▶06 Look at photograph B. It shows people cooking. Read what a student said about the photograph. Find and correct three mistakes with vocabulary. Then listen to check your answers.

In the photograph I can see a family cooking in their kitchen. There is a mother, father and two children. They are standing at the table and they are all cooking together. I think they are making cakes. The children are both wearing aprons. I can see some milk and fruit on the table, and some other things for making little cakes. Behind the family there are other things to use in a kitchen and quite a lot of plates and cups. The kitchen is modern and on the left there is a window with a curtain. There is also some food – I can see peppers and a bag of bread. The family look happy and they are all smiling.

A

B

Reading
Multiple choice, long text (Part 3)
▶ CB page 20

About the exam:
In this part of the exam you read a text and answer five multiple-choice questions. There are four options to choose from. The last question may ask about the general meaning of the text or the writer's purpose or opinion.

Strategy:
- Look at the text quickly to get an idea of what it is about. Read the questions carefully.
- Read the whole text again carefully and identify the parts of the text where you can find the answers to the first four questions.
- Check every option carefully, then choose the one that answers each question.
- Before you answer the last question, read the whole text again.
- Check every option carefully, then choose the one that answers the question.

1 Read the text and questions. For each question, choose the correct answer.

1 Why does the writer decide not to follow the Mediterranean diet?
- A He doesn't particularly like olive oil.
- B He doesn't think it's very healthy.
- C He found out about another diet.
- D He wanted to lose some weight.

2 What problem does the writer have with the Caveman diet?
- A the range of foods you have to eat
- B the types of food you can't eat
- C the amount of meat in it
- D the lack of fruit in it

3 What does the writer say about eating crisps and chocolate?
- A He is surprised such an unhealthy diet exists.
- B He wouldn't try it because he wants to give up eating crisps and chocolate.
- C He thinks it would be really good if you could also eat biscuits and ice cream.
- D He is planning to try it by eating small amounts of crisps and chocolate.

4 What is the writer's opinion about special diets?
- A They can be unexpectedly bad for us.
- B They don't usually include food people want to eat.
- C They offer lots of different options to choose from.
- D They stop people eating a range of food.

5 What would be the best summary of this text?
- A We get lots of useful information about diets. However, we should also eat what we enjoy.
- B We should eat to stay healthy rather than following a special diet.
- C We should go back to eating a traditional diet and give up processed foods.
- D We shouldn't worry about trying to eat like our ancestors. Times have changed.

Diet doubts

Every time I open a newspaper, there's another article about changing the way we eat. First we were told it should be the Mediterranean **diet**, with its **emphasis** on tomatoes, olive oil and fish. I love all these foods so I really thought the Mediterranean diet was the one for me. Then I read that the Japanese diet would be even better, especially if I wanted to lose weight. Rice, seaweed, soya bean products and fish are the key **ingredients** here. I think sushi is delicious so the Japanese diet sounded like a good idea.

Then I read an article about something called the Caveman diet. This time it's meat that is the most important food, but our **ancestors** also ate eggs, fish and seafood. They enjoyed eating fruit and vegetables too, so that's good news. The trouble is, if I decide to eat like a caveman, I'll have to give up all **processed** foods like chocolate and crisps. And I love them!

Believe it or not, there really is a chocolate and crisps diet, but it can't be very healthy unless you eat other foods as well. Anyway, you're actually more likely to lose weight if you do eat chocolate and crisps apparently, but not too often. Maybe I can keep eating them after all.

Mediterranean, Japanese or Caveman? They all sound healthy, **nutritious** and quite tasty but what really matters is variety. There are too many things you are not allowed to eat on these diets. I think we should have a little of all the things we love.

2 Complete the sentences with the words in bold in the article on the previous page.

1 Some of my .... left Ireland in the 1840s because they couldn't get enough to eat.
2 Doctors put a lot of .... on eating healthy food.
3 I'll have to go on a .... I'm putting on loads of weight!
4 I was going to make sushi but I don't have all the ....
5 Soya bean products are supposed to be very ....
6 .... foods often have a lot of artificial colouring.

3 Match questions 1–4 to answers A–D.

1 Do you often go on a diet?
2 Do you like food advertisements?
3 Do you buy food because it is cheap?
4 What's your favourite food?

A Not much, because they make food look better than it is.
B No, because it may not be good quality.
C Fruit, because it's good for me!
D No, because I never put on weight.

Vocabulary
suffixes ▶ CB page 21

1 Add a suffix from the box to the words in brackets to complete the sentences. You may need to make the nouns plural.

-able   -ful   -less   -ment

1 I won't buy tablecloths unless they're .... (wash). Dry-cleaning is so expensive!
2 I love the .... (advertise) for food on television. They're so funny!
3 I'm very .... (care) when I cook – I always make a big mess in the kitchen!
4 Eating in a restaurant can be very .... (enjoy) if the food is good.
5 I'm trying to put less sugar in my coffee; now I only have one .... (spoon) instead of three!
6 I'm a terrible cook but I'm .... (hope) that I will get better with practice.

7 I try to measure ingredients when I cook – you need to be .... (care) if you want the food to taste good.
8 He's a .... (hope) cook! I can't eat his food!

2 Find and correct the mistakes with suffixes in the sentences.

1 I only wear clothes that are washful when I cook.
2 I'm very careless when I cook. I always make sure everything is exactly right.
3 I love cakes. I often buy a bagless from the local shop!
4 I think that people get a lot of enjoyable from good food.
5 I love cooking. I find it very enjoyment.

Grammar
modals of possibility ▶ CB page 22

1 Complete the sentences with *must*, *might* or *can't* and the verbs in brackets.

1 That .... (be) an apple – it's the wrong shape. It .... (be) a banana.
2 It .... (rain) tonight so maybe we'd better take a taxi to the restaurant.
3 You .... (be) hungry. You haven't had anything to eat all day.
4 This .... (be) the right restaurant. Joe said it served Indian food and this is Italian.
5 I think I .... (eat) chicken tonight – I had fish last night.
6 This .... (have) garlic in it – I can taste it.

2 Find and correct the mistakes with verb forms in the sentences.

1 He must be on a diet because I saw him eating a large chocolate pudding at lunchtime.
2 It can't be time to leave the restaurant. It's after midnight and we're the only people here!
3 That might be a strawberry. It's the right shape, size and colour so there's nothing else it can be.
4 I can't decide what to eat. I must have fish or I must have chicken – they both look good.
5 It's good to eat local food when you travel, though sometimes it must not be something you like!
6 This might not be the price! It's far too expensive!

Listening
Multiple choice, long text (Part 4)
▶ CB page 23

About the exam:
In this part of the exam you hear an interview in which a person answers questions. There are six multiple-choice questions each with three options to choose from. You hear the recording twice.

Strategy:
- Before you listen, read the context sentence and all the questions and options carefully.
- The first time you listen, mark the option you think answers each question.
- When you listen again, check that the option you have chosen really answers the question.
- Don't choose an option just because you hear the same word or words – it may not answer the question.

1 ▶07 **For each question, choose the correct answer.**

You will hear an interview with a young man called Chris Jones, who has his own restaurant and also works as a chef on a television cookery show.

1 Why did Chris decide to become a chef?
   A His family encouraged him.
   B His friends shared his interest.
   C His teachers said he had talent.
2 Chris opened his own restaurant because
   A he liked the idea of working for himself.
   B he wanted to share his own dishes.
   C he hoped to make money.
3 Chris's favourite food is fish because
   A it is healthy and nutritious.
   B he can cook it in different ways.
   C it's different from the food he ate as a child.
4 How did Chris feel about working on a television series?
   A He was happy when he became famous.
   B He was pleased to be working with other chefs.
   C He was surprised to have got the opportunity.
5 Before the first television programme, Chris felt
   A worried about cooking bad food.
   B certain he would make a mistake.
   C afraid of forgetting something.
6 What does Chris say is most important to him for the future?
   A opening more restaurants
   B travelling to other countries
   C writing a book

2 Match verbs 1–5 to phrases A–E to make collocations.

1 shop   A the quality of food
2 find   B products to a person's home
3 check   C online
4 scan   D special deals
5 deliver   E a product at the supermarket

3 Complete the sentences with the collocations in Activity 2 in the correct form. Make any other changes necessary.

1 I think I get a better deal by .... instead of going to a supermarket myself and they .... so I don't have to carry them home on the bus..
2 At the supermarket the assistant .... you want to buy at the checkout.
3 I always .... by looking at advertisements in the newspaper – you can save money!
4 I always look carefully at fruit before I buy it – it's important to .... so that you don't buy anything bad.

Writing
Story (Part 2) ▶ CB page 24

About the exam:
In Part 2 of the Writing paper you choose to write one task from two options, an article or a story. For the story, you are given the first line and you must finish the story in about 100 words. You should try to make your story as interesting as possible.

Strategy:
- Read the task and the first line of the story carefully.
- Plan your story. Think about what happens at the beginning, the middle and the end of your story.
- Think of ways to make your story interesting for the reader, for example by using a variety of language and time linkers.
- Write your story using about 100 words. Organise it into paragraphs.
- Check what you have written, especially spelling, punctuation and grammar.

1 Look at the exam task. Then put the sentences A–G in the correct order to make a story.

> Your English teacher has asked you to write a story.
> Your story must begin with this sentence.
> *My parents were out and I decided to make spaghetti for dinner.*
> Write your **story** in about **100 words**.

- A I went to answer it.
- B When my parents came home, they had no idea anything had happened.
- C He had gone to get a glass of water and had seen that the kitchen was on fire.
- D My parents were out and I decided to make spaghetti for dinner.
- E My brother started shouting from the kitchen.
- F We put the fire out.
- G The phone rang.

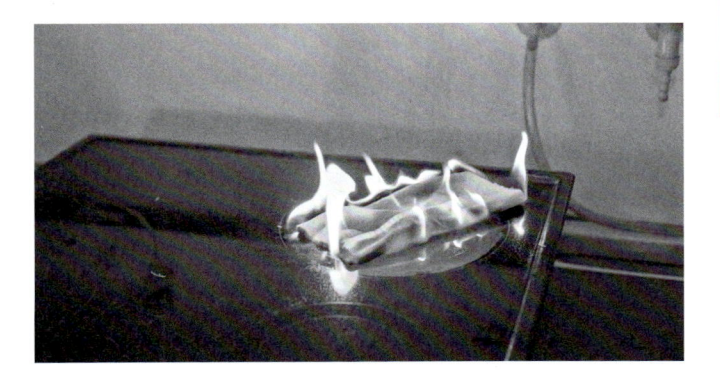

2 Read the full story and choose the correct time linkers to complete it.

It could have been worse!

My parents were out and I decided to make spaghetti for dinner. I put some water on to boil but, unfortunately, I turned on the wrong burner. **(1)** *Eventually/Just then*, the phone rang. I left the cloth I had been using on top of the cooker and went to answer it.
I must have been talking for quite a while when, **(2)** *suddenly/finally*, I heard my brother shouting from the kitchen. **(3)** *A few moments earlier/Finally*, he had gone to get a glass of water and had seen that the cloth was on fire.
Luckily, we managed to put the fire out but there was a lot of smoke. **(4)** *Eventually/Suddenly*, we got rid of it by opening all the windows. When my parents came home, they had no idea anything had happened.

3 Look at the exam task and the notes a student has written. Put the notes in the correct order for the story.

> Your English teacher has asked you to write a story.
> Your story must begin with this sentence.
> *It was one of the worst experiences I have ever had in a restaurant.*
> Write your **story** in about **100 words**.

- A didn't have enough money to pay bill
- B invited my friend to dinner for her birthday
- C only had £5 in my pocket
- D she ordered the most expensive things on menu
- E realised I didn't have my wallet
- F wanted her to have a good time so told her to choose anything she wanted
- G friend had to pay
- H got home and found my wallet on bed
- I waiter brought bill – £50!!

4 Use the notes in Activity 3 to write the story.

3 Mind your manners

Vocabulary
describing feelings ▶ CB page 27

1 Complete the sentences with the words in the box.

| amused | annoyed | bored | confident | embarrassed |
| excited | nervous | satisfied | surprised | tired |

1 I get very .... if I'm travelling and I forget to take a book with me.
2 I feel quite .... when I have to meet new people – I find it quite scary.
3 I often feel .... after walking around a supermarket for a long time – my feet hurt!
4 I love birthdays – I get very .... about getting lots of presents!
5 I often feel .... when people thank me – I never know what to say and I usually go red.
6 I feel very .... when something I do goes well – it makes me feel good.
7 When I play tennis, I'm always .... that I can win because I play very well.
8 I am often .... by things I read in the newspapers – I definitely don't believe everything!
9 We were all .... by his jokes – he really made us laugh.
10 I get very .... when people talk loudly on their mobile phones on trains – it's incredibly rude.

Listening
Multiple choice, short texts (Part 2) ▶ CB page 27

About the exam:
In this part of the exam you hear six short conversations. There is one question for each conversation with three options to choose from. You decide which option answers the question.

Strategy:
- Before you listen to a conversation, read the sentence that tells you who the people are and what they are talking about and the question and possible options.
- The first time you listen, choose the option you think is correct.
- The second time you listen, check your ideas.

1 ▶ 08 For each question, choose the correct answer.

1 You will hear two friends talking about a visit to a restaurant.
   What was the man disappointed about?
   A the quality of the food
   B the speed of the service
   C the atmosphere

2 You will hear a woman telling a friend about a visit to the theatre.
   How did she feel about it?
   A annoyed with someone in the audience
   B upset by the position of her seat
   C bored by the play she saw

3 You will hear two friends talking about a class they both attended.
   What do they agree about it?
   A The teacher was rather impolite.
   B The point of the lesson wasn't clear.
   C The lesson wasn't well planned.

4 You will hear two friends talking about a party they both went to.
   What did the man like best about it?
   A the people who were there
   B the music that was played
   C the food and drink

5 You will hear a woman telling a friend about a tennis match she played in.
   The woman wants the man to
   A help her get more physically fit.
   B play more matches with her.
   C practise with her more often.

6 You will hear two friends talking about a new cinema.
   What do they agree about it?
   A It's rather messy.
   B It's very expensive.
   C It's quite uncomfortable.

Grammar

-ing forms and infinitives
▶ CB page 28

1 Complete the table with the verbs in the box.

arrange   can't stand   can't wait
expect   involve   learn   mind   practise

verb + -ing form	verb + infinitive

2 What is a friend? Choose the correct alternatives.

A friend is someone who
1 always supports you without *to ask/asking* questions.
2 wants *to show/showing* you kindness and respect.
3 enjoys *to spend/spending* time with you.
4 is happy *to tell/telling* you the truth at all times.
5 keeps *to make/making* you laugh.
6 decides *to stay/staying* with you when times are difficult.
7 accepts who you are without *to try/trying* to change you.
8 dislikes *to hurt/hurting* you.

3 Find and correct six mistakes with verb forms in the text.

> **Friendship**
>
> Friends are an important part of most people's lives. According to research, to have quality relationships makes you feel happier.
>
> If it's difficult seeing your friends every day or if you can't wait meeting them, you can always arrange keeping in touch online.
>
> Friends choose loving you for who you are, not what you look like – it's what's on the inside that they are interested in. To keep a friendship going, you have to decide doing as much as you can for them too – friendship is a two-way street!

3

Speaking
Individual long turn (Part 2)
▶ CB page 29

1 Look at photograph A and decide if the sentences about it are true or false.

1. The customer is waiting to pay in a supermarket.
2. Both people are wearing winter clothes.
3. There are a lot of shelves with bread on.
4. It is a modern shop.
5. The customer looks annoyed.
6. The customer is carrying a bag.

2 Read what a student said about photograph A. Complete the text with the words in the box. There is one word you don't need to use.

annoyed   apron   baker's
bread   change   coat   coffee machine
happy   old-fashioned

I can see a woman in a small **(1)** .... shop. She looks **(2)** .... because she has just bought something that she is pleased with. I can see a lot of loaves of **(3)** .... on the shelves. The shop assistant is wearing a white **(4)** .... over a T-shirt. She looks kind and is giving the customer her **(5)** .... The customer is wearing a winter **(6)** .... and she is carrying a bag. The shop is **(7)** .... and I can see chocolates on the counter. There's a **(8)** .... at the back on the right, so you can buy take-away drinks.

3 ▶09 Listen and check your answers to Activity 2.

4 Read what a student said about photograph B. Complete the text with the words in the box. There is one word you don't need to use.

bag   bored   cardigan   embarrassed
mobile phone   newspaper   outdoor
standing up   tired

There are a lot of people travelling on a train. Some people are sitting down and they all look **(1)** .... They're not talking to each other. They're all wearing **(2)** .... clothes. The woman in the foreground on the right is looking at her **(3)** .... The man opposite her is reading a **(4)** .... A woman near him looks **(5)** .... and she has her eyes closed. At the back of the train some people are **(6)** .... There aren't any seats for them to sit down. One woman is wearing a long **(7)** .... and trousers. She's carrying a **(8)** .... and she's wearing glasses.

5 ▶10 Listen and check your answers to Activity 4.

Vocabulary
phrasal verbs ▶ CB page 30

1 Rewrite the underlined parts of the sentences using the correct form of the phrasal verbs in the box.

> clean up   get along well   give up   hand in
> hang out   hurry up   keep on   look after
> look up   turn up

1 I don't know what this word means – I must <u>check it</u> in the dictionary.
2 I hate it when people <u>play their music very loud</u> when they're listening to it on the train.
3 I <u>have a very good relationship</u> with my sister.
4 I refuse to wait in a queue for anything – I just <u>stop waiting</u> and go home.
5 I love <u>taking care of</u> my neighbour's children – we have such fun together.
6 I never mind what people think about me. I just <u>continue</u> behaving in the same way.
7 Come on – we're late! Please <u>get moving</u>!
8 I hate <u>tidying</u> my bedroom. I have so much stuff in it!
9 I must finish my homework soon. I've got to <u>give it to the teacher</u> tomorrow morning.
10 I love <u>spending time</u> with my friends at the weekend.

Grammar
modals of obligation ▶ CB page 31

1 Complete this conversation between two friends with the correct form of *have to*, *must* or *should*.

A: Are you going to that speed-dating event on Saturday?
B: I can't go this weekend after all but I want to go the following weekend. I (1) .... remember to tell them I want to change the day.
A: Can you do that?
B: Yes, basically. But you (2) .... tell them four days in advance and you also (3) .... pay €5 extra.
A: Perhaps I could go this weekend in your place.
B: No, I'm afraid that's not possible. You (4) .... be registered with FastDate, and you're not a girl!
A: Oh! So if someone takes your place, they (5) .... be the same gender as you? Tell me more about it. (6) .... (you) wear special clothes?
B: No, but everyone wants to make a good impression so you (7) .... try and look your best. I usually wear jeans and a smart jacket.
A: How long do you get to talk to each person?
B: Five minutes. Then a bell rings and you (8) .... move to the next table. That should be enough time to decide if you might want to see that person again.
A: What happens if you run out of things to say?
B: Well, it's a good idea to prepare some questions in advance, just in case, but not too many – you (9) .... try to be natural and spontaneous.
A: If you like someone, what (10) .... (you) do next?
B: After each conversation you put a tick next to the person's name if you want to see them again. I think you (11) .... try and make a few notes as well to help you remember the person. Then, the next day, you (12) .... go to the FastDate website and enter your ticks online. If the other person has ticked you too, you get each other's contact details so you can arrange a date.
A: It sounds great! You (13) .... (not) forget to email me the website address so I can register too.

2 ▶ 11 Listen and check your answers to Activity 1.

Reading
Open cloze (Part 6) ▶ CB page 32

About the exam:
In this part of the exam you read a short text with six gaps. It focuses on grammatical features such as tenses, pronouns, prepositions, linkers and articles.

Strategy:
- Read the title and the text quickly to get an idea of what it is about.
- Read the text again. Look at the words both sides of each gap.
- Think about what type of word is missing and decide what the missing word is.
- Read the whole text again to make sure it makes sense with the words you have written in the gaps.

3

1 Complete the sentences by writing one word in each gap.

1 It was rude of you to go .... talking after the teacher had told us to be quiet.
2 Would you please turn the music .... ? I'm trying to study.
3 Susan decided to unfriend Toby because all .... posts were selfies of him and his friends at parties.
4 I've accepted friend requests from people I don't really think of .... friends.
5 I'm really grateful to you .... helping me choose a gift for Simon.
6 I don't know .... she doesn't answer my emails.

2 For each question, write the correct answer. Write one word for each gap.

VIRTUAL GOOD MANNERS

You might not think so, but most of us are quite polite. We thank the people **(1)** .... give us gifts or help us. We apologise if we hurt them, damage **(2)** .... belongings or annoy them. This behaviour is second nature in real life, but we may have to think more carefully about **(3)** .... polite we should be on social networking sites.

For example, it's better to send a personal message instead **(4)** .... posting a comment on a friend's wall if it's something they might not want other people to see. It's also better to think before accepting friend requests rather **(5)** .... hurting that person's feelings later on by unfriending them.

Finally, if you decide to close your social media account, make sure you warn your friends first. You don't have **(6)** .... explain yourself. Just say goodbye and tell them that they can use other methods to contact you if they need to.

3 Complete these definitions with the correct form of words and phrases from the text.

1 .... are things that you own, especially things you carry with you.
2 Something that is .... to you is something you have done so often that you do it almost without thinking.
3 If you put a comment on a social media site you .... it.
4 .... is another way of saying 'instead of'.
5 If you .... to someone who is angry or upset with you, you tell them the reasons why you did something.
6 .... are planned ways of doing something.

Vocabulary

phrasal verbs ▶ CB page 32

1 Match 1–8 with A–H to form sentences.

1 You don't just go for it
2 You hang up
3 You call someone back
4 You switch your mobile off
5 You carry on
6 You turn your mobile on
7 You give up
8 You don't take out your mobile phone

A when you've finished talking or if you get very angry.
B a conversation or a phone call.
C when you're not allowed to use it or if you don't want to be interrupted.
D when it's okay to use it and you want to make and receive calls.
E if you couldn't talk to them earlier or if you didn't finish your conversation.
F if you think someone might try and steal it from you.
G if someone tells you they don't want you to take their photograph.
H if the phone keeps ringing but the other person doesn't answer.

Writing
Email (Part 1) ▶ CB page 34

About the exam:
In this part of the exam you have to write an email in reply to an email you have received. There are some notes on the email to help you. You write about 100 words.

Strategy:
- The notes and the other email tell you the sort of information you need to write.
- Write your email using full sentences.
- Check that you have included all the information from the notes.
- Check what you have written, especially spelling, punctuation and grammar.

1 Look at the exam task below and decide if these sentences are true or false.

1 You need to think of something you had in common with Jaden.
2 You can say that you don't want to meet up with Jaden.
3 You can say you don't want to meet for breakfast.
4 You should think of a day to meet.
5 You have to say which café you would prefer.
6 You need to ask Jaden to suggest something to do afterwards.
7 You must write exactly 100 words.

Read this email from your new English-speaking friend Jaden and the notes you have made.

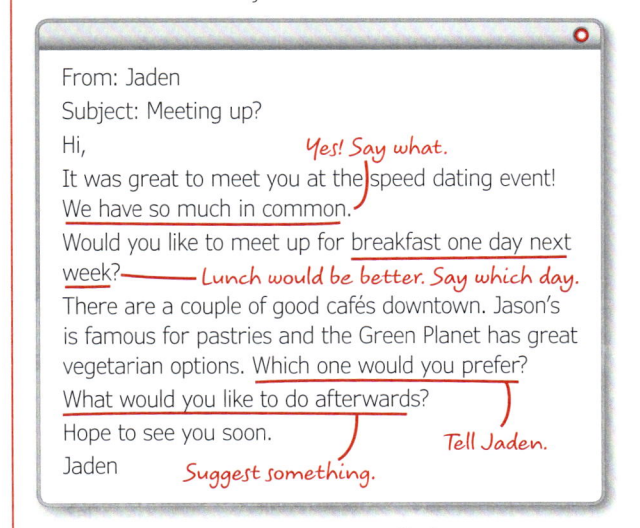

From: Jaden
Subject: Meeting up?
Hi,
It was great to meet you at the speed dating event! — *Yes! Say what.*
We have so much in common.
Would you like to meet up for breakfast one day next week? — *Lunch would be better. Say which day.*
There are a couple of good cafés downtown. Jason's is famous for pastries and the Green Planet has great vegetarian options. Which one would you prefer?
What would you like to do afterwards? — *Tell Jaden.*
Hope to see you soon.
Jaden — *Suggest something.*

Write your **email** to Jaden using **all the notes**.
Write about **100 words**.

2 Look at the emails two students wrote for the exam task in Activity 1. Which student, Stefan or Kristian, wrote the friendlier message?

Hi Jaden,
It was good to get your email. I like people with a cool sense of humour and you laughed at all my jokes. We can meet next saturday. I don't eat usually breakfast and I'm not a vegitarian. Lunch at the other café would be okay as long as the pastries are not expensive. I need to buy a new jacket so we can go shopping after lunch. There are some good shops near Jason's. See you there at about 1.
Stefan

Hi Jaden,
It was great to get your email. I agree completely. We do have a lot in common! You're the first person I've met who is a fan of K-pop like me.
How about meeting up next Saturday? Breakfast would be fun but I think lunch it would be more easy for me because I have to help my father paint the bathroom in the morning. Would that be okay for you? Both cafés sounds great, by the way. I love vegetarian food so maybe Green Planet would be better.
We could go to a movie in the afternoon. What you think?
Kristian

3 Find and correct the mistakes with spelling and grammar in the emails in Activity 2. There are three mistakes in each email.

4 Plan and write your answer to the exam task below. Remember to use all the notes.

Read this email from your English-speaking friend Pamela and the notes you have made.

Hi, — *Yes please! Bring something to eat or drink?*
It's always good to chat online but I'd really like to see you. I wondered if you'd like to come to an English conversation evening I'm having at my place next Saturday. I'm expecting quite a few friends to come along and most people are bringing someone else they know. It should be fun and it's a great way to practise your English.
See you there around 7.30? — *Will bring Lucy. Say why.*
Pamela — *Might be a bit late. Explain why.*

Write your **email** to Pamela using **all the notes**.
Write about **100 words**.

4 Then and now

Speaking
Collaborative task (Part 3) ▶ CB page 39

About the exam:
In this part of the exam you and your partner speak to each other. The examiner gives you and your partner a situation to discuss. There are some pictures to help you in your discussion. Once the examiner has introduced the task, they don't join in your discussion.

Strategy:
- Discuss each picture with your partner. Make sure you say all you can about each picture before you move on to the next one.
- Listen to your partner and make comments on their ideas. If your partner is quiet, encourage him or her to speak by asking questions. You won't lose any marks yourself if your partner doesn't answer your questions.
- Don't hurry to reach a decision. You don't have to come to an agreement before the examiner stops you.

1 ▶ 12 Look at the exam task and then listen to a conversation between two students. Do they reach a decision?

Some students want to make a time capsule so that people who live a hundred years from now can learn about life today.

Here are some things they can put in the capsule.

Talk together about the different things the students could put in the time capsule and say which would be most interesting.

Things to put in the time capsule

Time capsule: not to be opened until the year 2119

2 Complete these sentences from the conversation in Activity 1.

1 Do you .... we should choose small things?
2 How .... the mobile phone?
3 We .... put different kinds of music on it.
4 .... do you think about the money?
5 .... we could just use the front page.
6 So .... would be most interesting?

3 Listen again and check your answers to Activity 2.

Listening

Multiple choice, pictures (Part 1)
▶ CB page 40

1 ▶ 13 For each question, choose the correct answer.

1 Where is the art gallery?

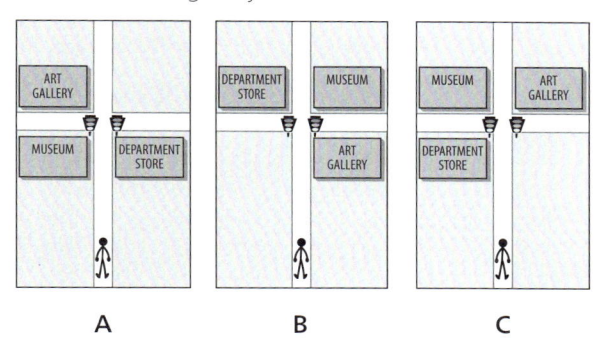

A   B   C

2 What did the woman like best in the museum?

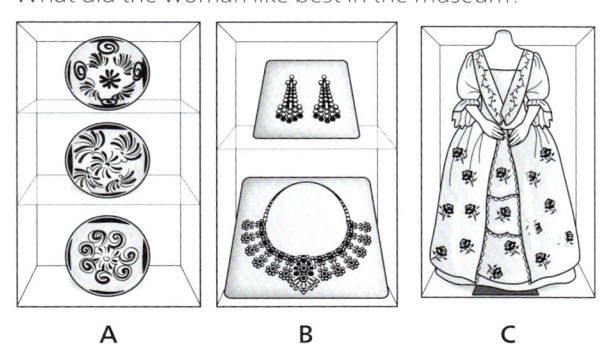

A   B   C

3 When is the best day for students to visit the museum?

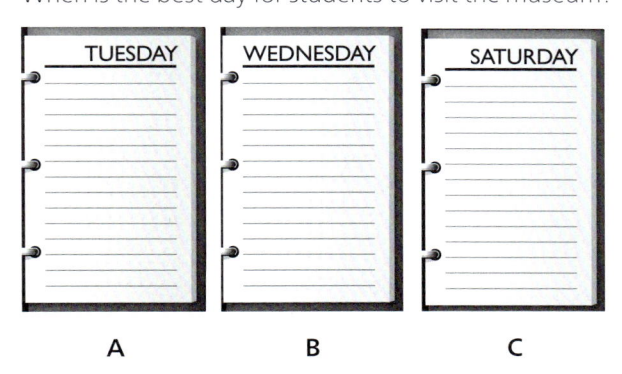

A TUESDAY   B WEDNESDAY   C SATURDAY

4 What did the man buy in the museum shop?

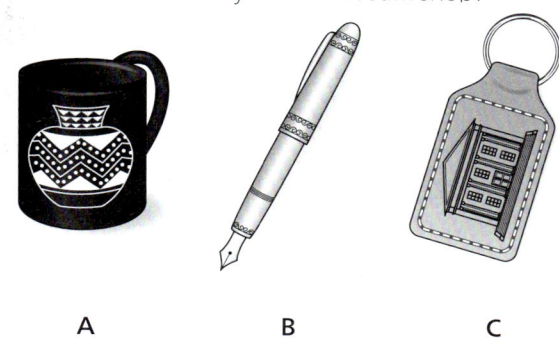

A   B   C

5 What does the woman say is most useful to her?

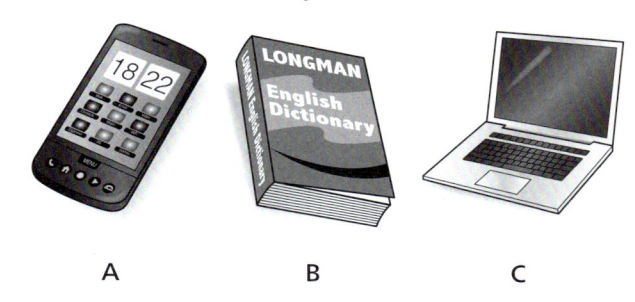

A   B   C

6 What has the man kept the longest?

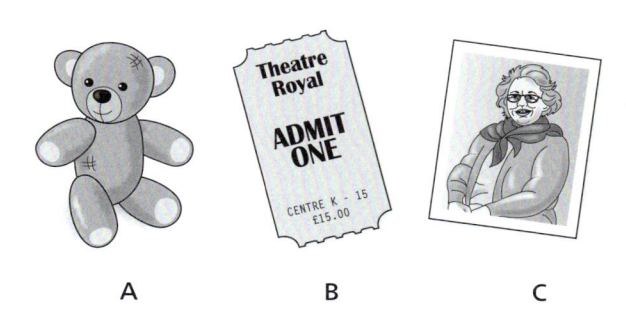

A   B   C

7 Where does the woman want to go at the weekend?

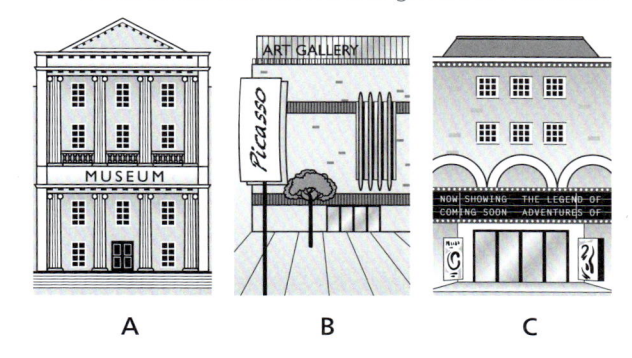

A   B   C

4

Grammar
used to ▶ CB page 41

1 Complete the sentences with *used to* and the verbs in the box.

| go | have | live | make | see | tell |

1 I .... in Melbourne but now I live in Sydney.
2 I .... a next door neighbour in Melbourne called Diana.
3 We .... each other every day but now we talk on social media.
4 We .... to a café to have coffee and talk but we can't now.
5 Diana .... very funny jokes and I miss those.
6 She .... me laugh so much it hurt and nobody else can do that.

2 Put the words in the correct order to make a conversation.

1 in / winter / you / didn't / go / skiing / use / to / ?
2 Yes. / Switzerland / used / two / weeks / we / always / to go / for / to / .
3 use / did / go / to / in / always / you / January / ?
4 Yes. / same / used / see / the / people / to / we / always / there / .
5 what / most / did / you / use / enjoy / to / ?
6 Everything! / falling / over / only / was / thing / use / didn't / to / I / enjoy / the / .

3 Complete the sentences with *used to* and a suitable verb.

In the past
1 A lot of people .... the train to work.
2 Most men .... hats.
3 Women .... trousers or jeans.
4 People only .... one TV and programmes were in black and white.
5 The whole family .... TV together.

Reading
Multiple-choice cloze (Part 5)
▶ CB page 42

About the exam:
In this part of the exam you read a short text with six words missing. There are four options for each missing word. You choose the option which correctly fills the gap. The options test vocabulary including words with similar meanings, common collocations and phrases and phrasal verbs.

Strategy:
- Read the title and the text quickly to see what it is about.
- Read the text again carefully. At each gap think about what kind of word is missing
- Look at the four options and choose the one that fits the gap.
- Read the whole text again to make sure it makes sense with the options you have chosen in the gaps.

1 Choose words or phrases from the box to describe the photographs.

collar   fashion parade   jeans   leather jacket
make-up   sleeveless top   sunglasses   T-shirt

A   B

2 Complete the sentences with your own ideas.

1 The kind of retro fashions I like best are ....
because ....
2 When I look at some the contemporary fashions I think ....

3 Choose the correct option to complete the sentences.

1 I think some contemporary fashions have .... too extreme.
   A become   B turned   C gone   D developed
2 That jacket .... really good on you.
   A suits   B looks   C goes   D fits
3 My friend is .... growing a beard.
   A considering   B wondering   C thinking   D questioning
4 A lot of people grew their hair .... in the 1970s.
   A big   B long   C large   D wide
5 One of the things I .... fun doing is looking at old photos.
   A get   B have   C enjoy   D make
6 My parents have some photos of .... taken in the 1980s – they look so young!
   A theirs   B they   C their   D themselves

4 For each question, choose the correct answer.

The styles that keep coming back

Have you ever bought something you thought was the latest fashion, only to have a parent or grandparent say 'Oh, I had one of those when I was your age'?

The **(1)** .... this happens is that fashion trends are endlessly recycled. Styles that were popular in the 80s, 70s, 60s and 50s and even **(2)** .... than this, continue to inspire today's designers. Even people involved in producing top fashion labels **(3)** .... back to the clothes of the past. They often find their best ideas in things **(4)** .... by the young people from previous generations, and reproduce these rather than creating something completely new. This means that if a style looked good and was popular before, there is every **(5)** .... that it will be again.

So take a look at photos of your parents or grandparents when they were your age. They might **(6)** .... you some ideas for your own wardrobe!

1 A reason   B cause   C explanation   D excuse
2 A longer   B older   C later   D earlier
3 A see   B watch   C look   D consider
4 A dressed   B carried   C used   D worn
5 A opportunity   B risk   C chance   D option
6 A provide   B give   C get   D present

5 Find words in the article in Activity 4 to match definitions 1–4.

1 continually, something that keeps happening all the time
2 give someone else good ideas
3 make something again
4 all the clothes you like to wear

Vocabulary

linkers of addition and contrast
▶ CB page 43

1 Choose the correct alternatives to complete the sentences.

1 *Although/However* I am not interested in history, I like watching historical films.
2 I love going to museums *as well as/too* art galleries.
3 I'd love to go to Egypt *although/in spite of* it's very hot in the summer.
4 I learn about history from books and *also/too* from the internet.
5 I haven't read a history book in years *although/in spite of* the fact that I studied it at school.
6 *Despite/Though* the rain, we still went to the museum.
7 My brother hates visiting museums. He came with us *despite/though*.
8 We visited a number of historical sites and quite a few museums *as well as/too*.

2 Complete the sentences with linkers from Activity 1.

1 I love visiting old buildings .... the fact that some of them are not very well kept.
2 My best friend enjoys visiting old places .... going on beach holidays.
3 .... the high cost, we decided to buy tickets to the exhibition.
4 I don't like spending time on the internet .... I can find lots of information there.
5 I really enjoy reading history books. .... , my friend doesn't.
6 I'm not really interested in watching historical films .... – they seem so unreal.
7 He loves watching historical films. He .... enjoys visiting museums and historical sites.

Vocabulary
town and city ▶ CB page 44

1 Do the crossword.

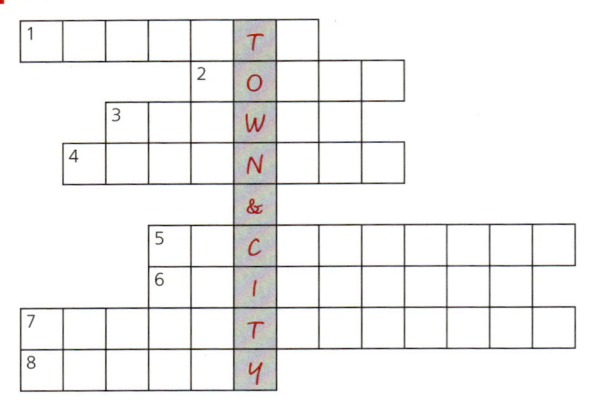

(Crossword with vertical word: T O W N & C I T Y)

1. typical weather conditions in an area
2. in a place near where you live
3. when something gets bigger or develops
4. adjective from 'friend'
5. services that are available in a place
6. a person who lives in a house very near you
7. films, concerts, etc. that people like to watch
8. full of activity

2 Complete the text with the words in the box.

facilities   fresh   friendly   growth   lively   local
mild   playgrounds   spaces   transport

Santa Cruz de Tenerife, where I live, has been described as one of the world's most liveable cities in a recent article. The journalist commented on the (1) .... climate, excellent public (2) .... for getting around the city and the wide range of entertainment (3) .... There's a concert hall, a theatre, several museums and an art gallery. If you prefer to spend your time out in the (4) .... air, there are plenty of open (5) .... and parks, even in the centre of the city. Some of the parks have (6) .... for young children.

Though there has been quite rapid population (7) .... over the last few years, you can still find (8) .... neighbours and a sense of community. My own neighbourhood is very (9) .... – there's always something going on – and the (10) .... shops are great too.

3 Complete the sentences with *fresh*, *work* or *public*.

1. One of the nice things about living in the country is all the .... fruit you can buy there.
2. It's a really good idea for young people to get some kind of .... experience before they leave school.
3. It's always better to use .... transport than to drive your own car in a city.
4. Monday is a .... holiday so none of the shops will be open.
5. I try to .... out whenever I can, just to keep fit, but it's not always easy to find the time.
6. I'm moving abroad next month – I need a .... start.

Grammar
past simple and present perfect
▶ CB page 45

1 Complete the sentences with *for* or *since*.

1. I've known my closest friend .... about ten years.
2. I've been a student here .... three weeks.
3. I've had my mobile phone .... February.
4. My friend has had the same hairstyle .... he was 14.
5. I've liked my favourite singer .... a really long time.
6. We've lived in our house .... 2002.

2 Make questions with *How long …?* to which the sentences in Activity 1 are the answers. Then answer the questions about yourself.

3 Complete the sentences with the past simple or present perfect form of the verbs in brackets.

A It's great but I'm thinking about getting a different one that .... (come out) last month.
B I .... (not make) many new friends yet.
C He thinks it's time for a change though so he .... (decide) to let it grow. Finally!
D A couple of months ago I .... (see) her play in London.
E My parents .... (buy) it after we .... (move) here from Buenos Aires.
F We .... (do) so many different things together.

4 Match the sentences in Activity 1 to the sentences in Activity 3.

Writing
Article (Part 2) ▶ CB page 46

1 Look at the exam task below and decide if these sentences are true or false.

You have to
1. identify your most treasured possession.
2. explain why it is so important to you.
3. describe how much it cost.
4. explain why you don't want to throw it away.

> You see this notice on an English-language website.
>
> **Articles wanted!**
> **Something I would never throw away!**
> What is your most treasured possession? Why is it important to you?
> Why don't you want to throw it away?
> Write an article answering these questions and we will put it on our website.
>
> Write your **article** in about **100 words**.

2 In an article it is important to give interesting details. Below are some ideas students had for their articles. Read the sentences in Activity 3 from the introductions they wrote in answer to the exam task. Which two ideas are not mentioned?

- a gift from someone they love
- a musical instrument
- a photograph
- something another person had dropped
- something that was used by a famous sportsperson
- something they read
- something they wear
- something very valuable

3 Match the first sentences (1–6) with the reasons (A–F) that students have given to make introductions to the article.

1. I know it sounds strange but one object I would never throw away is something I actually found in the street. It's a really old dirty coin.
2. I would never throw away the soft teddy bear my grandmother gave me when I was born.
3. I've always enjoyed exciting fantasy stories, and there's one in particular that I love.
4. I will never throw away the used tennis ball I caught at an international tennis match.
5. No matter how old I get I will never throw away a fantastic T-shirt I was given for my fourteenth birthday.
6. I just couldn't live without playing the guitar, though mine is quite old.

A It's called 'Harry Potter and the Philosopher's Stone'. I would never throw away my copy.
B It's already looking a bit worn out but I still love wearing it.
C I'm saving up for a better one now I can play more music, but that first one will always be my favourite.
D Novak Djokovic hit the ball into the crowd at the end of the match. Just having that ball inspires me to keep training.
E He is still sitting on my bed today and I hardly ever go away without taking him with me.
F The date is 1947 and that's the year when my grandfather was born.

4 Underline the interesting adjectives students have used in their first sentences (1–6) in Activity 3.

5 Write an introduction for each of the two ideas in Activity 2 that were not mentioned.

6 Look at two conclusions to the article. Which one is more interesting? Why?

A That is why I would never throw away something like this. You should get one too. They're really wonderful.
B So, whatever happens, I don't think I could ever throw away something that has meant so much to me throughout my life. I look at it every day and I will treasure it forever.

7 Plan and write your own answer to the exam task in Activity 1. Remember to use interesting adjectives and give interesting details.

5 Share and share alike

Vocabulary
sharing ▶ CB page 48

1 Choose the correct words to complete the sentences.

1 I love going out with friends and *sharing/exchanging* a meal with them.
2 It's a good idea to *exchange/hire* clothes for a special occasion if you might only wear them once.
3 I don't often *lend/borrow* my things to other people in case they lose them.
4 It's good to *exchange/divide* information with friends about reliable shopping websites.
5 I often *sell/hire* my unwanted household goods on the internet to make money.
6 Would you *rent out/hire* your spare room to a friend?
7 I often *divide/swap* clothes with my sister because we're the same height.
8 I always *hire/lend* a car when I'm on holiday so I can get around easily.

Vocabulary
clothes ▶ CB page 49

1 What's the difference? Complete the sentences with the pairs of words in the box.

| blouse/shirt   hat/cap   jacket/overcoat   shoes/boots |
| tie/scarf   trousers/jeans |

1 Men wear a .... when they wear a suit but women wear a .... on the top part of their bodies..
2 Men wear a .... round their neck when they want to look smart but anyone can wear a .... to keep their neck warm.
3 If it's cold, people wear an .... to go out but in the spring a .... is warm enough.
4 A .... keeps your head warm but a .... keeps the sun out of your eyes.
5 It's not a good idea to wear .... on your feet in the snow – it's more sensible to wear ....
6 It's very fashionable for men to wear .... instead of .... when they go out but it's not good to wear them to work because they're not smart enough.

2 Match the first half of the compound adjectives (1–3) to the second (A–C).

1 second-   A fashioned
2 old-   B date
3 up-to-   C hand

3 Complete the sentences with the compound adjectives in Activity 2.

1 The jeans I bought last year look really .... now. The styles have changed completely.
2 If you want to look .... , buy your clothes at Trendsetter Fashions.
3 You can get some really great .... stuff in that charity shop on the corner.

4 ▶ 14 You will hear a conversation between a man called Joe and his friend Helen about buying clothes. Listen and decide if the statements are true or false.

1 Joe has to buy clothes for a special occasion.
2 Helen has a great interest in fashion.
3 Joe doesn't buy clothes very often.
4 Helen is not pleased that Joe doesn't like some colours.
5 Joe doesn't want to look old-fashioned.
6 Helen recommends buying clothes from a second-hand shop.

verbs related to clothes
▶ CB page 49

5 Complete the sentences with the verbs in the box.

| take off | fit | go with | iron |
| put on | suit | try on | wear out |

1 It's very important to .... clothes in the shop to check the size.
2 Some colours don't .... each other – like orange and red.
3 If clothes don't .... you because they are too big or too small, they look terrible.
4 I never buy clothes made of linen because I have to .... them after washing.
5 I get dressed very quickly in the mornings – it doesn't take me long to .... my clothes.
6 Children's clothes .... very quickly because they don't take care of them.
7 I hate all the clothes in the shops at the moment. These bright colours don't .... me at all.
8 I don't want to .... my new leather jacket. I'd wear it all the time if I could – I love it so much!

order of adjectives ▶ CB page 49

6 Choose the correct option to complete the sentence about the order of adjectives.

We put adjectives in the following order in sentences:
A opinion, size, colour, material.
B size, opinion, material, colour.
C colour, material, size, opinion.

7 Find and correct the mistakes with the order of adjectives in the sentences.

1 I've just bought a beautiful silk blue dress but it was really expensive!
2 I love my cotton short skirt – it's great for hot weather.
3 My friend gave me a red horrible woollen sweater for my birthday!
4 I'm hoping to buy a cotton cheap blue dress to wear on the beach.
5 Max is wearing a velvet trendy red jacket – he looks very cool!
6 I'm going to the sales today. I want to buy a leather smart black jacket because my old one is worn out.

Listening
Gap-fill (Part 3) ▶ CB page 50

About the exam:
In this part of the exam you hear one person giving information (e.g. to a group of people or speaking on the radio). You complete notes or sentences about what they say. You hear the recording twice.

Strategy:
- Read all the notes or sentences to get an idea of what the topic is.
- Try to guess what kind of information is missing from each gap: a noun, a verb, a time, a date, etc.
- The first time you listen, fill in as much as you can.
- The second time you listen, check your answers and fill in any remaining gaps.
- Make sure your spelling is correct, the notes or sentences make sense and your writing is easy for the examiner to read.

5

1 You will hear a man talking about a club for pet lovers. Before you listen, read the leaflet and decide if the sentences are true or false.

1 The club is for people who already have a pet.
2 You have to pay to join the club.

Pet Share Club

Who can join the club?
You must be at least **(1)** .... to join.

What kind of pets are there?
The most popular pets are **(2)** ....

How does the club work?
Most people rent a pet for a **(3)** ....
It is better to make a booking **(4)** .... because it's quicker.
It's important to have a **(5)** .... near your home.

What does it cost?
Annual membership costs **(6)** ....

---

2 Look at the leaflet in Activity 1. What kind of word or information is needed to fill each gap?

3 ▶ 15 Look at the leaflet in Activity 1 again. For each question, write the correct answer in the gap. Write one or two words or a number or a date or a time.

Grammar
comparatives and superlatives
▶ CB page 51

1 Complete the sentences comparing pets with the correct form of the adjectives in brackets.

1 Cats are usually .... dogs. (small)
2 They are .... dogs. (independent)
3 Dogs are often .... cats. (noisy)
4 Tortoises are much .... to look after .... cats. (easy)
5 Cats are definitely .... tortoises. (affectionate)
6 Rabbits usually have .... fur .... dogs. (soft)

2 Some words are missing from this text. Complete it with the words in the box. Use one word in each sentence.

as   less   more   most   than   the (x2)

Dogs make best pets, in my opinion. They're much more fun cats, rabbits or tortoises. Tortoises have to be the boring pets in the world. My friend has a tortoise and he says they're interesting than I think. They're also a lot expensive to feed than other animals. They're not nearly friendly and affectionate though. Some people who don't have time to look after a pet themselves share other people's pets, or dog-walk them, which seems best idea to me.

Reading
Multiple matching (Part 2)
▶ CB page 52

About the exam:
In this part of the exam you:
- read eight short texts that describe things like activities, books, films, etc.
- read descriptions of five people (or groups of people)
- match each person to one of the short texts.

Strategy:
- Read about the people first. Underline key information.
- Read through the short texts to find one that matches the first person. Look for key words or information.
- Continue reading the texts and matching the rest of the people.
- Check that each text you choose matches all the needs of the person you have matched it to.

1 The young people below are looking for somewhere to stay when they come to the UK. Underline the important information in the descriptions. The first one has been done for you.

1. Noelia <u>loves small children</u> and <u>enjoys cooking</u>. She is <u>studying architecture</u> and it is important for her to be able to <u>see famous buildings</u>. <u>She doesn't want to spend too much money</u>.

2. Piotr plays the drums. He would like to live with other students with similar interests. He loves animals and would like to have a pet.

3. Lakshmi is studying nursing. She wants to specialise in looking after old people. She loves classical music. She can have her meals at the hospital where she will be working.

4. Anneline needs to be near the university so she can study at weekends. She wants to make new friends while she is in the UK, especially people from other parts of the world.

5. Nourridine is studying to be a chef. He would like to be able to cook his own meals. He plans to bring his car to the UK. He would like to live with an English person.

2 Read the advertisements for accommodation and underline the important information.

A. We are a young couple with a baby, a cat and a lovely spare room in our flat. The room has wonderful views of many famous places in London, like Saint Paul's Cathedral. We offer a lower rent to someone who can prepare meals and help look after the baby at weekends.

B. My husband and I live with our 14-year-old son, Simon, in a beautiful country house. Our other son is studying abroad and we would like to have a student to stay in his room, join us for family meals and also help Simon with his school work.

C. There are still shared flats available in our International Student Lodge. You will have access to the library and car park at the university, which is across the road. Students from all over Europe, Asia, Africa and America have made Student Lodge their home. Why not join them?

D. I'm a nurse with a flat near the hospital. I'm looking for an older person, possibly a quiet student, to share with me. I often work at night so you'll be on your own a lot of the time. I eat my meals at the hospital so my kitchen is not very well-equipped.

E. I am offering free accommodation in exchange for help with my mother, who is now almost 90. You will have your own room but I'm afraid I cannot provide meals or let you use the kitchen. I have a season ticket for the opera, which you are welcome to borrow from time to time.

F. I'm looking for someone to share my flat with me. I'm a 22-year-old man from Manchester. You will have your own room, use of the garage and access to the kitchen and laundry. No pets or smokers, I'm afraid.

G. We have a spare room in our house in a village near Cambridge. We're a family with three teenage children who live at home, a fourth who is studying abroad and two very friendly cats. My wife's father also lives with us and does most of the cooking.

H. We have a room to rent in our house. There are three of us sharing. I'm from Sweden, Julio's from Argentina and Eddie, the dog, is from England! We are keen guitarists and we play together most evenings. I mean, Julio and I play; Eddie sometimes sings!

3 Decide which kind of accommodation would be the most suitable for the people in Activity 1.

5

Vocabulary
house and home
▶ CB page 53

1 Read the definitions. What are they describing?

1 Modern flats often have these at the window instead of curtains.
2 You hang them to cover windows.
3 You cover the floor with it.
4 It's the place you keep the car.
5 You turn it on in the summer to keep you cool in the house, although it can be expensive.
6 You put it over you in bed to keep you warm at night.

2 Choose the correct alternatives to complete the sentences.

1 I appreciate old things – I always buy *antique/modern* furniture when I can afford it.
2 It's nice to have outdoor space – I eat breakfast on my *floor/balcony* every morning.
3 I love growing flowers but, unfortunately, my house doesn't have *an entrance/a garden*.
4 I live in a very hot country so it's important to have cen*tral heating/air conditioning* in my house.
5 I have *blinds/glasses* on my windows for privacy.
6 I love having soft *cushions/pillows* on my bed – they help me sleep better.

Speaking
Individual long turn (Part 2) ▶ CB page 54

A

B

1 ▶ 16 Listen to a student describing one of the photos. Which one is he describing?

2 The second student is describing the other photo. Complete her turn. Use one word in each gap.

> I can see a father shopping for clothes with his young son. They are looking for clothes to buy. The father is sitting on the **(1)** .... and he is holding a striped **(2)** .... in front of his son to see if it is the right **(3)** .... They are both laughing, so they are happy about it and they think it will fit. In the shop there are different shirts hanging **(4)** .... the man and there are lots of other small T-shirts on the wall behind them. They're for children. The man is wearing **(5)** .... and a T-shirt, and the boy is wearing **(6)** .... on his feet. I can't see what kind of shoes the man is wearing because he is sitting down.

3 ▶ 17 Now listen and check your answers to Activity 2.

Grammar

too and *enough*, *so* and *such*
▶ CB page 55

1 Rewrite the sentences with the words in brackets in the correct place.

1. Nicolas always wears smart clothes. (such)
2. Most performance cars are expensive for someone like me. (too)
3. There are only about 340,000 people in Iceland. I didn't know it was a small country. (such)
4. I'm not hungry to eat a whole pizza! (enough)
5. We were tired that we went straight to bed. (so)
6. There are not open spaces for children to play in my town. (enough)

2 Choose the correct alternatives to complete the sentences.

1. It's *so/such* crowded on the bus in the evenings that I sometimes walk home instead.
2. Ana is *so/such* friendly – she smiles and says hello to almost everyone she meets.
3. That's *so/such* a pretty dress! It really suits you.
4. Tina has *so/such* many friends! She's really popular.

Writing

Email (Part 1) ▶ CB page 56

1 Look at the exam task below and the email a student has written. Which of the notes has the student <u>not</u> covered in their email.

Read this email and the notes you have made.

From: Chris
Subject: Clothes swap
Hi,
I saw on social media that you were interested in doing a clothes swap and that you want to get rid of some of your winter clothes. I want to swap some of my summer clothes, so it sounds as if <u>we could make an arrangement.</u> *Great!*
I'd like to see some of the things you want to swap and <u>I'm sure you want to see my clothes too.</u> We could do this by email or through social media. <u>Let me know which way you would prefer.</u>
<u>Do you have favourite colours or styles?</u>
All the best,
Chris

Yes, say why.
Tell Chris.
Describe them.

Write your **email** to Chris using **all the notes**.
Write about **100 words**.

Hi Chris,
Thanks for your email. It's a really good idea for us to do a clothes swap.
I'm moving to a place where it will be really cold so I would love to see some of your winter clothes. I can also send you photos of the summer things I'd like to swap. I think social media would be better. That way, we could share our photos with other people who might be interested in a swap too.
Alex

2 Read Alex's answer again. Write a sentence or two giving the answer for the note that Alex didn't cover.

3 Now look at the exam task below. Are these sentences about the task true or false?

1. You should arrange a day to talk to Carla.
2. You should say whether you like cats.
3. You should ask when Carla will be in France.
4. You should ask about Carla's cat.

Read this email and the notes you have made.

From: Carla
Subject: Cat sitting
Hi,
I saw your profile on the 'super pet-sitter' site. <u>You look like a really nice person</u> and you're obviously a cat lover like me. I think you would be ideal to look after our flat and our lovely cat Smokey. We need someone to look after him while we visit some friends in <u>France for five days.</u>
<u>What would you like to know about Smokey?</u> Could we speak <u>one day next week</u> so that I can tell you more about him?
Best wishes
Carla

Thank you!!
When?
Tell Carla.
Yes. Say which day.

Write your **email** to Carla using **all the notes**.
Write about **100 words**.

4 Plan and write your answer to the exam task in Activity 3.

6 You live and learn

Speaking
General questions (Part 1) ▶ CB page 59

About the exam:
In Phase 2 of Part 1 the examiner will ask you and your partner some general questions about yourselves and what you do. You answer these questions individually.

Strategy:
- Try to give interesting answers, and add some details and/or reasons to your answer.

1 ▶ 18 Listen to two students answering some questions in Phase 2 of a Part 1 speaking test. Tick (✔) the topics the examiner asks the students about.

1. what they did yesterday
2. their families
3. their habits
4. what they like doing in their spare time
5. their plans for the future

2 Which student, Sofia or Xin, gave better answers? Why?

3 Listen again and complete the extracts from the conversation with the words and phrases in the box. There is one word or phrase you don't need to use.

| actually | after that | because | by bus | first of all | really |

1. ...., I went to the cinema with my friends.
2. We saw a .... good film, which was very exciting, and .... we went to a pizza restaurant for a meal.
3. .... I eat a big breakfast.
4. Then I go to college ....

Discussion (Part 4) ▶ CB page 59

About the exam:
In Part 4 you answer questions about what you think. The questions are related to the topic of the discussion you had with your partner in Part 3.

Strategy:
- Try to say what you think clearly, and give interesting answers.
- Listen to your partner's questions and answers. The examiner may also ask you to comment on what your partner has said.

4 Look at some questions students were asked in Part 4. Choose the best answer to each question.

1 Do you prefer winter holidays, or summer holidays?
   A Winter holidays are much better for me because there are more things to do. In the summer people just go to the beach.
   B Winter holidays are not so good. It's too cold.
2 Is it important to do exercise when you're on holiday?
   A It's a good idea to visit interesting places instead of doing exercise.
   B It's very easy to sit and do nothing when you're on holiday, but I think this is a good thing because it helps you relax, so doing exercise is not important.
3 Do you think people have enough holidays?
   A I would like to have more holidays because I like them!
   B People work very hard and so it's important for them to have holidays. I think that two weeks is long enough though.

5 ▶ 19 Listen to two students answering two of the questions above. Complete the sentences with the words in the box.

| agree | also | because | disagree | perhaps |
| same | so | usually | | |

Examiner: Carlos, do you prefer winter holidays, or summer holidays?
Carlos: I love winter holidays **(1)** .... I really like skiing. **(2)** ...., I think the mountains are beautiful. The air is very fresh and it is very healthy.
Examiner: What do you think, Maria?
Maria: I **(3)** .... with Carlos. I prefer summer holidays. I **(4)** .... go to the beach in summer. I love hot weather, and I don't like being cold, so summer is better for me.
Examiner: Do you think people have enough holidays, Maria?
Maria: I think people work too hard and **(5)** .... they need to relax. They should have lots of holidays!
Examiner: Do you **(6)** .... Carlos?
Carlos: Yes, I think the **(7)** .... as Maria. I think people should spend more time with their family and have fun. So **(8)** .... we should have more holidays!

Reading
Multiple choice, short texts (Part 1) ▶ CB page 60

About the exam:
In this part of the exam you read five short texts. They may be signs, notices, labels, notes or messages. Each one has three different explanations (A, B, C). You choose the option that explains the meaning of the text.

Strategy:
- Look at the text. Think about where you might see it and what it means.
- Read the three options carefully and decide which one is closest in meaning to the text.
- Check the other options to make sure they are wrong.

1 For each question, choose the correct answer.

1
> Due to popular **demand**, the library will now stay open until 10 p.m. during the June examination preparation **period**.

A The library always closes after 10 p.m.
B There are exams in the library in June.
C Students have more time to study in the library in June.

2
> Angela,
> The clocks go forward tonight. I'm worried I might **oversleep** in the morning. Could you wake me up at 7 when you leave for work? I don't want to be late for college again!
> Sam

A Sam wants to persuade Angela to take him to college.
B Sam would like Angela to do him a favour tomorrow.
C Sam is reminding Angela that they have to get up early tomorrow morning.

3

Examination Rules

All mobile phones must be switched off and passed to the teachers in charge of the examination.

Your phone will be returned to you when you **hand in** the answer sheet.

A The teachers will switch all the phones off.
B The teachers will give you your phone back.
C You can keep your phone with you if you switch it off.

4

Mum, I'm still having trouble with my new laptop – someone needs to have a look at it. Can you take it back to the computer store on Saturday, please? They shouldn't **charge** anything as it's new.

The boy wants his mother to
A return the laptop to the store for repair.
B ask the store for a refund.
C collect a new laptop from the store.

5

15% discount for students who show a **valid** student card

A Students must use a card to pay for things.
B The card used to pay for something must be valid.
C If students show their card, they pay less money.

2 Match the words in bold in Activity 1 to the definitions.

1 sleep for longer than you planned
2 ask someone to pay money for something
3 a particular length of time with a beginning and an end
4 something that is correct and usable; not out of date
5 a strong request
6 give something to someone like a teacher

3 Complete the sentences with the correct form of the words in bold in Activity 1.

1 If you don't .... your work on time you can lose marks.
2 The computer shop didn't .... me any extra money for transferring data onto my new laptop.
3 The principal decided to agree to the students' .... for healthier food in the canteen.
4 Have you got a .... driving licence? If you have, we can rent a car.
5 He visited the UK twenty times over a .... of five years.
6 Tina is always forgetting to set her alarm and often ....

Vocabulary

prepositional phrases ▶ CB page 61

1 Choose the correct alternatives to complete the article.

Why cartoons are not a waste of time

I learnt English in an unusual way. But for me, it worked! When I was little, we had satellite TV at home with a good English language channel. My mum knew that English was an important language so even though I was only small, she made me watch it. She was **(1)** *in charge/on sale* of what I watched so because I was young she chose cartoons. At first they didn't mean much to me, and **(2)** *in case/in fact*, to be honest I understood nothing **(3)** *at all/at least*! However, as I started to enjoy the programmes, I understood a lot more.

My mother told me that I should learn English when I was young **(4)** *in case/at least* I needed it later in life, and that this was an excellent way of picking it up. I couldn't analyse the grammar **(5)** *at all/at the latest* so I couldn't explain it to anyone else, but I was able to use the most **(6)** *up-to-date/up-to-now* expressions naturally.

So later, when I started learning English formally at school, I already knew a lot. But I still did the homework exercises because they were fun, and it was helpful to keep my language **(7)** *at the latest/up-to-date* and to correct any small mistakes I made. I plan to learn **(8)** *at the latest/at least* one more language, maybe in a similar way, although I know there are many good online courses **(9)** *on sale/in fact*. I'm sure the key to success in the modern world is being multilingual, so I'm very grateful to my mother for encouraging me to watch those cartoons when I was young.

Grammar

past simple and past continuous
▶ CB page 62

1 Match sentences 1–3 to uses A–C.

1 I went to a fantastic college – the course was great and I made loads of friends.
2 While I was working on my project, my brother was studying for his English test.
3 I was studying in the library when my friend arrived.

A past continuous: two or more past actions in progress at the same time
B past continuous + past simple: a past action in progress when another action happened
C past simple: completed past actions

2 Find and correct the mistakes in the sentences.

1 I practised my English pronunciation when, suddenly, the telephone rang.
2 While I studied for my exam, my brother was playing football.
3 I was moving to Spain last year to learn Spanish.
4 My mother called me on my mobile while I spoke to my teacher.
5 I was passing my exam last week! I'm so happy!
6 I was watching television when my friend was calling me last night.
7 I was laughing when my friend told me the story!
8 I was taking a language course in England while my friend learnt French in France.
9 I saw my friend just as she walked past my window.
10 I knew the words but I wasn't understanding the grammar.

3 Complete the email with the past simple or past continuous form of the verbs in the box.

arrive   be   buy   cycle   discover   join
leave   meet   not know   rain   talk

Hi Jack,
My first week at university is over. Things **(1)** .... really well! From the moment I **(2)** .... at the university, there **(3)** .... loads of things to do every day! I **(4)** .... loads of people at the welcome disco last Friday and while I **(5)** .... to one girl there called Jenny, I **(6)** .... that she had attended the same primary school as me – although I **(7)** .... her then. Last Wednesday I **(8)** .... into town and **(9)** .... some clothes. It **(10)** .... and I got very wet! Yesterday I **(11)** .... the university tennis club with Jenny. OK, that's enough for now. Write soon!
Jon

Vocabulary

education ▶ CB page 63

1 Complete the sentences with the words in the box.

course   curriculum   homework
lecture   report   research   teacher

1 I love my .... at school – her classes are fun.
2 I hate doing .... every night – I'd rather spend time after school with my friends.
3 I'm enjoying taking my .... in history at college – I have to do a lot of .... on the internet but it's interesting.
4 I'm a bit nervous about my end-of-year .... from my teachers – it may not be very good!
5 The school .... includes German, art and music classes.
6 The .... on art history will take place in the main hall on 15 October.

adverbs ▶ CB page 63

2 Complete the sentences with adverbs formed from the words in brackets.

1 I .... wanted to be a dancer but now I'd like to be a teacher instead. (origin)
2 .... I worked as a teacher but now I'm a holiday rep – it's more fun! (previous)
3 .... my friend didn't pass his driving test, so he'll have to take it again. (fortunate)
4 It's difficult to explain the problem but, ... , it's because of a computer breakdown. (basic)
5 The project is .... going to involve the whole department. (probable)
6 The lecturer is good – she .... explains everything well. (general)
7 He worked .... to pass the exam. (hard)
8 My friend .... works harder than I do – he gets better marks! (obvious)

Listening

Multiple choice, short texts (Part 2)
▶ CB page 64

1 ▶ 20 For each question, choose the correct answer.

1 You will hear two friends talking about a history lesson.
   They both think that
   A it's a good thing to learn about the past.
   B the lesson was difficult to understand.
   C studying the subject can often be boring.

2 You will hear a woman telling a friend about her music lessons.
   What does she find difficult about them?
   A what she has to play
   B the instructions she has to follow
   C the amount of preparation she has to do

3 You will hear two students talking about a lecture they went to.
   They agree that it was
   A difficult to follow in places.
   B helpful for their coursework.
   C fun to listen to.

4 You will hear a woman telling a friend about learning to drive.
   How does she feel about it?
   A disappointed with the instructor
   B worried about taking the driving test
   C unhappy about the cost of the lessons

5 You will hear a man telling a friend about a college course he's going to do.
   What does he say about it?
   A It looks rather difficult.
   B It's too expensive for him.
   C It could be useful for his future.

6 You will hear two friends talking about playing tennis.
   The man wants the woman to help him to
   A become healthier.
   B eat better food.
   C play more often.

Grammar

past perfect ▶ CB page 65

1 Choose the correct alternatives to complete the text.

As soon as I **(1)** *got / had got* to university, I remembered that my classmates **(2)** *told / had told* me there was going to be an exam that day. I **(3)** *felt / had felt* really nervous because I **(4)** *missed / had missed* lots of lectures and I really **(5)** *didn't know / hadn't known* much about the subject at all.

By the time I **(6)** *got / had got* to the lecture hall, the lecturer **(7)** *already gave out / had already given out* the exam papers. I **(8)** *didn't have / hadn't had* anything for breakfast and I **(9)** *didn't feel / hadn't felt* very well. Most of the other students **(10)** *seemed / had seemed* to be finding the exam quite easy. I **(11)** *barely looked / had barely looked* at the questions when I **(12)** *saw / had seen* that the boy next to me **(13)** *wrote / had written* almost a page.

When the lecturer **(14)** *said / had said* to stop writing, I **(15)** *only answered / had only answered* two of the three questions. I **(16)** *was / had been* sure I **(17)** *failed / had failed* but when the results **(18)** *came out / had come out*, I **(19)** *saw / had seen* that I **(20)** *got / had got* quite a good mark!

2 Join the sentences. Begin with the words in brackets and change the verbs to the correct form.

1 I woke up. I missed my doctor's appointment. (by the time)

2 Adam collected his luggage. He went to look for a taxi. (as soon as)

3 Heather finished doing her homework. She went out. (when)

4 We did the shopping. We came home and cleaned the house. (after)

5 Christine got to the beach. It started to rain. (by the time)

6 He blew out the candles on the birthday cake. He started opening his presents. (as soon as)

7 Stephen finished his breakfast. His sister left for school. (by the time)

8 The teacher arrived. The students already stopped talking. (when)

Writing

Story (Part 2) ▶ CB page 66

1 Look at the exam task and the story a student has written. Find and correct six mistakes with the past simple and the past perfect.

> Your English teacher has asked you to write a story. Your story must begin with this sentence:
> *It was my first day and I was nervous.*
> Write your **story** in about **100 words**.

> It was my first day and I was nervous. My mother hung my new school uniform in the wardrobe the night before. She put my new school shoes next to the chest of drawers. I got up, and after I had my shower, I started to get dressed. Suddenly, I realised that my school shoes hadn't been there. Then I had remembered that I had left my bedroom door open the night before. I ran downstairs and out into the back garden. There was our new puppy, Eddie, with one of my shoes in his mouth! He already destroyed the other shoe.

2 Divide the story in Activity 1 into paragraphs.

3 Complete sentences 1–9 to make a story. Use one idea from each of the boxes on the right.

1 It was my first day …
2 I was feeling …
3 In fact, something rather strange had happened …
4 I had been …
5 I decided …
6 I was still thinking about what had happened when I …
7 I tried …
8 Finally, I …
9 We …

4 Write a final sentence for your story.

1
- at university.
- in a completely new job.
- on holiday with my friends.

2
- nervous because I'd never had a proper job before.
- a little bit anxious but also curious about the other students, the lecturers and the course.
- really great because I knew we were going to have a really fantastic time.

3
- a few days before.
- the night before.
- exactly a year before.

4
- looking at clothes in a shop I really like when I saw a boy I know trying to steal a leather jacket.
- in bed for about an hour when I heard someone outside the house calling out my name.
- on my way to the airport when I realised I had left my passport at home.

5
- to ignore it and soon after I fell asleep.
- to call out his name and he was so embarrassed that he put the jacket back.
- not to go and get it because I knew I could travel on my national ID.

6
- realised that the lecturer was asking me a question.
- realised that I had left my small backpack at home with all my favourite clothes in it.
- saw the boss standing in front of my desk.

7
- to phone my mother but I didn't have enough credit on my phone to make an international call.
- to pretend I had been thinking about the latest sales figures but I don't think he believed me.
- to remember the last thing I had heard her say but my mind was a complete blank.

8
- decided to admit that I hadn't been listening.
- managed to send her a text message and she promised to post it to me the next day.
- asked him a question about the company and he seemed to be pleased about that.

9
- went on talking about company policy for the next 20 minutes or so.
- finished the lecture and she smiled at me as she went out of the room.
- went to the post office every day for a week but the backpack never arrived.

7 Water

Vocabulary
weather ▶ CB page 71

1 Do the crossword.

Across
1 white frozen water that falls from the sky and lies on the ground
7 a storm with thunder and lightning
8 a short period of rain or snow
10 frozen water
11 very strong winds

Down
2 a general word for air that blows about
3 another word for 'rainy'
4 bright light from the sun, good for sunbathing
5 a soft gentle movement of air
6 a word that means 'extremely cold'
9 cloudy air near the ground which is difficult to see through

2 Complete the sentences with words from the crossword in Activity 1 in the correct form.

1 There'll be some .... tonight so drive slowly – you won't be able to see very far ahead.
2 There is often a .... at the end of a hot summer day, with bright lightning.
3 It had been hot all day so she was happy to feel a gentle .... on her face in the evening to cool her down.
4 When I'm on holiday, I want lots of .... so that I can get a tan!
5 I hate very strong .... – they can often cause damage to houses.
6 We can't go out yet – the rain has made all the roads very ....

3 Which is the odd word out in these groups of words?

1 breeze wind dry gale
2 shower rain wet temperature
3 heat thunder lightning storm
4 degrees mild freezing snowfall

Listening
Multiple choice, long text (Part 4)
▶ CB page 72

1 Match verbs 1–6 to phrases A–F to make collocations.

1 run   A the flowers in the garden
2 pour   B your clothes
3 have   C a hot bath
4 rinse   D with rain
5 water   E your hair after using shampoo
6 wash   F a shower

2 ▶ 21 For each question, choose the correct answer.

You will hear an interview with a woman called Nadia Winters, who presents the weather forecast on television.

1 How did Nadia feel about science at school?
  A She enjoyed all aspects of it.
  B She liked it better than other subjects.
  C She needed to do it for her future work plans.

2 What does Nadia say about appearing on television?
  A Her parents encouraged her to try it.
  B She had always wanted to do it.
  C She was nervous about it.

3 Nadia says that she got her first job presenting the weather on television because
  A she worked hard.
  B another presenter left.
  C she knew the right people.

4 What does Nadia like best about her job?
  A being famous
  B meeting different people
  C travelling around the country

5 What does Nadia say about being a TV weather presenter?
  A It's important to be confident.
  B It's easier if you are an actor as well.
  C It's necessary to understand the technology.

6 Nadia says that it's hard to give detailed forecasts
  A in the early months of the year.
  B during very heavy storms.
  C when it is a long way in the future.

Grammar
countable and uncountable nouns
▶ CB page 73

1 Choose the correct alternatives to complete the sentences.

1 *Many/Much* people enjoy going on cruises because they are very relaxing.
2 Cruise ships have *a lot of/much* activities on board.
3 People on cruise ships sometimes think there is too *many/much* to do!
4 *Few/Little* people dislike going on cruises.
5 Some people spend *a lot of/many* time on cruises.
6 The ship's engines didn't make *much/few* noise.

2 Put the words in the box into the correct sentence. You may need to change the form of some words. There is one word you do not need to use.

| bread   coffee   glass (x2)   noise (x2)   painting |

1 At night you can hear some very strange .... on a ship!
2 It's important to keep the .... in the portholes clean so that passengers can see out.
3 I can't see anything if I don't wear my ....
4 I often buy .... at the supermarket even though it's not as good as the baker's.
5 I sometimes buy .... I like in art galleries – and they often sell art on cruise ships.
6 I really hate it when there's a lot of .... at night – I can't sleep!

Reading
Gapped text (Part 4) ▶ CB page 74

1 You are going to read an article about how to survive on a deserted island. Read the article quickly and put these items in the order in which they appear in the text. Number them 1 to 8.

- A leaves
- B sunburn
- C waterfalls and streams
- D sea water
- E insects
- F a message
- G passing ships or boats
- H the beach

2 Read the article again. Five sentences have been removed. For each question, choose the correct answer. There are three extra sentences which you do not need to use.

- A You probably won't feel like eating these on your first day.
- B You could put it in a bottle as well.
- C You can drink the liquid inside it to prevent dehydration.
- D Whatever you write should be visible from the air.
- E Apart from protecting you from the sun, wind and rain they can also be used as blankets.
- F Most people are not willing to try it.
- G The water in these will be purer and less likely to make you sick.
- H You could also try to find a cave.

3 Look at the words in bold in the article and choose the correct definition for each word as it is used in the article.

1 *tips*
   - A money you give to a waiter
   - B useful pieces of advice
2 *grab*
   - A take quickly
   - B hold tightly
3 *hut*
   - A a small simple building
   - B something you wear on your head
4 *chilly*
   - A a bit cold
   - B frightening
5 *choosy*
   - A careful
   - B fussy
6 *soothe*
   - A make something feel better
   - B protect something

SURVIVING ALONE ON AN ISLAND

Would you know what to do if you found yourself alone on a tropical island? It can happen so it's worth being prepared. Here are some **tips**.

Your first priority is to look for drinking water. You will die in only a couple of days if you don't get enough liquid. Go inland from the beach and look for waterfalls or streams. **(1)** ....

Since this is a tropical island, there are probably loads of coconut palms around. Climb a tree and **grab** a green coconut. **(2)** .... Whatever you do, don't drink sea water, because it's full of salt and so it will make you even thirstier than you were before.

Next you should try to collect some palm leaves. Use them to make a little **hut**. **(3)** .... You'll need these at night as it can be **chilly**. Build your hut close to the beach so you can still see any passing ships or boats that might come to your rescue.

After building your hut you will be getting hungry. You can try fishing or hunting but insects are also food. **(4)** .... Eventually, however, you'll be very hungry and you won't be so **choosy**. Coconuts are full of protein too and their oil can be used to **soothe** sunburnt skin.

Your main task now is to attract attention. Use large stones to write a message on the sand. **(5)** .... Keep your fingers crossed that someone in a plane will see it and come to your rescue!

Vocabulary
adjectives and prepositions
▶ CB page 74

1 Match 1–10 to A–J to form sentences.

1 Cats are not very keen
2 I'm not very familiar
3 Chicago is known
4 Why are so many people attracted
5 The lake near my house is very similar
6 When she was at college, Tina got involved
7 I'm sometimes surprised
8 A lot of people get very stressed
9 My father is very fond
10 I think the students might be feeling anxious

A with the water park in the city.
B in a research project about saving water.
C on water – in fact, they hate it.
D by how much my friends enjoy sailing.
E to holidays by the sea?
F out by having to work long hours in the office.
G to one I visited last year on holiday.
H about their exam results – they should get them very soon.
I for being called the windy city.
J of swimming in the lake – he goes every morning.

2 Find and correct the mistakes with prepositions in seven of the sentences. Tick (✔) the sentences that are correct.

1 Thailand and Greece are known for their many beautiful islands.
2 I was anxious in flying, but actually I loved it.
3 I'm very keen about swimming.
4 I was very disappointed for the standard of the hotel on my last holiday.
5 One of the beaches on Fuerteventura is similar to a beach I used to go to when I was a child.
6 That website you told me about was really useful by finding the best beaches.
7 I know the north of the island quite well but I'm not as familiar on the south.
8 My friend who lives there is very involved about a campaign to keep the beaches clean.
9 She's very attracted to the idea of doing voluntary work with animals.
10 We're both very fond with animals too.

Grammar
articles ▶ CB page 76

1 Choose the correct alternatives to complete the sentences.

1 Do you ask your friends for *advice/the advice*?
2 There was *a thunderstorm/the thunderstorm* last night and *a noise/the noise* woke me up.
3 *Glass/The glass* is made from sand and other minerals.
4 Where there's *smoke/a smoke*, there's *fire/the fire*.
5 Could you get *bread/a bread* and some butter when you go out?
6 *Coffee/The coffee* they make here is always very strong.
7 Save *water/the water* and turn off *tap/the tap*.
8 I love *cheese/a cheese* but I don't like *milk/the milk*.

2 Complete the text with *a*, *an*, *the* or – for no article.

Nobody knows exactly when (1) _____ people first started to build (2) _____ boats but it seems that (3) _____ history of sailing goes back thousands of years. (4) _____ very first boats were probably log canoes. (5) _____ boats capable of making (6) _____ long sea voyages are more recent but (7) _____ surprising discovery in (8) _____ unlikely place has provided more information. (9) _____ world's oldest sea-going boat was found in (10) _____ middle of (11) _____ desert in (12) _____ Kuwait. (13) _____ archaeologists who found it think it was used to carry goods from (14) _____ Mesopotamia to (15) _____ southern shores of (16) _____ Persian Gulf. This would explain why some Mesopotamian pottery was found thousands of miles from where it was made.

3 Look at this postcard a student has written. The student has not used any articles. Put an article where necessary before the words in bold.

Dear Marina,

We had **wonderful time** in **Egypt**. As you know, we took **cruise** down **Nile**. We started in **Cairo**. **Boat** was really luxurious and **itinerary** was amazing. We saw all **most famous** archaeological sites like **Pyramids of Giza** and **Valley of the Kings**. **Guides** were great and **other people** on **boat** were good fun. I tried to learn **bit** of **Arabic** but everyone spoke good English. On **last night** there was **special party** with **fantastic food** and **wonderful music**. By **time** we got to **bed**, **sun** had already come up!

Love,

Carla

7

Speaking
Collaborative task (Part 3)
▶ CB page 77

1 Look at the exam task and decide if these sentences are true or false.

1 You have to choose the activity you like best.
2 You have to decide which activity would be best for the friends to do.

> Some friends are planning to spend a day together at the beach. They want to have fun, but they don't want to spend much money.
>
> The pictures below show some things they could do.
>
> Talk together about the different things they could do and decide which would be best.

2 ▶22 Read the comments an examiner wrote about two students. Then listen to the students, Martin and Ana, talking about the activities in the exam task. Are the comments about Martin, Ana or both of them?

1 used some good vocabulary
2 in too much of a hurry to reach a conclusion
3 didn't really ask the other student for their opinion

3 Here are some extracts from a conversation about the same task between two other students. Complete them with the words in the box. There is one word you do not need to use.

agree   and   how about   right
think   what   why

1 I think that swimming would be a good activity. Do you .... ?
2 So you don't like the idea of surfing. .... do you say that?
3 Do you .... swimming or walking would be more interesting?
4 I see what you mean about the cost of the café. .... fishing, then?
5 Maybe they could think about doing several different things. .... do you think?
6 So we both think sitting on the beach is not a good idea. Is that .... ?

46

4 Now match extracts 1–6 from Activity 3 to responses A–F below.

A Perhaps, but they can't talk while they're in the water and it isn't very exciting.

B Yes, that's a good point, but don't forget they haven't got much money to spend so they can't do more than one expensive activity.

C Yes, I think we definitely agree on that point.

D Well, they could do it, but to be honest it seems boring and not exciting – they just sit there waiting for the fish.

E I prefer walking myself, because they can discover new places along the beach. It's good exercise too.

F Well, they'll have to spend money to rent the surfboards, and maybe they can't all surf very well.

Discussion (Part 4) ▶ CB page 77

5 ▶ 23 Read the Part 4 questions and listen to students answering four of them. Match the speakers to the questions they answer.

A What do you enjoy doing with friends at the beach?

B What do you usually spend money on when you're at the beach?

C Do you prefer a beach holiday or a winter holiday?

D Do you buy a lot of souvenirs when you go away on a trip?

E Do you enjoy sightseeing when you're in a new place?

F Do you think people spend enough time relaxing these days?

Writing
Email (Part 1) ▶ CB page 78

1 Which two statements below do <u>not</u> refer to a cruise?

1 We visited many different ports.
2 It was great for relaxing.
3 We travelled on our own.
4 It was difficult to get around.
5 There was lots of food available all the time.
6 There were days when we didn't stop anywhere.

2 Look at the email that Analise has written. She has made nine mistakes in her email. Match the underlined mistakes (1–9) to the comments (A–F). You need to use some of the comments more than once.

> Subject: Holiday news
>
> Hi Sara,
>
> How are you? We've just got back from a **(1)** <u>cruze</u>. It was great! **(2)** <u>We sailed from Barcelona</u> around the Canary Islands. I loved seeing all **(3)** <u>different places</u>. On one island there was **(4)** <u>fantastic market</u>. I **(5)** <u>buy</u> some lovely earrings. There **(6)** <u>was</u> really nice people on board the ship and we made lots of friends. **(7)** <u>If you want to relax</u>, a cruise is perfect, and I can recommend ours although you may get bored with the days **(8)** <u>sea</u>.
>
> Well, write soon and **(9)** <u>say</u> me if you book a trip!
>
> Analise

A You should start a new paragraph here.
B Spelling.
C Something missing here.
D Wrong tense.
E Wrong form.
F Wrong word.

3 Rewrite the email in Activity 2, correcting the underlined mistakes.

4 Plan and write your own answer to the exam task below. Make sure that you check your work for mistakes when you have finished.

> Read this email from your English-speaking friend Jordan and the notes you have made.
>
> From: Jordan
> Subject: Meeting up?
> Hi,
> Guess what – I'm coming to your town next weekend and I'd love to meet up with you. *Explain.*
> Where's the best place to meet and when? *Tell Jordan?* Is there anything interesting we could do this weekend? I'd like to go out for a meal, so where would you recommend? *Tell her and say why.*
> I love swimming, so could we do that as well? *No, because …*
> Hope to hear from you soon!
> Jordan
>
> Write your **email** to Jordan, **using all the notes**.
> Write about **100 words**.

8 Nearly famous

Listening
Gap-fill (Part 3) ▶ CB page 81

1 Read the advertisement for a new television show. Are the sentences true or false?

> **New reality show** coming to **Channel 10** later in the year! **Watch ordinary people** interview **celebrities** when they are **off-guard** and ask them **difficult questions**. See how they react!
>
> *The fun starts in August – make sure you're tuned in!*

1 The celebrities are expecting an interview.
2 The presenters are professional actors.
3 The programme begins in the summer.

2 ▶ 24 You will hear Paul Johnson, the producer of the new television show, talking about ways of getting on the show. For each question, write the correct answer in the gap. Write one or two words or a number or a date or a time.

New reality TV show!

We're looking for new presenters to interview celebrities.

People required:
- Must be outgoing and good at communication.
- The best age for presenters is **(1)** ....

Qualifications and experience:
Presenters
- get training on how to **(2)** .... and speak in a natural way.
- are given **(3)** .... to wear.
- must speak **(4)** .... as well as other languages.

How to apply:
Send an email with a **(5)** .... and your phone number.

Dates for auditions:
Auditions will be held from 23 April to **(6)** .... April.

Vocabulary
entertainment ▶ CB page 82

1 Match each word in the first box to a word in the second box to make compound nouns.

ballet	chat	designer	film	magazine
radio	rock	show	soap	stadium	stage
talent	television

actor	broadcast	business	clothes
commercial	concert	cover	dancer	opera
show	show	star	studio

2 Complete the conversation with compound nouns from Activity 1 in the correct form. The first letter of each word is given.

Mike: Did you see that TV programme last night – the **(1)** c............... s............... where the presenter talked to that **(2)** b............... d...............? She's an interesting person.

Sara: Yes – she left classical dancing to become a **(3)** r............... s..............., didn't she? Imagine going from a classical stage with other dancers to giving a **(4)** s............... c............... in front of thousands of rock music fans!

Mike: But ballet is so different from rock music. I could have understood it if she had become a **(5)** s............... a............... in a theatre – after all, ballet involves acting, so that would be logical, and she's used to being on stage.

Sara: Yes. And sometimes dancers have chosen to appear in television **(6)** s............... o............... – just one episode, for the fun of acting in a popular series.

Mike: And, of course, other celebrities make **(7)** t............... c............... – they make a lot of money by appearing in advertisements like that.

Sara: On top of that, their photograph appears on **(8)** m............... c............... all over the world – it must be a great life. They get to wear expensive **(9)** d............... c............... and stay in five-star hotels!

Mike: I'd love that! Some people seem to have all the luck.

Sara: Well, there's nothing stopping you! Why don't you enter a **(10)** t............... s...............? You might win, and then you could have that lifestyle.

Grammar
reported speech ▶ CB page 83

1 Rewrite the sentences in reported speech.

1 'I saw Miley Cyrus in an airport once.'
 He said ....
2 'I met Emma Watson in a café in March!'
 He said ....
3 'I don't believe him though.'
 She said ....
4 'He's never met anyone famous.'
 She said ....
5 'He's always saying that he's seen someone famous somewhere or other.'
 She told me ....
6 'I've been to the Academy Awards ceremony a couple of times.'
 She said ....
7 'It was amazing!'
 She said ....
8 'I can't go this year because there's something really important I have to do that day.'
 She told me ....
9 'I'll tell you if I'm going next year.'
 She said ....
10 'You can join me!'
 She said ....

2 Find and correct the mistakes in the sentences. Tick (✔) the sentences that are correct.

1 He told us that he could speak Japanese.
2 She said me she didn't like having her photo taken.
3 She told she would be at home on Saturday night.
4 My singing coach said I had to practise more.
5 I told them that I didn't want to be on a TV show.
6 Carla said us she had tried to get a part in a movie.
7 Liam said I could borrow his camera.
8 Luke said me he would be late for the interview.
9 She told to me that she was going home.
10 Tim said he had been late for school the day before.

3 What were the people's actual words in Activity 2? Rewrite the sentences in direct speech.

4

Read part of an interview with Sean, an Australian actor, and the article Kim, the journalist, wrote based on the interview. Then complete Kim's article below.

Kim: So, Sean, you grew up in Melbourne, Australia.

Sean: Not exactly. My family moved out of the city to a place called Apollo Bay. It was a great place to grow up!

Kim: And why was that?

Sean: My dad and all my brothers have always surfed but down there we surfed every day before and after school. Also, it's a small community and I've always loved places where you know everyone.

Kim: So how did you get into acting?

Sean: My brother Raori got into it first. As a kid, I always loved movies but it wasn't like I dreamt of being an actor. It wasn't until I was about 17 and I watched my brothers doing TV shows that I wanted to act myself. I started doing acting classes after school and then got a part in the series *Home Town*.

Kim: And what do your surfing friends think about your acting career?

Sean: They've never really shown much interest in it, actually. They just want to go and surf so they don't treat me any differently.

Sean's still surfing!

I'm really impressed by Sean O'Sullivan! He hasn't forgotten where he comes from, even though he's now world famous. Sean told me that he **(1)** .... in a small town near Melbourne called Apollo Bay. Apparently, his family moved there to get away from the city. Sean loved living there. He said that his father and his brothers **(2)** .... and that in Apollo Bay they **(3)** .... every day!

Another thing he loves is the sense of community. He told me that because it was such a small place, he **(4)** .... everyone there.

I wasn't surprised to hear that Sean **(5)** .... movies as a child. But it did surprise me to learn that acting hadn't been one of his dreams. He told me that he **(6)** .... doing acting classes after school, when his brothers began appearing on TV shows.

He's stayed friends with his surfing mates over the years. Sean said they **(7)** .... much interest in his acting career and that all they **(8)** .... to do was surf. For them, Sean's still just one of the guys.

Speaking
General questions (Part 1)
▶ CB page 84

1
Choose the best answer to the questions.

1 Do you enjoy watching soap operas on television?
  A I don't watch much television because I prefer sport. I watch a lot of football.
  B I watch some of them, but not many – I do enjoy the ones about hospitals though because I think they're interesting.

2 Do you often watch films at home with friends?
  A I think it's much better to watch a film on a big screen – it's more fun, so no I don't do that often.
  B I go to a restaurant with friends or I meet them to go shopping. Sometimes we meet at my home.

3 Tell us about your favourite film.
  A I love the whole *Star Wars* series – they're exciting. I've seen them all many times.
  B The film I love most is actually one of *The Avengers* series. The story is fun and there's lots of action.

4 What did you do last weekend?
  A I'm sorry I can't remember, but I probably met my friends somewhere.
  B I went to the beach for the day with my family and in the evening we went to the cinema.

Individual long turn (Part 2)
▶ CB page 84

A

B

2 Look at the photographs and the extracts from students' descriptions. The students can't remember some of the words they want to use. Match the underlined words in the sentences to the words in the box.

actors   autographs   remote control   rug
shelves   spectators   sports bag   tidy
tournament   uniform

Photograph A

1 He's wearing the special clothes that officials wear.
2 He must be playing in a competition where people play against each other because I think he's won a game.
3 People must like him because he's signing his name for his fans to keep.
4 He's carrying a thing that has his sports kit in it.
5 The people watching look happy to see the player and talk to him.

Photograph B

6 One of them is holding the thing you use to change the channels on TV.
7 There's a cupboard on the left of the television with things inside to put stuff on.
8 The people on the television are people in soap operas.
9 The living room looks very neat and it's not in a mess.
10 There is a thing like a small carpet on the floor.

3 Read what a student said about photograph A. Complete the student's description with *in* or *on*.

(1) .... the middle of the photograph there is a tennis player and he's wearing sports clothes. He's also carrying two sports bags and signing autographs. (2) .... the background there are a lot of spectators who have been watching the game. There are men and women and they're wearing summer clothes. It must be quite hot, because they're not wearing sweaters or coats. Lots of them are holding cameras and taking photographs of the tennis player. They all look excited. (3) .... the left of the photograph there's a man in a uniform – he's watching what's happening. There's another man in a uniform standing (4) .... front of the people, looking at them. (5) .... the right of the photo I can see a woman showing the man next to her the photo she has taken. (6) .... the middle of the photo by the tennis player's feet I can see a board with writing on it.

4 Read what a student said about photograph B. Complete the student's description with the phrases in the box.

above   I can see   on the right of   there's
they're   underneath

(1) .... the photograph there are two people sitting together on a sofa in a living room. They could be a mother with her daughter. (2) .... both wearing casual clothes. The woman is wearing jeans and a shirt and flat shoes. The girl isn't wearing shoes but she's got socks on. They're both smiling and they look happy. They're watching television together. One of them is holding a remote control to change the channel. On the screen (3) .... two actors – a man and a woman. They're wearing formal clothes and the woman is holding a microphone. It could be a talent show. (4) .... the television there are some shelves with a black box, which looks like a DVD recorder. On the left of the television (5) .... a cupboard with some enormous glasses in it. (6) .... the television there's a picture in a frame and two potted plants. The room is very tidy!

5 ▶ 25 Now listen and check your answers to Activity 4.

8

Grammar
reported questions
▶ CB page 85

1 Rewrite the questions in reported speech. Begin with *He asked me …* .

1 'Do you find Brad Pitt attractive?'
2 'What do you like most about him?'
3 'Do you think he is more attractive than Johnny Depp?'
4 'What did you think of his latest film?'
5 'Was Angelina Jolie in it too?'
6 'Who else was in it?'
7 'Have you seen any of her films?'
8 'Are you going to the cinema this weekend?'
9 'Can I come with you?'
10 'How much will the tickets cost?'

2 A student wrote these sentences about an interview he had. Find and correct the mistakes with reported questions in them. There are mistakes in six of the sentences. Tick (✔) the sentences that are correct.

1 She asked me where did I live.
2 She asked me have you always lived there.
3 She wanted to know what it was like living there.
4 She also asked me what I am studying at the moment.
5 She asked me what I had done during the summer holidays.
6 She wanted to know if I had enjoyed myself.
7 She asked if I have got any special plans for the future.
8 She wanted to know what was I going to do when I finished studying.
9 She also asked me what I enjoyed doing with my friends in the evenings.
10 She wanted to know do I enjoy watching television or listening to music.

Reading
Multiple-choice cloze (Part 5)
▶ CB page 86

1 Read the article in Activity 2 quickly and choose the best title for it.

A Why people are interested in celebrities
B The secret life of celebrities
C A celebrity lifestyle

2 For each question, choose the correct answer.

Our **fascination** with celebrities is nothing new. The musicians and silent film stars of the **past** also had thousands of fans. But why do the rich and famous **(1)** .... to us so much? Psychologists tell us that news about celebrities **(2)** .... us believe that anything is possible. Our dreams can come **(3)** .... and we too can become hugely **successful** and have everything we want. **Curiosity** about celebrities isn't necessarily **harmful** but it may **(4)** .... that we don't feel very closely connected to our friends, family and community. That's why we sometimes use information about celebrities on social media to **(5)** .... a gap in our lives. This is why we **(6)** .... so **upset** about the deaths of famous people. We can feel very sad about the loss of someone we didn't actually know personally. Fortunately, our **grief** doesn't usually **last** more than a couple of weeks.

1	A	attract	B	appeal	C	draw	D	catch
2	A	makes	B	shows	C	keeps	D	means
3	A	real	B	right	C	exact	D	true
4	A	tell	B	say	C	mean	D	be
5	A	fill	B	complete	C	answer	D	shut
6	A	go	B	turn	C	get	D	develop

3 Find words in the article in Activity 1 to match definitions 1–8.

1 damaging
2 the time before the present
3 the state of being very interested in something
4 great sadness
5 unhappy and worried because something bad has happened
6 the desire to know about something
7 continue
8 getting the results you want

Vocabulary

-ed and -ing adjectives
▶ CB page 86

1 Choose the correct alternatives to complete the rules.

1 When an adjective describes a person's feelings, it ends in *-ed/-ing*.
2 When an adjective describes a thing that affects a person's feelings, it ends in *-ed/-ing*.

2 Complete the sentences with adjectives formed from the verbs in brackets.

1 It's rather .... (depress) when things keep going wrong.
2 I am .... (fascinate) by the lives of celebrities – I can't stop reading about them!
3 I find it .... (surprise) that so many people read about celebrities.
4 I get very .... (frighten) if I watch horror films on television on my own.
5 There's a very .... (interest) programme on television tonight about celebrities.
6 It's very .... (encourage) when people tell you that you're doing things well.
7 I'm .... (amaze) you've never heard of her – she's really famous!
8 It's .... (worry) that such talentless people are role models for so many young people nowadays.

3 Complete the sentences with adjectives formed from the verbs in the box.

| amaze | depress | encourage | fascinate |
| frighten | interest | surprise | worry |

1 I feel rather .... when the newspapers are full of pointless articles about celebrities.
2 The lives of rich people are .... – they are so different from mine!
3 I get very .... when celebrities do a lot of charity work.
4 I'm not at all .... in what rich people do.
5 People who run marathons for charity are .... – I couldn't do it!
6 It's .... how many young people are only interested in becoming famous.
7 I was pleasantly .... when I read about the charity work celebrities often do.
8 Are you at all .... by the intense media interest in celebrities?

Writing

Article (Part 2) ▶ CB page 88

1 Look at the exam task. Which of these tips should you follow when you write an article?

1 Have a clear introduction.
2 Use lots of adjectives.
3 Have clear paragraphs.
4 Give reasons for your ideas.
5 Answer all the questions in the task.

You see this notice on an English-language website.

> **Articles wanted!**
> Who is your favourite celebrity?
> What qualities do you think a celebrity should have?
> Would you like to be a celebrity?
> Write an article answering these questions and we will put it on our website.

Write your **article** in about **100 words**.

2 Read a student's answer and choose the best linkers to complete it.

> **My favourite celebrity**
> My favourite celebrity is (1) *actually/completely* someone who is only famous locally. He is a man who does a lot of good things for charity, and he helps people as much as he can.
> (2) *In my opinion/However* a celebrity should be someone who everyone can respect. (3) *In fact/On the other hand*, a celebrity should be a good role model for all young people, (4) *despite/so that* they have a good example to follow.
> I don't think that I would make a good celebrity, (5) *because/so* I think it must be difficult to behave well all the time – (6) *and/although* it might be fun if people asked me for my autograph!

3 Plan and write your answer to the exam task in Activity 1. Remember to give examples to support your ideas and make sure that you have a clear introduction and conclusion.

9 Creativity

Grammar

modals of ability ▶ CB page 91

1 Choose the correct alternatives to complete the sentences.

1 I *can/manage* to play the guitar but I *can't/couldn't* sing.
2 This painting is fantastic! *Can/Could* you paint in oils as well as draw?
3 I *could/managed to* get a ticket for tonight's concert at the last minute.
4 Ben *can't/couldn't* hear the phone ringing because he was watching a film on TV.
5 I *could/managed to* get quite a good photo of Jamie even though he never sits still.
6 *Will you be able to/Could you* join us tomorrow?

2 There is one extra word in each of these sentences. Find it and cross it out.

1 They were be able to see an island in the distance.
2 Did you could manage to finish that painting?
3 Could you to tell me where I can buy art materials?
4 Will you be able to manage come to the meeting?
5 My cousin is able to can design web pages.
6 We won't be not able to send you the tickets until next week.

3 Complete the article with *can, can't, could, couldn't* or *able*.

The very young artist

If you ask most children to paint a street scene, they are usually only **(1)** .... to produce triangle-topped boxes for houses, stick trees and animals or people that are the wrong size. But one young boy is different. Although he is only six, Jamie **(2)** .... paint in a way that many adults **(3)** .... only dream of. At first he painted boats and sea scenes but then he realised he **(4)** .... also paint rural landscapes and animals. One art expert said it was unusual to find someone so young who **(5)** .... paint in this way.

Jamie says he likes painting because it's fun and because it helps him imagine places he **(6)** .... visit because they're too far away. He is hoping that he'll be **(7)** .... to have his own exhibition before he feels he is too old – that means at least before he is eight! I **(8)** .... imagine doing that myself when I was six!

Reading
Multiple matching (Part 2)
▶ CB page 92

1 The people below all want to take an art course. There are descriptions of eight courses. Decide which course would be the most suitable for the people below.

1 Carmen hasn't tried to paint or draw anything since she was a child. She doesn't have any of her own **materials**. She would like to take her time and go to the course once a week for a few months.

2 Adam wants to start making clothes for his friends. He would like to be able to show them pictures of what he plans to make first. He loves all the styles from the 1940s and often watches films from that time.

3 Paula learnt to paint at school and is very good at it. Recently she started a painting of her husband that she is having **trouble** finishing. She would prefer a course that only lasts a couple of days.

4 Daniel has been drawing for many years. He would like to try something new. He loves music and often uses it to give him ideas.

5 Sam has always wanted to paint people. He can draw but he needs to learn how to use materials. He has his own **studio** at home.

Art courses

A Drawing from scratch
For absolute beginners, the course is a relaxed introduction to basic drawing skills. No experience needed, and paper and pencils supplied. Weekly sessions from January to June.

B Express yourself through drawing
Draw confidently and develop your ability to express yourself while learning about design. Draw from life or from your imagination.

C Fashion design
Learn to create attractive clothes. Find out how to draw an **outfit** and get inspiration from nature and from old movies. Great for students with a general interest in fashion design.

D Hat making
Learn to produce your own absolutely fabulous and original hat to match your favourite outfit! Course tutor Maggie da Silva designed the hats for Channel 2's hit period drama *Upton Castle*.

E Oil painting
Learn to use oil paints like a professional artist. This course covers the main oil painting **techniques**. Your finished painting will be shown in the end-of-course exhibition.

F Painting portraits
By the end of this six-week course you will have made a good start on your first portrait, which you can then finish at home. You will learn about the relationship between colour and light, how to mix paints and how to use paintbrushes.

G Painting school
Over two consecutive days, experienced students develop their skills and find new artistic directions. Are you a bit **stuck** with something you've started to work on? Bring it along or start a new piece of work.

H Watercolour world
This course is suitable for experienced artists. Explore the possibilities that watercolour painting offers. Work from your own photographs or be inspired by nature or music.

9

2 Match the words in the box to the definitions. The words also appear in bold in the texts on page 55.

> materials   outfit   stuck   studio
> techniques   trouble

1. a set of clothes that you wear together
2. unable to continue with your work because it is too difficult
3. a room where a painter or photographer works
4. special skills or ways of doing things
5. problems or difficulties
6. things you use in order to do an activity

Vocabulary

formal language ▶ CB page 93

1 Find less formal synonyms for these words in the texts on page 55.

1. attempted (text 1)
2. intends (text 2)
3. skilful (text 3)
4. required (text A)
5. exhibited (text E)
6. complete (text F)

2 Rewrite the sentences to make them less formal.

1. Sonia is not a very good sculptor but she's an extremely skilful painter.
2. She has exhibited her work all over Europe and Asia.
3. She required a visa for some of the countries she visited.
4. I attempted to enrol in a course at the art college but my application arrived too late.
5. I hope to complete my studies early next year.
6. I intended to study painting and drawing.

3 In the sentences below, both alternatives have a similar meaning. Choose the more formal alternative.

1. If you *want/would like* to know more about the job, *tell us/let us know*.
2. The bus for London *sets off/departs* at 6 a.m.
3. For *further/more* information, please visit our website.
4. Any student who *has finished/completed* their task can leave now.
5. We *request/ask* that people close the windows when they leave the room.
6. We think that our course *provides/gives* a good introduction to the workplace.

Listening

Multiple choice, long text (Part 4)
▶ CB page 94

1 Match the verbs (1–6) to the words and phrases (A–F) to make collocations.

1	work	A	realistic
2	get	B	your time
3	waste	C	a character
4	create	D	a job
5	have	E	in a team
6	look	F	a problem

2 ▶ 26 For each question, choose the correct answer.

You will hear an interview with Brian Wentworth, a computer games designer.

1. Brian became a computer games designer because
   A his family encouraged him.
   B he got a job after graduation.
   C he learnt a lot about it at college.
2. The thing Brian finds most difficult about his job is
   A getting original ideas.
   B working with others.
   C staying motivated.
3. What Brian enjoys most about designing games is
   A making them look beautiful.
   B producing them technically.
   C seeing people playing them.
4. What does Brian think about *Village Games*?
   A It was impossible to write the story.
   B It was important to get the level right.
   C It was the most popular game he designed.
5. What does Brian think about children playing computer games?
   A They can develop important skills.
   B They should try other things like sport.
   C They spend too much time playing them.
6. What does Brian say about good games designers?
   A They have a lot of patience.
   B They are good players themselves.
   C They understand people's personalities.

Grammar
relative clauses ▶ CB page 95

1 Choose the correct alternatives to complete the article.

Drawing on the brain

In the late 1960s Betty Edwards, **(1)** *who/that* was an art teacher, began to wonder why her students, **(2)** *who/which* had successfully learnt languages, mathematics and other skills, found it so hard to learn to draw. She had also noticed that some students **(3)** *who/what* had found it really difficult at the beginning suddenly seemed to be able to draw perfectly well. She began to explore the research on the brain **(4)** *who/that* had been done by a famous scientist called Roger Sperry. Sperry was one of the people **(5)** *who/which* were responsible for discovering that the brain is divided into two halves, or hemispheres. Edwards developed a theory based on the research **(6)** *who/that* Sperry had done and in 1979 she wrote a book, **(7)** *that/which* she called *The New Drawing on the Right Side of the Brain*. The book, **(8)** *who/which* you can still buy today, has helped thousands of people learn to draw.

2 Join the sentences using non-defining relative clauses. Use the underlined sentence for the relative clause.

1 <u>Joseph Conrad is one of the world's greatest writers in English.</u> He was not a native speaker of that language.
2 His father died when Joseph was only 11. <u>His father had translated Shakespeare's plays into Polish.</u>
3 Joseph then lived with his uncle. <u>His uncle was a very careful man.</u>
4 However, he let Joseph go away to sea. <u>Joseph was only 16 at the time.</u>
5 His experiences on board ships inspired many of his novels. <u>The ships sailed to countries like India, Africa and Australia.</u>

Vocabulary
job skills ▶ CB page 96

1 ▶ 27 Listen to three people talking about their jobs. What do they do? Match each speaker to a job from the box.

dentist   DJ   firefighter   games designer
pilot   politician   scientist   secretary
surgeon   teacher

2 Listen again. What skill does each person like using most in their job? Choose a skill from the box for each speaker. There are two skills you do not need to use.

attention to detail   communication skills
leadership skills   problem solving   teamwork

prefixes ▶ CB page 96

3 Choose a meaning from the box for each prefix.

about yourself   again   not (x4)

1 im- ....
2 un- ....
3 re- ....
4 dis- ....
5 ir- ....
6 self- ....

4 Write the opposites of these words using the prefixes in Activity 3.

1 happy ....
2 agree ....
3 well ....
4 regular ....
5 employment ....
6 like ....
7 exciting ....
8 possible ....
9 patient ....
10 advantage ....

9

5 Complete the conversations with words using the prefixes in Activity 3.

1. **A:** Do people say that you are not very patient?
   B: Yes, they think I'm very _____ !
2. **A:** Would you like to do my job?
   B: No, I'd really _____ it!
3. **A:** Are you feeling okay?
   B: No, I'm feeling rather _____ , I'm afraid.
4. **A:** Would you like to work for yourself one day?
   B: Yes, I'd love to be _____ !
5. **A:** Would you like to change your job, even if you had to train again and get new skills?
   B: Oh yes, I'd love to _____ and get new skills!
6. **A:** I don't think it's possible to finish this project.
   B: I agree – it's _____ .
7. **A:** I never know when you're at work – your hours are not at all regular.
   B: No, I work very _____ hours, I know.
8. **A:** You don't look very happy about the news.
   B: No, I feel very _____ about it.

Speaking
Collaborative task (Part 3)
▶ CB page 97

1 Complete the phrases for introducing opinions with the words and phrases in the box. There is one word or phrase you do not need to use.

| idea | not sure | opinion | personally | seems |
| speaking | suppose | | | |

1. I _____ it's true that sport is popular – it's certainly on television a lot!
2. _____ , I think that going to a restaurant with friends is great.
3. I'm _____ how easy it is for people to make decisions about their career when they're still at school.
4. _____ for myself, I love playing tennis at the weekend.
5. In my _____ , everyone should relax at the weekend.
6. It _____ to me that sport is a great way to spend our free time.

2 Look at the exam task. What should you talk about?

A The advantages and disadvantages of the different activities for the friends.
B What each activity is and what to do.

> Some friends want to do something together at the weekend but they're not sure what the weather will be like. They all enjoy sport but don't want to spend much money.
>
> The pictures on the opposite page show some things they could do.
>
> Talk together about the different things they could do together and say which would be most fun.

3 Read the discussion below. Are these sentences true or false?

1. Carlos suggests going to a restaurant.
2. Carlos likes the idea of a restaurant.
3. Maria prefers the idea of shopping to jogging.
4. Carlos thinks that the friends should not run together.
5. Maria likes the idea of watching football.

4 Underline the expressions Maria and Carlos use to give their opinion.

Maria: I don't think that it's a good idea for them to go to a restaurant – it would be very expensive.

Carlos: That's a good point, but they can talk together in a restaurant and have a nice time. In my opinion, that's a great thing for them to do. I suppose it's nice to buy new things but I'm not sure that shopping is fun. Speaking for myself, I actually hate it! It's expensive too.

Maria: They all like sport, so I guess they could buy sports clothes if they went shopping. They might enjoy that, even though you don't! What do you think of the idea of jogging? That's sport, which they like, and it doesn't cost any money so it would be better than shopping.

Carlos: But they may all run at different speeds, so they wouldn't be doing it together. Personally, I think that watching sport is better for them – like going to a football game.

Maria: Okay – that's a good idea. It seems to me that we should choose something that is connected with sport but they can also share the experience. What about cycling?

Writing

Story (Part 2) ▶ CB page 98

1 Look at the exam task and the stories two students have written. Which of these tips for making your writing more interesting does each student follow?

1 Set the scene.
2 Include the main events.
3 Write a good ending.
4 Divide your story into paragraphs.
5 Add some dialogue to make your story more exciting.
6 Use adjectives, adverbs and verbs to make your story more interesting.

Your English teacher has asked you to write a story.
Your story must begin with this sentence.
I had always wanted to be famous until one day in March.
Write your **story** in about **100 words**.

2 Rewrite both stories. Improve them by following all the tips in Activity 1.

Student A

I had always wanted to be famous until one day in March. A few weeks earlier I had been chosen to read one of my short stories on a radio programme. As soon as I arrived a woman came up to me and said 'Come straight into the studio. You're on in five minutes. Watch the red light.' 'But what about the sound check?' I asked. 'There's no time for that!' she said, and went off. I realised that I'd left my glasses at home. I saw the red light come on but I couldn't see what I had written.

Student B

I had always wanted to be famous until one day in March. I sent a short story I had written about a horrible murder on a train in to a competition. The prize was €100 and the chance to read the story aloud on the radio.

When the competition results came out I was really disappointed. I hadn't won! Then that night I saw an exciting movie on TV about a murder on a train. It was exactly the same as my story. I felt really embarrassed and relieved that I hadn't won the competition.

10 What's it worth?

Grammar

passive voice ▶ CB page 103

1 You are going to read about some things that were sold on the internet. Read the article below and choose the best answer to the questions.

1 Who might find the cookie jar useful?
   A cooks
   B people on a diet
   C science fiction enthusiasts
2 What is the biggest selling point of the USB typewriter?
   A It was invented a long time ago.
   B It combines features of the past and the present.
   C It is easy to use.

2 Read the article again and decide if the sentences are true or false.
1 The cookie jar can be bought on the internet.
2 The cookie jar was designed to stop people taking biscuits.
3 Normal typewriters are still being widely used.
4 The USB typewriter can be attached to any computer.
5 The USB typewriter can be transported easily.
6 The USB typewriter was made in the USA.

3 Find and underline 11 passive verb forms in the article.

Articles
Politics | Obits | Education | Earth | Science | Defence | Health | Art

Necessary or just fun?

There are many strange things available to buy on the internet. But how useful are they? If you've bought something strange, did you find you needed it or has it never been used? Here are two things that might fit either category.

First, the UFO cookie jar. It is shaped like a spaceship with an alien sitting on top. The alien's eyes light up to frighten anyone who is tempted to open the jar. Once the biscuits have been placed in the jar, they are protected from anyone trying to lose weight but who tries to get a biscuit secretly! Any type of biscuit can be stored in the jar and the unusual design makes it a talking point.

Second, a 'back to the future' gadget! Typewriters may be things of the past but this invention means they can be brought back. It's the USB typewriter and it can be plugged into any computer with a USB port. It then becomes the computer's keyboard and is equipped with all the functions of a normal keyboard, although obviously it can't be carried around like a laptop! The typewriter was made in the USA.

10

4 Rewrite the sentences below in the active voice.

1. Advertisements are seen by many people before they buy a product.
2. Spring and summer fashions are presented by their designers in Fashion Weeks in London, Paris and Milan.
3. Models are helped with their hair and make-up by hair stylists and make-up artists.
4. The jewels were put on sale last week by the person who stole them.
5. The spring collection was designed by a famous Italian model.
6. This jacket has already been worn by somebody else.

5 Complete the second sentence in each pair using the passive voice.

1. People often advertise things they don't want on the internet.
   Unwanted things .... on the internet.
2. It's said that somebody buys a mobile phone every six seconds.
   It's said that a mobile phone .... every six seconds.
3. It's important to check the security of a site if you're buying something online.
   It's important that the security of a site .... if you're buying something online.
4. They have sold 12,000 tickets online.
   12,000 tickets .... online.
5. People often find good deals on cars on the internet.
   Good deals on cars .... on the internet.
6. They sold this antique painting to the highest bidder.
   This antique painting .... to the highest bidder.
7. They've pulled down those old shops in the High Street since last month.
   Those old shops in the High Street .... since last month.
8. They gave the owners of the old shops some money as compensation.
   The owners of the old shops .... some money as compensation.
9. People sometimes make mistakes when they buy clothes online.
   Mistakes .... by people when they buy clothes online.
10. Once I nearly bought a car that the owner was advertising for £5!
    Once I nearly bought a car that .... by the owner for £5!

Reading

Open cloze (Part 6)
▶ CB page 104

1 A student has written the right part of speech (e.g. prepositions, relative pronouns) but the wrong word to fill each gap in the exam task. Correct the student's mistakes.

> For each question, write the correct answer. Write **one** word for each gap.
>
> **Finders keepers**
> Have you ever thrown something away and then **regretted** it? How would you feel if the thing you threw away turned **(1)** _up_ to be worth thousands or even millions of euros? There are many stories of lucky people **(2)** _which_ lives were changed completely when they came across extremely valuable **items** someone else **(3)** _has_ thrown away. Things like lottery tickets, paintings or antiques **estimated** to be worth thousands of euros have all been found in rubbish. Once someone even found a large **(4)** _number_ of **cash concealed** inside an old car tyre.
>
> In many countries, anyone who finds something that has **(5)** _be_ thrown away or lost has the right to keep it after a certain amount of time has gone by. That's **(6)** _how_ you should always go through the pockets before you throw away an old jacket or pair of jeans. You might be throwing away more than you **intended**!

2 Find words in the text with similar meanings to the underlined words in these sentences.

1. I hadn't <u>planned</u> to stay up so late.
2. The jewels were <u>hidden</u> inside an old handbag.
3. She <u>guessed</u> the value of the antique to be over a thousand pounds.
4. He always <u>felt sorry about</u> breaking up with Susan.
5. Some of the <u>things</u> in the auction were quite cheap.
6. I don't like carrying around a lot of <u>money in notes and coins</u>.

61

10

Vocabulary
verbs and prepositions ▶ CB page 105

1 Choose the correct alternatives to complete the sentences.

1. Have you bought anything *from/on* that new department store in town?
2. When I'm shopping with friends I insist *on/to* having coffee breaks so we can chat.
3. The shop assistant apologised *by/for* the slow service.
4. I don't like lending clothes *from/to* my sister – I never get them back!
5. I hate companies that charge a lot *for/with* delivery.
6. I approve *about/of* companies that don't use a lot of plastic in their packaging.
7. I never succeed *about/in* getting discounts – I'm not good at bargaining!

2 Find and correct the mistakes with prepositions in the sentences.

1. I often borrow books for my friends.
2. I always listen at my friends when they tell me what clothes suit me.
3. My friend Carla always insists about good service in the local restaurant.
4. I often forget when I've made an appointment to a haircut and then I feel embarrassed.
5. My local library provides activities with children in the school holidays.
6. I lent my book for a friend but he lost it.
7. I think we recycle more plastic now compared by people in the past.
8. I gave a book for my aunt as a birthday present.

3 Complete the conversation by writing a preposition in each gap.

Sam: What are you going to do in the summer holidays?

Adam: I'm planning to go on a camping trip with some friends. Camping is cheaper compared (1) .... staying in a hotel because hotels charge a lot (2) .... a room in the summer.

Sam: Where are you going?

Adam: Well, I've been searching (3) .... information on the internet. There are loads of places we could go but I haven't succeeded (4) .... finding the perfect place yet. My friends insist (5) .... being near a beach.

Sam: Don't listen (6) .... them – it's more fun to go camping in the countryside. There are loads more activities to do there, like horse-riding and hiking.

Adam: I suppose I could just choose somewhere myself and hope they approve (7) .... it. By the way, can I borrow a tent (8) .... you?

Sam: Sorry, but I've already promised to lend my tent (9) .... my cousin Ana.

Vocabulary
shops and services ▶ CB page 106

1 Match products 1–8 to shops A–H.

1	sofa	A	sports shop
2	dictionary	B	bookshop
3	football	C	greengrocer's
4	sausages	D	butcher's
5	plants	E	shoe shop
6	boots	F	jeweller's
7	bracelet	G	furniture store
8	vegetables	H	florist's

2 Identify these shops not mentioned in Activity 1. You have been given the first letters to help you.

1. I buy all my clothes in small b.................... – I don't like big chain stores.
2. I spend all my time in my local c.................... s.................... because my laptop's always going wrong!
3. I get fresh bread from the b.................... every morning.
4. My local n.................... sells sweets and other things, as well as papers and magazines.
5. The s.................... outside my town is huge. It sells almost everything, including petrol.
6. I like shopping in d.................... s.................... because I can buy so many different things in one place.

3 ▶ 28 Listen and match each of the speakers (1–8) to a shop from Activities 1 and 2.

1. ....   5. ....
2. ....   6. ....
3. ....   7. ....
4. ....   8. ....

4 Listen again and match the speakers (1–8) to the replies (A–H).

A Oh, now we're here let's do our shopping – it might be better by the time we've finished.
B We have a good choice here. How big is the space you have for it?
C Of course. Would you like it sliced?
D Certainly. These are on special offer today – and they're very tasty.
E I have this but if you pay more it'll be better quality and you'll improve your game.
F No problem. Which operating system are you using?
G Just a minute and I'll measure your finger.
H Would you like red ones or a mix of red and yellow? They all smell beautiful.

5 ▶ 29 Listen and check your answers to Activity 4.

Grammar
get/have something done
▶ CB page 107

1 Correct the mistakes in five of the sentences.

1 I had my hair cut last week by an excellent hairdresser.
2 We are have our house repainted next week.
3 Julio will getting his jeans cleaned very soon – they're so dirty!
4 We are planning to get the car repaired as soon as possible.
5 It's so great that you can get everything deliver directly to your door!
6 When I travel I make sure that I have got films downloaded on to my tablet to watch on the flight.
7 My friend always having her shoes made by hand in Italy.
8 I'd love to have all my food cook for me by a chef!

2 Put the words in the correct order to make questions.

1 get / your / where / hair / do / cut / you / ?
2 car / often / serviced / how / get / you / do / your / ?
3 why / tattoo / done / get / did / you / a / ?
4 old / how / your / were / when / ears / pierced / you / got / you / ?
5 teeth / whitened / when / get / your / did / you / ?
6 shirt / made / get / you / did / that / where / ?
7 often / how / your / you / get / eyes / do / tested / ?
8 did / she / portrait / when / her / painted / have / ?

3 Match the questions in Activity 2 to the answers (A–H).

A Last month. I brush them well now to keep them looking good.
B Oh, I just ordered it online.
C I don't know. I just thought it looked good.
D I haven't had them pierced yet.
E Once a year, otherwise I don't think it's safe to drive.
F Every year – I think it's a good thing to do, especially if you wear glasses.
G At the hairdresser's on the corner. Do you like it?
H Last week. The artist was Italian, I think, and she's very pleased with it.

4 ▶ 30 Listen and check your answers to Activities 2 and 3.

Listening
Gap-fill (Part 3) ▶ CB page 108

1 ▶ 31 Listen and write the words you hear. Then check the spelling of the words in a dictionary.

1 .... 6 ....
2 .... 7 ....
3 .... 8 ....
4 .... 9 ....
5 .... 10 ....

2 ▶ 32 For each question, write the correct answer in the gap. Write one or two words or a number or a date or a time.

You will hear a man giving information on the radio about a sale taking place at a hotel.

The sale will take place at the **(1)** .... Hotel.
The cheapest parking costs **(2)** £ ....
(3) .... will be the most popular items for sale.
The sale starts at **(4)** .... a.m. on Saturday.
Older people should bring their **(5)** .... card.
Detailed information can be found in the local
(6) ....

10

Speaking

Collaborative task (Part 3) ▶ CB page 109

1 Look at the exam task. What should you **not** do?

A talk about possible free gifts
B explain which free gift you would like yourself
C discuss your ideas with your partner

> A new sports shop is opening in town. The owner wants to attract customers by giving each one a free gift that will also help to advertise the shop in the town.
>
> The pictures below show some gifts he could give his customers.
>
> Talk together about the different gifts the shop owner could give the customers, and say which would be best.

2 ▶ 33 Listen to Lena and Jakub doing the exam task in Activity 1. Are the statements true or false?

1 Lena thinks the shop should give expensive gifts.
2 Jakub suggests giving sports tickets.
3 Lena disagrees about the cost of the tickets.
4 They both like the idea of the bag, but Lena rejects it.
5 Jakub doesn't like the scarf as the free gift.
6 Lena agrees with Jakub about the scarf.
7 They both think the baseball cap is a good free gift.
8 They mention all the gifts before making a choice.

3 Listen again and complete the phrases the students used to respond to each other's opinions.

1 Jakub: That's .... – so we need to choose something cheap.
2 Lena: Yes, I ...., and also they don't really advertise the shop, do they?
3 Jakub: That's .... – I hadn't thought of that.
4 Jakub: I'm not sure that's the best choice, although I .... customers might like it.
5 Lena: You're ....! I hadn't noticed that.
6 Jakub: I'm not .... – my sister hates them!

Discussion (Part 4) ▶ CB page 109

4 ▶ 34 Look at the questions the examiner asks the students in Part 4. One student has answered the question, and the examiner has asked the other student to respond to what their partner has said. Match the answers (A–E) and the responses (F–J) to the questions (1–5). Then listen and check your answers.

1 Would you like to have a free gift from a shop?
2 Do you think giving a free gift is a good way to advertise a shop?
3 Do you often buy things you see advertisements for?
4 Do you like to buy the same things as your friends?
5 Do you think it's better to watch sport in a stadium or on television?

A I like to go shopping with my friends, and we do buy the same things quite often.

B That's easy – it's much better to watch it on television because it's more comfortable and it's not so noisy.

C Yes, it would be great! I love getting something for nothing.

D I don't think it's a very good idea, really. I think it would be better to have big advertisements in the town centre so that lots of people see them.

E Absolutely not! I only buy things I choose for myself, not things I see in advertisements.

F I don't agree – it's much more fun to be with lots of people watching a live game! You don't get any excitement on television.

G I agree with Lena. I don't think that people will notice the logo on any free gift, and also the gift might just get thrown away.

H I agree – I don't like advertisements at all, especially on television so I try not to watch them.

I No, it's not the same for me – even if I go shopping with my friends, we often buy different things.

J Actually I think it's better to pay for something you really want instead of just being given something you might not use.

Writing

Article (Part 2) ▶ CB page 110

1 Look at the exam task below and the answers two students have written and their teacher's comments on the right. Match the teacher's comments (1–2) to the students' answers (A–B).

> You see this advertisement on an English language website.
>
> **Articles wanted**
> **The perfect gift**
> How can we choose the perfect gift for a friend?
> Does the money we spend matter most or is it the thought that counts?
> Write an article answering these questions and we'll put it in our website.
>
> Write your **article** in about **100 words**.

2 Correct the grammar and spelling mistakes in the students' answers.

3 Rewrite the students' answers so that they follow their teacher's advice.

Student A

> Choosing the perfect gift for a friend is never easy. It's good to remember things your friend has said they are keen on. Maybe your friend have mentioned something they would like to have but can't afford to buy.
>
> For my birthday last year, my friends all get together and bought me some really great headphones I'd said them I wanted. I didn't have enough money to buy them myself so I was really pleased to get them as a present.

Student B

> It's not neccesary to spend any money at all on a gift for your friend. Use your imagination and creativity. For example, you could paint or draw a picture of part of your town your friend really likes.
>
> Some other good ideas are cooking your friend a delisious meal or getting together with others to record a video. Everyone can say what makes your friend special for them or tell a funny story.
>
> Things like these make really special gifts. In the end, it's the thought and not the money that counts.

1 Your article has a very good opening sentence that introduces the topic. Although it's fine to talk about your own experience, try to summarise the main idea of your article in the final sentence. There are also three grammar mistakes.

2 You've written a good article with some great suggestions for perfect gifts. Your article has a good final sentence that summarises your main idea but it would be better to turn your first sentence into a question to interest the reader. There are also three spelling mistakes.

4 Plan and write your answer to the exam task below.

> You see this advertisement on an English language website.
>
> **Articles wanted**
> **The perfect gift**
> Is there something you would really like to receive as a gift?
> What is it and why have you just got to have it?
> Write an article answering these questions and we'll put it in our website.
>
> Write your **article** in about **100 words**.

11 A small world

Vocabulary

travel and transport ▶ CB page 113

1 Choose the correct alternatives to complete the sentences.

1 When I visit another country I love to *go/take* sightseeing.
2 It's great when you can *share/take* photos with friends through the internet.
3 If you go to a popular restaurant it's a good idea to *put/make* a reservation before you go.
4 I love buying *memories/souvenirs* when I'm on holiday.
5 Some friends read *guidebooks/manuals* before they travel to a new country but I prefer to use the internet.
6 I'd love to take a *journey/trip* to the USA one day!

phrasal verbs of travel ▶ CB page 113

2 Read the sentences and match the phrasal verbs in sentences 1–4 to the patterns A–D.

1 I love **catching up with** news about my friends on email.
2 I usually **pick** my friend **up** from the station when she comes to visit me.
3 I often **set off** on holiday on a Friday night because there's less traffic.
4 It's always a good idea to **look for** cheap flights on the internet.

A verb with no object
B verb + preposition + object
C verb + object + preposition
D verb + preposition + preposition

3 Replace the underlined verbs in the sentences with the correct form of the phrasal verbs in the box.

end up	get rid of	look for	set off	set up	turn into

1 I hate <u>starting</u> on a journey early in the morning – I'm never awake!
2 On one holiday I got lost and <u>found myself</u> in a forest!
3 I <u>try to find</u> cheap hotels but they are often not very good.
4 I never <u>throw away</u> old photographs – they hold happy memories.
5 It's useful when people <u>place</u> webcams in different locations – it's easy to find out about the weather.
6 My last holiday <u>became</u> an absolute nightmare – everything went wrong!

66

Reading

Multiple choice, long text (Part 3)
▶ CB page 114

1 Read the article quickly and decide if this sentence is true or false.

The writer has never travelled to a foreign country.

2 Read the article in Activity 1 again. For each question, choose the correct answer.

1 How does the author feel when foreign tourists speak to him in their language?
  A pleased
  B confused
  C annoyed
  D ashamed

2 What does the author do if he is only going to visit a country for a short time?
  A He doesn't bother to learn the language.
  B He learns how to say the things that are absolutely necessary.
  C He tries to be polite to people even if he doesn't understand them.
  D He studies the language for a few weeks before he leaves home.

3 According to the author, why can knowing only a few words and phrases be a problem?
  A You can't have a proper conversation with anyone.
  B You might get an answer that is too difficult for you to understand.
  C You might look as if you have not tried hard enough to learn the language.
  D You might seem to know more of the language than you actually do.

4 According to the author, what might a local person think when a tourist tries to speak the local language?
  A 'I'll try and help them since they've obviously tried to learn my language.'
  B 'Even if I try and answer their question, I don't think they'll understand.'
  C 'I'm in a hurry and I can't waste time trying to talk to these people.'
  D 'They should learn my language properly if they want to try and speak it.'

5 What is the author trying to do in this article?
  A complain about foreign tourists
  B admit that he is not good at learning languages
  C tell you what to study when you learn a foreign language
  D persuade travellers that learning languages has benefits

On the road in a foreign language

How often have you had the experience of a tourist in your country asking you a question in their language and just expecting you to understand them? How do you feel when this happens? Perhaps you don't have any idea what they're saying and you hurry away in **confusion** and **embarrassment**. Maybe you know the language and feel proud that you are able to respond. If, on the other hand, you're anything like me, you probably feel **irritated** or even a little angry.

When this happens to me, I do feel irritated, especially if the person just repeats whatever they have said in a louder voice. Nevertheless, I try to be polite and friendly, of course, even if I still don't understand. I use the experience to remind myself how important it is to try and learn the language of the places I visit. I know that I'm **unlikely** to be able to learn much if I'm only going to be there for a few days rather than a few weeks but I can at least try to learn the things I will almost certainly need to say. I mean **greetings** like 'hello' and 'goodbye', the words for 'please' and 'thank you', how to ask politely for goods or services, how to ask how much they cost and how to ask for directions.

You might be thinking that there's not much point knowing how to ask a question like that if you are not going to be able to understand the reply. That has happened to me sometimes, but I still believe that trying to say something in the local language is a good thing. At least you've shown you are willing to make an effort and that often makes all the difference. Perhaps the person you ask will show you where to go or even take you there. If you just ask them in your language, they might not even bother to answer and you will almost certainly have failed to make a new friend.

67

3 Complete the sentences with words formed from the words in bold in the text.

1 I'm .... ! What do we have to do here?
2 I've never been so .... in my life! I went bright red.
3 I find it really .... when people talk in loud voices on their mobile phones.
4 It's .... to rain later. Take an umbrella.
5 The new teacher .... the class and told us her name.

Vocabulary
compound adjectives ▶ CB page 115

1 Match 1–8 to A–H to make compound adjectives.

1 one-   A made
2 self-   B fashioned
3 energy-   C way
4 hand   D lit
5 old-   E minute
6 world-   F service
7 brightly-   G famous
8 twenty-   H efficient

2 Complete the compound adjectives with the words in the box.

assured   confident   paid   painted
sewn   written

1 hand- ...., hand- ....
2 self- ...., self- ....
3 well-/badly- ...., well-/badly- ....

3 Complete the sentences with compound adjectives from Activities 1 and 2.

1 I hate eating in .... restaurants on holiday. I prefer to have a waiter who brings me my food.
2 I'd love to buy a .... ticket to Australia and never come back.
3 I like to buy .... pictures of places I visit. They are much nicer than mass-produced souvenirs.
4 My aim in life is to have a .... job so that I have plenty of money.

Grammar
future forms ▶ CB page 116

1 Complete the conversations with the most appropriate future form of the verbs in brackets.

1 A: I don't think Georgina .... (get on) with Ryan. They're too different from one another.
   B: I don't know about that. I'm sure she .... (like) him.
2 A: Where .... (you /meet) Chrysa?
   B: Outside the main post office in Athens.
   A: When?
   B: We .... (meet) at 1.30 and .... (have) lunch with some friends of hers.
3 A: What shall we get Ahmed's mother? We .... (have to) give her something since she's invited us to stay.
   B: We could get her something typical from here.
   A: I know my sister .... (get) her some of those earrings we saw last week, so we could buy her a matching bracelet.
4 A: What are your plans for the future?
   B: I .... (study) tourism but before that I .... (take) six months off to travel. I .... (visit) some relatives in Australia.

2 Choose the correct alternatives to complete the sentences.

1 What *do you do/are you going to do* this summer?
2 What time *does your plane leave/will your plane leave*?
3 Look at those huge dark clouds. It looks like *it rains/is going to rain* later.
4 Next Monday *I have/I having* a French lesson in the evening. After that *I probably study/I'll probably study* for the test on Wednesday.
5 A: *Are you having/Do you have* a dessert?
   B: No, *I just have/I'm just going to have* tea now because I never drink coffee late at night.
6 The meeting *starts/will starting* at 8.00 – let's meet at the station at 7.15.
7 A: What *do you do/are you going to do* with all this paint?
   B: Paint my bedroom!
8 *I'll have/I'm having* lunch with Pete tomorrow. *We meet/are meeting* at Wendy's Diner at noon. Would you like to join us?
9 What time *does the lesson start/is the lesson starting*?
10 I'm sure *you'll have/you're having* a great time at Lee's party on Saturday.

Speaking
General questions (Part 1)
▶ CB page 117

1 ▶ 35 Listen to an examiner asking two students questions in Phase 2 of Part 1. Which student gives the better answers, Maria or Juan? Choose the best reason for your answer.

A The student gives short answers without any reasons or details.

B The student answers the questions fully and gives interesting details.

Individual long turn (Part 2)
▶ CB page 117

2 Look at the photographs. Complete the descriptions of the photographs using the words and phrases in the boxes. There is one word or phrase in each box you do not need to use.

Photograph A

classroom hair happy jeans maps pencils pictures sweater T-shirt

I can see two girls who are studying together in a (1) .... On the wall behind them there are some (2) .... The girls are sitting at a table and working together. The girl on the left is wearing a (3) .... with long sleeves but the girl on the right is wearing a (4) .... which has short sleeves. They both have long (5) .... which is tied back in a kind of ponytail. They're both looking at a big book which has (6) .... in it, like an atlas. The girl on the left is making notes on a piece of paper and the other girl is watching her. They both look quite (7) .... and interested in what they're doing. There are two pencil cases on the table and a lot of (8) .... on the table in front of them. The girl is writing with one of the pencils.

Photograph B

bag bridge buildings casual clear jeans river suitcase T-shirt

I can see a city, and there are a group of students who are standing near a big (9) .... which goes over a wide (10) .... It's a very famous place and it looks very old. There are a lot of (11) .... on the other side of the river but I can't see any near the students. The students are sightseeing together in the city. In the middle of the group there's a woman wearing (12) .... and a (13) .... with short sleeves. She's carrying a (14) .... on her left shoulder. On the other hand, two other students on the right are also carrying bags but they're wearing clothes with long sleeves. All the students are wearing (15) .... clothes. They're all talking to each other and some of them are looking at the view. They're enjoying themselves. The sky is (16) .... and I can't see any clouds so it's a nice day.

3 ▶ 36 Listen and check your answers to Activity 2.

4 Listen again and decide if these sentences are true or false.

1 Only Maria uses prepositions of place.
2 Only Juan uses linking words.
3 Only Maria describes the clothes the people are wearing.
4 Both students describe the photographs in detail.

Listening

Multiple choice, pictures (Part 1)
▶ CB page 118

1 ▶ 37 For each question, choose the correct answer.

1 Which activity does the woman decide to do?

2 Which photograph are they talking about?

3 When will the new leisure centre open officially?

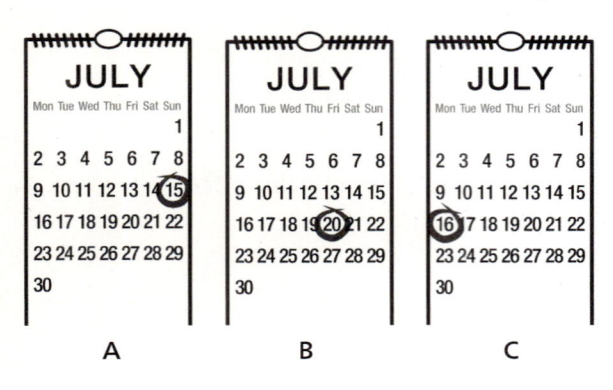

4 How will the family travel to their holiday destination this year?

5 What does the man decide to eat for lunch?

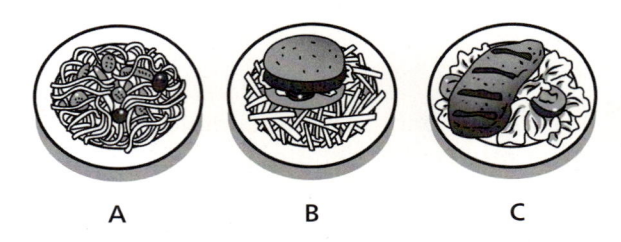

6 What did the woman like best about being on holiday?

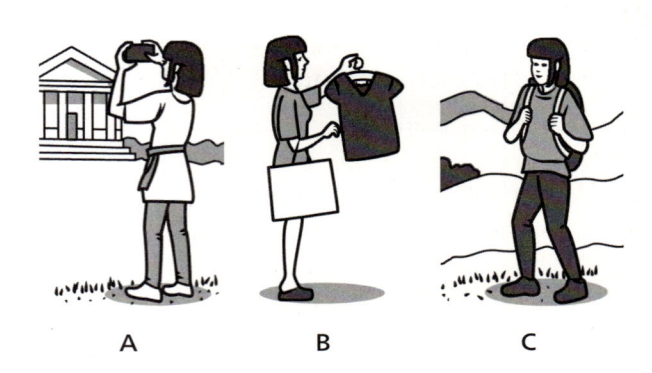

7 When will the plane take off?

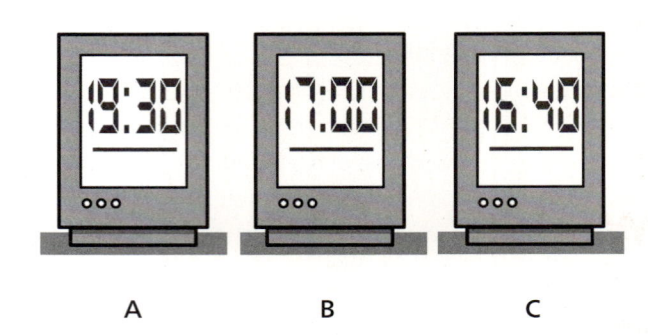

Grammar

will and be going to ▶ CB page 119

1 Complete the conversation with the most appropriate future form, *will* or *be going to*.

A: You **(1)** .... be pleased to hear that I **(2)** .... get a dog.

B: At last! I'm sure you **(3)** .... be glad you did. You **(4)** .... be able to take him for walks. Have you decided what kind you **(5)** .... get?

A: Well, I've been looking at some websites on dogs and I can't make up my mind. I think I **(6)** .... get either a cocker spaniel or a golden retriever if I can.

B: When **(7)** .... buy it?

A: I **(8)** .... (not) buy one, actually. I **(9)** .... get a dog from an animal refuge. Do you want to come with me? Maybe you **(10)** .... find a friend for Eddie.

2 Find and correct the mistakes with *will* and *be going to* in the sentences. Tick (✔) the sentences that are correct.

1 You can't carry those heavy boxes on your own. I'm going to help you with them.
2 I can see you're very busy. I'll come back later.
3 Naira has decided that she will not get a dog after all.
4 Alberto bought those new jeans. He'll wear them to the party tonight.
5 A: Do you want to share a pizza?
   B: I think I'll just have a salad, actually.
6 I don't feel very well. I think I'll go and lie down for a minute.
7 Pablo made an appointment at the hairdresser's. He'll have his hair cut.
8 In ten years' time most of my friends will be married.

Writing

Email (Part 1) ▶ CB page 120

1 Look at the exam task. What do you have to do?

A Tell your friend you've got a job too. Explain why you can't talk to her. Describe a place in your country and say why your friend should visit it.

B Tell your friend you're pleased about her job. Tell her when you can talk to her. Suggest a place she should describe and mention something that has changed there.

Read this email from your English-speaking friend Daphne and the notes you have made.

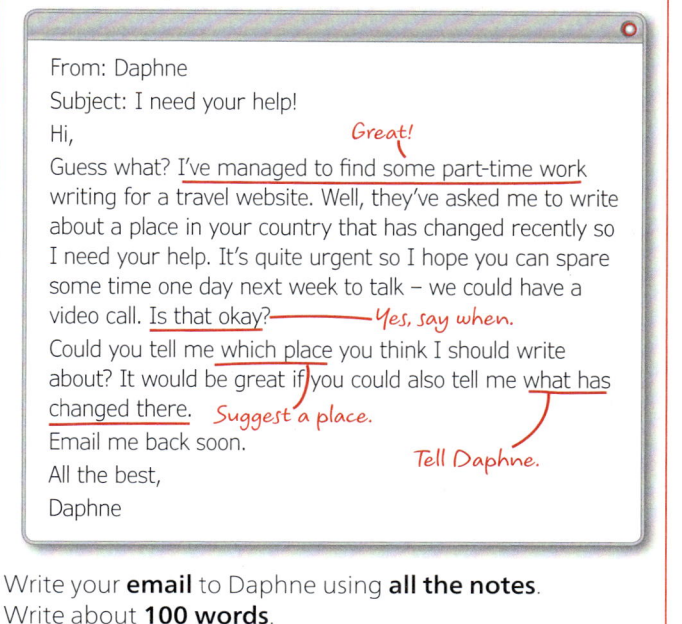

From: Daphne
Subject: I need your help!
Hi,
Guess what? I've managed to find some part-time work — *Great!*
writing for a travel website. Well, they've asked me to write about a place in your country that has changed recently so I need your help. It's quite urgent so I hope you can spare some time one day next week to talk – we could have a video call. Is that okay? — *Yes, say when.*
Could you tell me which place you think I should write about? It would be great if you could also tell me what has changed there. — *Suggest a place.* / *Tell Daphne.*
Email me back soon.
All the best,
Daphne

Write your **email** to Daphne using **all the notes**.
Write about **100 words**.

2 Look at the email a student wrote. In some places he has used very formal language. His teacher has underlined these parts of the email. Replace them with the informal expressions in the box.

all the best   but   I can   it's great to hear
let me know   too

Hi Daphne,

Thanks for your email. **(1)** It is excellent to know that you got a job. **(2)** I would be able to talk to you next Tuesday. I've been thinking about which place you should describe. Why don't you write about my town? Some people complain about the city council, **(3)** however, they've banned cars in the centre of the city, which is a big improvement, in my opinion. They've started organising all sorts of cultural events **(4)** as well. Last month there was even a Moroccan craft market!

(5) I look forward to hearing what time you would like to speak on Tuesday.

(6) Yours sincerely,
Nilo

---

3 Plan and write your answer to the exam task in Activity 1.

12 Extreme

Listening
Multiple choice, short texts (Part 2) ▶ CB page 123

1 ▶ **38** For each question, choose the correct answer.

1 You will hear two friends talking about a website.
   What do they both think about it?
   A It's very easy to use. **B** It's popular with many people.
   C It's useful for getting instant news.

2 You will hear a woman talking to a friend about sky diving.
   What does she enjoy most about it?
   A the team she's part of **B** the excitement she feels
   C the different places she goes to

3 You will hear a man talking to a friend about the travelling he does.
   What surprised him about his latest trip?
   A how cheap it was **B** how kind the local people were
   C how easy it was to get to places

4 You will hear two friends talking about a television documentary they both saw.
   What was the woman disappointed about?
   A the people who were in it **B** the lack of information
   C the time it was shown

5 You will hear two friends talking about a cycling race they took part in.
   What do they agree about it?
   A It was well organised. **B** It took a long time to complete.
   C It was an exciting experience.

6 You will hear two friends talking about an adventure holiday they've heard about.
   The man wants the woman to
   A find out more about it. **B** help him get fitter.
   C persuade their friends to join them.

Grammar
zero and first conditionals ▶ CB page 124

1 Match 1–6 to A–F to form zero conditional sentences.

1 When people eat the wrong type of food,   **A** she cries.
2 If you heat ice,   **B** they stay healthy.
3 When my baby sister is hungry,   **C** they get ill.
4 If people take regular exercise,   **D** they get hurt.
5 If people go out in the rain,   **E** it melts.
6 Unless people take care on mountains,   **F** they get wet.

2 Write a zero conditional sentence with *if* for each pair of sentences.

1. I don't have anything to do on Saturday mornings. I have breakfast in a café.
2. I have a match. I have something quick to eat at home.
3. I walk to the park. It's a nice day.
4. It's raining. My friend drives me to work.
5. The coach tells us off for playing badly. We lose.
6. We win. He takes us all out for a pizza.

3 Find and correct the mistakes in the sentences.

1. You'll never swim fast if you practise a lot.
2. I tell you if I decide to take that climbing course.
3. If we'll miss the last train, we'll have to walk home.
4. Unless you will work hard, you won't be successful.
5. You feel very proud if you get to the top of the mountain.
6. If you ask me to do something, I do it for you.

4 Complete the article with the correct form of the verbs in the box.

change   get (x2)   look   respond
roll   speak   stop   treat

The lion whisperer

What do you think a lion will do if you walk up to it and kiss it on the nose? Eat you for breakfast or purr like a pussycat? According to animal behaviourist Kevin Richardson, if you **(1)** .... down to the lion's level, **(2)** .... into its eyes and **(3)** .... softly, it **(4)** .... over and go to sleep. What's more, Kevin, who is also known as the 'lion whisperer', gets so friendly with the lions he works with that he can actually sleep with them.

But what will happen if the lion **(5)** .... hungry during the night? Will you become his next snack? Not at all, apparently. Kevin says that if you **(6)** .... lions with respect, they **(7)** .... with respect, affection and even love. He thinks we've been getting it wrong with animals like lions. Perhaps if we **(8)** .... trying to dominate them, they **(9)** .... their attitudes to humans and begin to see us as friends.

Vocabulary
sport and leisure
▶ CB page 125

1 Match verbs 1–8 to nouns A–H to make collocations connected with different sports.

1	kick	A	a goal
2	throw	B	a sport
3	run	C	a football
4	enter	D	a competition
5	do	E	a bike
6	hit	F	a marathon
7	score	G	a javelin
8	ride	H	a hockey ball

2 ▶ 39 Listen to four people talking about their sport. Match each speaker (1–4) to a sport from the box. There are two you do not need to use.

athletics   cycling   football   hiking   surfing
tennis

1 ....   2 ....
3 ....   4 ....

3 A student has completed these sentences about sport and leisure with the words in the box, but they have made some mistakes. Find and correct the mistakes.
Tick (✔) the words that are correct.

compete   enter   experienced   fitness
instructor   join in   practice   prize   safety
train

1. Tobias has decided to *join in* a surfing competition next month but he doesn't expect to win a *prize*.
2. She's a wonderful *instructor*. She always shows us what to do and encourages the shy, less confident members of the group to *enter* too.
3. Kim has started to *compete* for the marathon next year. She runs a couple of kilometres every day and does exercises to develop her overall *safety*.
4. If you are not an *experienced* climber, you need to use a lot of *fitness* equipment.
5. I haven't had enough *practice* rollerblading to *train* against other people in races or competitions.

do, go, play ▶ CB page 125

4 Complete the sentences with the correct form of *do*, *go* or *play*.

1 Have you ever _____ baseball? It's a great game.
2 My grandfather _____ dancing at a local club a couple of times a month.
3 A lot of young people _____ golf nowadays. It's become quite fashionable.
4 We all had to _____ gymnastics when I was at school. Some students loved it but a few of us hated it.
5 My sister cracked a tooth when she was _____ hockey. She got hit in the mouth by the ball.
6 Let's _____ horse-riding next weekend.
7 A lot of people wear headphones and listen to music whenever they _____ jogging.
8 Tina's been _____ karate for six months now.
9 My grandmother has been _____ yoga all her adult life. She's incredibly flexible.

Grammar
second conditional ▶ CB page 126

1 Find and correct the mistakes in the sentences. Tick (✔) the sentences that are correct.

1 If I were bitten by a poisonous spider, I will go straight to the hospital.
2 If I see a big vicious dog coming towards me, I would run away.
3 If I were lost in a forest, I would stay where I was and wait for help.
4 If a friend of mine fell into the water, I would cover them with a blanket after I had pulled them out.
5 If I saw a shark while I was swimming, I will try to swim away.
6 If a bear comes up to me while I was hiking in the woods, I would try to frighten it away.

2 Complete the sentences with the correct form of the verbs in the box.

| hit | lie | put | stand | tell | walk |

A I wouldn't. I _____ downhill.
B I wouldn't. I _____ face down and keep still.
C I would too but I _____ them to take their wet clothes off first.
D I wouldn't. I _____ still and look away.
E I wouldn't. I _____ it on the nose.
F I would too but I _____ some ice on the bite first.

3 Match the sentences in Activity 1 to the responses in Activity 2.

4 Match the responses in Activity 2 to these reasons.

1 It might lose interest and go away.
2 They wouldn't get warm quickly enough otherwise.
3 It would stop the poison spreading.
4 It might frighten it away.
5 They just get more aggressive if you make eye contact with them.
6 You are more likely to find a river or stream there.

5 Complete the blog entry. Write one word in each gap.

Indoor skydiving

Have you ever wondered what it (1) _____ be like if you (2) _____ fly like a bird, but you didn't know how to find out? Indoor skydiving centres have vertical wind tunnels that let you experience what the world (3) _____ be like if there (4) _____ no gravity. What (5) _____ it be like? Well, you (6) _____ certainly feel you were able to fly! So before you start real skydiving, try the indoor version. It's amazing!

Speaking
Collaborative task (Part 3) ▶ CB page 127

1 Look at the exam task. Are the statements about it true or false?

1 You must talk about the advantages of hiking.
2 The man can take whatever he wants with him in his bag.
3 The man has to carry the bag so he doesn't want it to be heavy.
4 You must talk about which thing or things would be most useful for him.

A young man is going hiking for the day with friends in the countryside. He wants to take a small bag with him that is not too heavy.

The pictures on the next page show some things he could take in his bag.

Talk together about the different things he could take in his bag, and say which would be most useful.

2 ▶ 40 Listen to two students discussing the task. Did they

1. discuss all the items?
2. give their own opinions?
3. ask their partner for their opinions?
4. say which item or items would be most useful?
5. sound interested in each other's ideas?

3 Complete the expressions the students used to agree, disagree and make suggestions with the words in the box. Then listen again to check your answers.

| already | agree | disagree | don't | guess | let's |
| opinion | point | right | think | understand |

1. What do you .... about the camera?
2. The book will be heavy too, ... you think?
3. You're .... – that's a good ....
4. I .... – the hat won't cover his arms and legs.
5. We've .... said he must take the phone and a cap.
6. In my .... it's essential to have something to eat.
7. I .... he mustn't leave that behind.
8. I .... what you're saying.
9. So .... say just the phone and the food and drink.
10. Okay – I .... with you.

Discussion (Part 4) ▶ CB page 127

4 Match the answers to the questions.

1. Do you enjoy hiking or do you prefer to travel around by car?
2. When you go on holiday, do you take a lot of bags or do you travel light?
3. Do you enjoy doing lots of activities when you're away or would you rather take it easy?
4. Who do you usually like to go on trips with?

A   I hate carrying a lot of stuff when I go away, so I usually only take a rucksack. My friends all take more than me, and then they have to pack it and unpack it all the time. I think it's better to travel light!

B   I love relaxing when I'm on holiday, so I never plan to do much. I think I need a break from everyday life! But if I'm visiting a new city then I do enjoy sightseeing because I think it's important to understand the history of a place.

C   It's different every time. I generally go on trips with my friends, because we share the same interests and we have fun together. Sometimes though I do go away with my family – like one year we all stayed in a big villa near the beach, and my cousins and lots of other relatives came to join us. That was great fun.

D   I think that hiking is good when there aren't too many hills but you need to be fit if you want to walk a long way. You can see more places if you travel by car and travel longer distances, but you don't really see the countryside.

12

Reading

Multiple choice, short texts (Part 1)
▶ CB page 128

1 Choose the sentence that best describes the meaning of the first sentence.

1 Sharp bend ahead!
   A Be careful because there is a dangerous corner in front of you.
   B Always look in front of you when there is a dangerous corner.
2 This door is alarmed.
   A Opening the door will set off the alarm.
   B Please ring the alarm before opening the door.
3 In case of fire, use the stairs.
   A Use the stairs in case there is a fire.
   B Use the stairs when there is a fire.
4 Don't leave your bag unattended in the airport.
   A Keep your bag with you at all times in the airport.
   B Leave your bag with an attendant, not in the airport.
5 Leave the building immediately if the fire alarm goes off.
   A Stay in the building unless there is a fire.
   B Don't stay in the building if the fire alarm sounds.

2 For each question, choose the correct answer.

1

This film contains scenes that may be unsuitable for children under 12.

   A Children under 12 are not allowed to see this film.
   B This film is not recommended for children under 12.
   C This film has scenes with children under 12.

2

DANGER: CLEANER AT WORK. FLOOR MAY BE WET.

   A Take care because you may fall.
   B The cleaner may be doing **dangerous** work.
   C If you make the floor wet, the cleaner will come.

3

STAND BEHIND THE YELLOW LINES WHEN A TRAIN IS APPROACHING.

   A Do not cross the yellow lines if a train is coming.
   B Passengers should always wait for trains behind the yellow lines.
   C There is danger behind the yellow lines if a train is coming.

4

To: Mr Jackson
From: Climbing International

Unfortunately, bad weather conditions are continuing to cause avalanches high on the mountain so the expedition has been postponed for at least a week.

The email from Climbing International
   A warns Mr Jackson not to go on the expedition.
   B explains why the expedition has been **delayed**.
   C rearranges the expedition for a date in the future.

5

EXTREME ACTIVITY DAY
AT WESTFIELD PARK, SATURDAY 15 MAY

Tickets available on the gate or in advance with 10% discount. Everyone **welcome** but you must be over 18 to do parachuting.

The advert says that the activity day
   A can be fun for all the family.
   B is cheaper if you buy tickets before 15 May.
   C has some activities that are for children.

3 Complete the sentences with the words in bold in Activity 2. There is one word you do not need to use.

1 Of course you can bring your dog. Pets are always .... here!
2 Our plane was .... for two hours because of a technical problem.
3 The train is now .... its final destination.
4 We asked the hotel receptionist and she .... a restaurant where they serve fresh fish.
5 ...., we won't be able to join you.
6 Everyone knows that lions are very .... animals.

Vocabulary
confusing words ▶ CB page 129

1 Choose the correct alternatives to complete the sentences..

1 I never *remember/remind* my friends' birthdays – it's very embarrassing!
2 Here, *bring/take* this with you – you might need it.
3 It's great to go on day *trips/travels* with my family.
4 Please *bring/take* your homework to the next class so that I can mark it.
5 I often need *remembering/reminding* about work I have to finish.
6 Would you like to *come/go* to my house and have dinner with me tonight?
7 Let's *come/go* to the cinema on Saturday.
8 I find that *travel/trip* is often very tiring.

2 Choose from the pairs of words in the box to complete the sentences. You may need to change the form of some of the words.

| learn/teach | lend/borrow | live/stay |
| lose/miss | work/job | |

1 I'd love to find .... in another country one day.
2 It's often a mistake to .... money to friends – it can cause problems.
3 If I .... the eight o'clock bus, I get to work late.
4 When I'm travelling, I love to .... in small family-run hotels.
5 I'm terrible with small objects – I keep .... my car keys!
6 I'd love to .... in a home in an extreme climate – it must be exciting.
7 Being a ski instructor is my ideal ....
8 I think that it's very hard to .... another language quickly.
9 It's getting more and more difficult to .... money from a bank nowadays.
10 It must be fun to .... people to ski – I'd love to do that!

Writing
Story (Part 2) ▶ CB page 130

1 Look at the exam task and the stories two students have written. Which of these tips for making your writing a story does each student follow?

1 Set the scene by saying what the situation is.
2 Include the main events.
3 Write an interesting ending.
4 Divide your story into paragraphs.
5 Add some direct speech to make your story more exciting.

> Your English teacher has asked you to write a story.
> Your story must begin with this sentence.
> *I didn't believe I could do it.*
> Write your **story** in about **100 words**.

Student A

> I didn't believe I could do it. When my friend suggested joining an indoor rock climbing gym, my immediate reaction was 'No way!' But one afternoon I went to watch him. Reaching the top of the wall obviously made my friend feel fantastic so I decided to give it a try. As I got further and further above the ground my arms and legs began to shake. I was terrified. I was just about to give up when a voice inside me said, 'Not this time!' Somehow I got to the top of the wall.

Student B

> I didn't believe I could do it. Speaking in public is very scary. Although everyone hates speaking in public, I'm really scared of it.
>
> My teacher told me I had to take part in a class debate. She said she was sure I would do it well.
>
> I spent weeks planning what I could say. I practised hundreds of times in front of the mirror and even recorded myself. Even so, I was still worried.
>
> The big day came. I got up to speak and somehow it all came out just as I had planned.

2 Write the stories again and improve them so that they both follow all the tips in Activity 1.

Vocabulary bank

Using a dictionary

What's in a dictionary?

A dictionary does not just tell you the definition of a word. It also gives you the information you need in order to be able to put the word into a sentence, how to spell it and how to pronounce it.

1 Match the different parts of the dictionary entry (1–8) to their explanations (A–H).

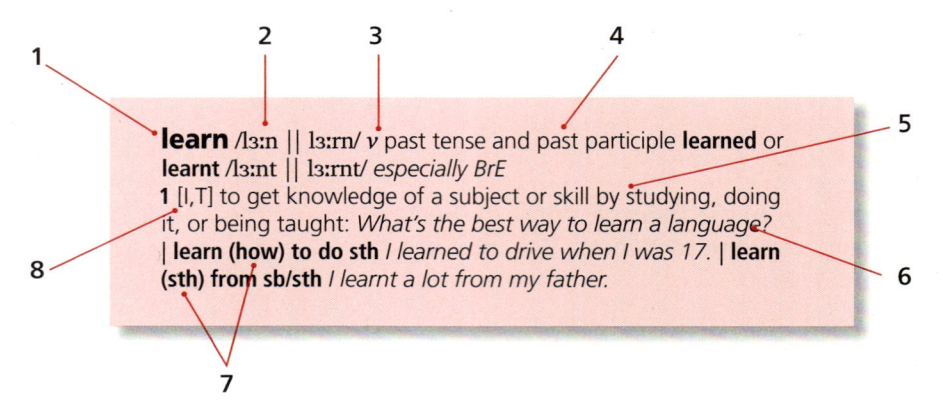

> **learn** /lɜːn || lɜːrn/ *v* past tense and past participle **learned** or **learnt** /lɜːnt || lɜːrnt/ *especially BrE*
> **1** [I,T] to get knowledge of a subject or skill by studying, doing it, or being taught: *What's the best way to learn a language?* | **learn (how) to do sth** *I learned to drive when I was 17.* | **learn (sth) from sb/sth** *I learnt a lot from my father.*

- **A** an example sentence that shows how the word is used
- **B** the pronunciation of the word in both British English and American English
- **C** what prepositions you need and how you use the word with an object or other verb
- **D** extra information about the word such as past forms, plural forms, whether it is countable or uncountable (for a noun), etc.
- **E** the word
- **F** the definition of the word
- **G** the type of word it is
- **H** for a verb, whether the verb is transitive (= needs an object) or intransitive (= does not need an object)

understanding pronunciation

You can listen to the pronunciation of a word using an online dictionary, although it can be helpful to be able to work out the pronunciation of a new word for yourself too. At the beginning of a dictionary you can find a list of phonemic symbols with example words which can help you to understand the pronunciation of a word. Word stress is shown by a ' symbol. This symbol appears just before the stressed syllable.

2 Which word is represented by the phonemic symbols?

1. /ɪmˈpɔːtənt/   *important / impossible*
2. /tʃɔɪs/   *choice / choose*
3. /ˈlɪtl/   *later / little*
4. /ɪkˈsept/   *expect / except*
5. /ˈrekɔːd/   *record (n) / record (v)*

VOCABULARY BANK

knowing a word

3 Look at the dictionary entry and answer the questions.

> **include** /inˈkluːd/ *v* [T]
> **1** If one thing includes another, the second thing is part of the first: *The price includes lunch.* | **be included in sth** *Service is included in the bill.*
> **2** to allow someone to be part of a group or activity [≠ **exclude**]: *The other children refused to include her in their games.*

1 How is the word spelt?
2 What kind of word is it?
3 Does it need an object?
4 How many different meanings does the word have?
5 What is the opposite of the word?
6 What preposition comes after the word?
7 Does the word have a short or long second vowel?
8 Is the stress of the word on the first or second syllable?
9 *A taxi to the airport is included in the cost of your trip.*
  Is the word used correctly in this sentence?
10 *When I sent out the invitations, I forgot to include. Sorry about that!*
  Is the word used correctly in this sentence?

recording a word

4 Think about the record you keep of new vocabulary and answer the questions.

1 Which items from the dictionary entries above do you include in your vocabulary records?
2 Which of these items do you think you should keep a record of? Why?
3 How often do you look at your vocabulary records? What do you do to try to learn some of those words? Which techniques work best for you?

It is important to keep good vocabulary notes so that they can help you to understand the meaning and how to use the word in future. Use your notes for revision but make sure you do more than just look at the notes. Try some of these things:

- **Think** about the meaning of the word. Is it positive or negative?
- **Think** about what words go together with this word.
- **Group** words in your list together, e.g. synonyms, same sound, same type of word.
- **Try** to connect to the word personally. Do you like it? Does it remind you of anything or anybody?
- **Try** to use the word in a sentence. Or try to use five words in a paragraph.

Collocations

prepositional phrases

1 Complete the table with the prepositions in the box.

at   by   for   in   on   out of

1	board fire foot purpose time	4	date order sight stock work
2	a hurry fact pieces private/public stock	5	accident car hand mistake name
3	all last least present the same time	6	a long time a reason ever example instance

2 Complete the sentences with words and phrases from Activity 1.

1 The plate was in .... on the kitchen floor. Perhaps the cat had knocked it off the table.
2 I'm afraid these shoes are out of .... We have a delivery tomorrow so they should be in .... then.
3 Please make sure you come to class on .... tomorrow. Don't be late.
4 Can I speak to you in .... , please? I don't want other people to hear.
5 She was very rude to him but at .... she apologised the next day.
6 My daughter watches TV and chats to her friends online at ....
7 My computer's broken so I've got to write my homework out by ....
8 The coffee machine's out of .... Hopefully, it'll be fixed tomorrow.
9 My car was in the garage on Tuesday so I came to class on ....
10 There were more than 300 passengers on .... the plane.
11 I haven't seen my friend for .... so I'm really looking forward to her visit.
12 I think that everything in life happens for ....

79

adjectives and prepositions

3 Complete the table with the prepositions in the box.

about   at   for   of   to   with

afraid fond jealous proud tired	1	famous grateful late responsible suitable	4 ....
confident curious happy sure worried	2	familiar kind married polite similar	5 ....
bad brilliant clever good terrible	3	angry bored happy satisfied upset	6 ....

4 Complete each sentence with an adjective and a preposition from Activity 3.

1 Kevin is .... maths. He started a maths degree when he was just 14!
2 My best friend met Justin Bieber. I'm so .... her! Why wasn't it me?
3 I'm .... my job these days. I'd like to do something more interesting.
4 This toy isn't .... children under three. There are too many small pieces.
5 My sister graduated top of her class. The whole family is really .... her.
6 We should all be more .... each other. It's not difficult to say 'please' and 'thank you'.
7 I'm the manager. I'm .... the whole company, including 20 staff.
8 Teresa was .... an important meeting today. Her boss wasn't happy about that.
9 I'm .... my girlfriend. How could she forget my birthday?
10 I'm .... cooking. I burn everything!
11 We're all very .... your help. We couldn't have done it without you.
12 Where have you been? Your mother was really .... you! Why didn't you call to say you were all right?

verbs and prepositions

5 Complete the table with the prepositions in the box.

at   for   from   of   on   to

apologise apply ask look wait	1	belong invite lend listen reply	4 ....
borrow choose prevent protect recover	2	approve consist dream remind take care	5 ....
concentrate decide depend plan insist	3	arrive laugh look point stay	6 ....

6 Complete each sentence with a verb and a preposition from Activity 5. You may need to change the form of the verb.

1 I usually .... my little sister when my parents go out.
2 I've left my purse at home. Can I .... some money .... you?
3 It can take two or more weeks to .... flu.
4 Kirsty doesn't have a car so she .... her brother to take her to class.
5 My parents don't .... my boyfriend. They want me to break up with him.
6 Please be quiet! I'm trying to .... my work.
7 You .... me .... your father. You have the same smile.
8 Noel sent me an email this morning but I haven't .... him yet.
9 Where have you been? We've been .... you for two hours!
10 This isn't my book. Do you know who it .... ?
11 When I am in London, I like to .... my favourite hotel in the Strand.
12 The flight was delayed so it took over six hours for us to .... our destination.

VOCABULARY BANK

verbs and noun phrases

7 Complete the table with the verbs in the box.

do   have   make   take

1	a photo a test/an exam a trip medicine	3	a coffee a shower a temperature fun
2	a mistake a noise money progress	4	homework the housework the washing-up your best

8 Complete the sentences with the verbs in the box. You may need to change the form of the verb.

break   do   gain   give   have   keep
make   pay   perform   print   run   save

1 When was the last time you .... a lot of fun?
2 Do you spend all your money or are you good at .... some of it?
3 Do you .... more noise than your neighbours or are they noisier than you?
4 Would you like to be an actor and .... on stage in front of hundreds of people?
5 Are you any good at .... a secret or do you tell everybody?
6 Would you like to .... your own business in the future?
7 Which world record would you like to .... ?
8 Do you read documents on your computer screen or do you prefer to .... them and read them on paper?
9 Have you ever offered your time for free in order to .... work experience?
10 In what situations do you have to .... a deposit in your country?
11 Do you mind .... housework?
12 Do you .... your parents a call every day?

9 Answer the questions in Activity 8.

Word formation

prefixes

1 Complete the table with the prefixes in the box.

dis-   im-   ir-   un-

1	2	3	4 ....
mature	regular	acceptable	loyal
patient	replaceable	avoidable	honest
perfect	responsible	fortunate	pleased
personal		pleasant	respectful
polite		reasonable	satisfied
possible		reliable	

2 Look at the underlined prefixes in sentences 1–4 and match them to questions A–D.

1 We won't all fit into one taxi. We need a <u>mini</u>bus.
2 David drove <u>non</u>-stop through the night to get here on time.
3 I forgot to save my report so I had to <u>re</u>type it.
4 William is very <u>self</u>-confident.

A Which prefix means *again*?
B Which prefix means *small*?
C Which prefix means *of, to, by* or *for yourself*?
D Which prefix means *not*?

3 Complete the words in the sentences with the prefixes in Activities 1 and 2.

1 Are young people more .... respectful than the previous generation?
2 Do you get angry easily or do you have .... -control?
3 Have you ever had to .... -do work on the computer because you forgot to save it?
4 Were you a mature or .... mature child?
5 Have you ever had a .... -break (a holiday for two or three nights)?
6 Do you prefer to read fiction or .... -fiction books?
7 Do you think it's a good idea to .... train when you're older and do something different?
8 Do you have a friend who's fun but .... reliable?

4 Answer the questions in Activity 3.

suffixes

5 Complete the table with the suffixes in the box.

-able   -ful   -less   -ly   -ment   -y

1 noun + ... → adjective	hair, fog, fun, noise, rain, sun
2 adjective + ... → adverb	annoying, calm, loud, patient, quiet, slow
3 verb + ... → adjective meaning *can*	accept, achieve, change, love, move, pleasure
4 noun + ... → adjective meaning *no*	care, colour, harm, hope, taste, use
5 noun + ... → noun meaning *full of*	care, colour, harm, hope, taste, use
6 verb + ... → noun	advertise, announce, disagree, disappoint, employ, involve

6 Use the suffixes *-or*, *-er* and *-ist* to form job words for the words in the box.

act   art   build   design   direct   farm
instruct   journalism   photograph   report
sail   science

7 Add a suffix to the words in brackets to complete the sentences.

1 Do you think that it is ever .... (accept) to hit someone?
2 Have you ever had to drive or travel when it's really .... (fog)?
3 Are you creative enough to be a .... (design)?
4 Would you make a good .... (act)?
5 Has anyone ever complained that you're playing music too .... (loud)?
6 Have you ever had a big .... (disagree) with one of your close friends?
7 What was the last .... (pleasure) experience that you had?
8 Are you a good driver or are you .... (care)?
9 Do you wait in queues .... (patient) or do you get annoyed?
10 What has caused you .... (disappoint) or regret this year?

8 Answer the questions in Activity 7.

compound nouns

9 Match 1–8 to A–H to form sentences.

1 She's a model and has been on magazine
2 We need a new light
3 When a judge walks into the law
4 Would you like to come to a fitness
5 There's live
6 Drivers should stop at a pedestrian
7 People are worried that global
8 The staff at this hotel need to improve their customer

A court, everyone must stand up.
B covers around the world.
C crossing and let people cross the road.
D class with me?
E warming will cause many problems in future.
F bulb in the lamp in the bedroom.
G service if they want to keep their guests.
H entertainment at the hotel every evening.

10 Use one word from each box to form compound nouns and complete the sentences. Be careful with spelling: some compound nouns are written as one word.

exchange   hard   information   music
railway   show   sign   snow

business   disk   festival   line   pack
post   storm   visit

1 I'd love to have a job in .... I think I'd be a good TV presenter.
2 What's the name of this street? Can you see a .... anywhere?
3 Coldplay are playing at a big .... near my house next month.
4 I need to delete some of the files on my computer because the .... is full.
5 The train had to stop because there were cows on the ....
6 Some French students came to our college as part of an ....
7 Please collect an .... from reception. It contains a map and guide to the college.
8 It's freezing outside. A .... is coming.

82

VOCABULARY BANK

compound adjectives

11 Match 1–8 to A–H to form sentences.

1 He's a good-
2 Both my parents have full-
3 We've just booked a last-
4 Using scissors is difficult for left-
5 The bag is expensive because it's hand-
6 I love my job. It's well-
7 Your children are polite and well-
8 Help yourself to food. This is a self-

A time jobs.
B minute trip to Paris. We're leaving tomorrow!
C service restaurant.
D behaved.
E paid and fun.
F looking man!
G made.
H handed people.

12 Use one word from each box to form compound adjectives and complete the sentences.

broken- energy- home- long-
never- one- two- world-

distance efficient ending famous
hearted hour made way

1 Is this film going to finish soon? It seems to be ....!
2 When my girlfriend broke up with me, I was ....
3 We've got a special .... lesson tonight, from 6 to 8 p.m.
4 I'm not sure I can afford the bus fare. How much is a .... ticket to Hull?
5 My brother has never been on a .... flight before.
6 Enrique Iglesias is a .... singer.
7 There's .... lighting all around our house to help us save money.
8 Here, try one of Carla's .... biscuits. They're delicious!

Phrasal verbs

phrasal verbs with *up*

1 Match the underlined phrasal verbs in sentences 1–8 to the definitions A–H.

1 She's decided to <u>give up</u> tennis after the tournament.
2 I arrive at the station at 10 p.m. Can you <u>pick</u> me <u>up</u>?
3 We couldn't find a restaurant that was open so we <u>ended up</u> getting a takeaway.
4 I can't believe she <u>hung up</u> without saying goodbye!
5 Andy was <u>brought up</u> by his aunt and uncle.
6 I'm sorry I'm late. I was <u>held up</u> by the traffic.
7 You're doing a really good job. <u>Keep up</u> the good work!
8 Do you have a dictionary? I need to <u>look</u> this word <u>up</u>.

A delay   E stop
B collect   F continue
C find information about G end a phone call
D raise   H finally have to

2 Complete the sentences with phrasal verbs from Activity 1. You may need to change the form of the verb.

1 Can you .... the train times on that website?
2 I'm going to .... my job. I hate it!
3 I want to .... my children in a big family.
4 No! Don't .... ! We need to talk!

phrasal verbs with *on*

3 Match the underlined phrasal verbs in sentences 1–8 to the definitions A–H.

1 I've never <u>got on</u> with my brother. We argue all the time.
2 If you <u>carry on</u> ironing, I'll make dinner.
3 How do you <u>turn on</u> the washing machine?
4 You'll need to <u>put</u> your coat <u>on</u> when you go out. It's cold.
5 I must go and <u>get on with</u> making dinner.
6 <u>Come on</u>! We're going to be late!
7 If you <u>get on</u> the train first, I'll pass your bags to you.
8 The family down the road <u>keeps on</u> having loud parties.

A make something work   E put clothes on your body
B continue   F hurry
C enter (transport)   G have a friendly relationship
D do something many times   H make progress with

4 Complete the sentences with phrasal verbs from

83

Activity 3. You may need to change the form of the verb.

1 We .... with our neighbours really well. They often come round for dinner.
2 Stop talking and .... your work!
3 My little sister .... taking my clothes without asking!
4 When her friend left, she .... working on her project.

phrasal verbs with *off*

5 Match the underlined phrasal verbs in sentences 1–8 to the definitions A–H.

1 We got up early so we could <u>set off</u> before the traffic got bad.
2 The plane <u>took off</u> at 5 a.m.
3 Don't forget to <u>switch off</u> the TV before you go to bed.
4 Kerry <u>got off</u> the bus at the wrong stop and had to walk for a mile!
5 Ewan's sick so we have to <u>put</u> the meeting <u>off</u> until next Friday.
6 Why have the lights <u>gone off</u>?
7 I had a terrible headache this morning but the pain's <u>worn off</u> now.
8 It's really hot in here. Why don't you <u>take off</u> your coat?

A exit (transport)
B stop working
C stop (something) working
D change to a later date
E remove (clothes from your body)
F start a journey
G move off the ground into the air
H disappear (feeling/effect)

6 Complete the sentences with phrasal verbs from Activity 5. You may need to change the form of the verb.

1 Is the TV broken? It just .... for no reason.
2 I felt great this morning but that feeling has .... Now I just feel tired!
3 I .... for work at 7.30 a.m. every morning.
4 The hall is booked next week so I've .... the party .... until the week after.

phrasal verbs with *out*

7 Match the underlined phrasal verbs in sentences 1–8 to the definitions A–H.

1 Sarah, please <u>hand out</u> a worksheet to everyone.
2 I want a hot drink but we've <u>run out</u> of coffee.
3 At the weekends I <u>hang out</u> with my friends.
4 We <u>set out</u> for the woods just after sunrise.
5 Jack is <u>going out</u> with Melissa.
6 We've got a problem that we need to <u>sort out</u>.
7 Can you <u>find out</u> who that woman is?
8 I thought I'd emailed everyone but I'd <u>left</u> Kevin <u>out</u>.

A start a journey
B not include
C give something to each person in a group
D spend time
E organise or solve
F use all of something so there's no more left
G get information about
H date

8 Complete the sentences with phrasal verbs from Activity 7. You may need to change the form of the verb.

1 Do you know how long Sun and Jin have been .... together?
2 Stu .... on his trip with a backpack and a tent.
3 We all sat down and the teacher .... the exam papers.
4 I got paid last week but I've .... money already!

phrasal verbs with other particles

9 Match the underlined phrasal verbs in sentences 1–8 to the definitions A–H.

1 Our car has <u>broken down</u> again!
2 Who is <u>looking after</u> your cat while you're away?
3 I <u>threw away</u> those old magazines.
4 I sometimes <u>call in on</u> my grandparents on the way home from college.
5 That shirt I bought was too small so I <u>took</u> it <u>back</u>.
6 I'm absolutely exhausted! I'm really <u>looking forward to</u> the weekend.
7 Does this shirt <u>go with</u> these trousers?
8 We <u>checked in</u> at the hotel at noon.

A visit someone while going somewhere else

VOCABULARY BANK

B stop working
C return
D be excited about something that's going to happen
E match
F put something in a bin
G go to the desk to say you have arrived
H take care of

10 Complete the sentences with phrasal verbs from Activity 9. You may need to change the form of the verb.

1 Don't worry about me. I can .... myself!
2 We're all .... seeing Mark again – we haven't seen him since high school.
3 I'll .... you on my way home and give you the money I owe you.
4 What's this rubbish doing here? Why haven't you .... it ....?

Different meanings of get

1 Match the verbs in the box to the different meanings of *get* in the sentences.

| arrive | become | buy | find |
| improve | move | prepare | receive |

1 When you go to the supermarket, could you <u>get</u> me a loaf of bread, please?
2 On my birthday, I <u>got</u> a book from my mother.
3 My sore throat isn't <u>getting better</u> – I may have to go to the doctor.
4 I'll call you when I <u>get</u> to the airport.
5 <u>Get</u> away from the edge of the pool – you'll fall in!
6 My friend's trying to <u>get</u> a new job – she really hates working in an office.
7 I'm going to put my coat on – I'm <u>getting</u> cold.
8 My sister takes ages to <u>get ready</u> to go out!

Easily confused words

1 Choose the correct alternatives to complete the sentences.

1 May I have a glass of orange juice, please, and a *package/packet* of crisps?
2 I don't believe she'd do something so stupid – she's usually very *sensible/sensitive*.
3 A lot of *strangers/foreigners* visit London every year from all over the world.
4 I often ask for *advice/advise* from my big sister.
5 He *told/said* me all about his weekend at the beach.
6 In my *opinion/idea*, people should take more exercise!
7 If you visit Scotland, you'll see some wonderful *nature/scenery*.
8 Please *remind/remember* me to send my brother a birthday card!
9 Can you *borrow/lend* me some money until tomorrow? I've left my purse at home.
10 Don't forget to *bring/take* me back a souvenir from your holiday!

Same sound, different spelling

1 Choose the correct alternatives to complete the sentences.

1 I love all sport *accept/except* football.
2 I love going to Italy – the food is so good *their/there*.
3 I'm sorry – I didn't *here/hear* what you said.
4 I hope the *weather/whether* is good on Saturday for our picnic.
5 I can't *see/sea* the screen very well – can we change our seats?
6 *Where/Wear* did you meet your friend?

85

Common errors: B1 Preliminary

1 Find and correct the mistakes with questions.
1 What your name?
2 Where you from?
3 What you do?
4 Where you going?
5 How many times you been outside your country?
6 What you enjoy most about the experience?

2 Find and correct the mistakes with the position of the adverbs of frequency.
1 I watch regularly films with my friends.
2 I'm good at getting things normally done but this week I've felt very tired.
3 I'm working always when my friends come round to chat.
4 I love going generally shopping but not when the shops are crowded.
5 I don't watch often television but sometimes I do at the weekend.
6 I try to do every day some exercise.

3 Find and correct the mistakes with the present simple and present continuous.
1 People who lives in glass houses shouldn't throw stones.
2 My sister ride her bicycle to college every day.
3 When do you coming to visit us again?
4 I going away for the weekend so I'll be a bit late on Monday.
5 My brother don't like hip hop music.
6 You takes the tram to La Laguna. It stop opposite the university.

4 Find and correct the mistakes with modals of possibility.
1 He must to be exhausted. The match has been going on for over five hours.
2 It mustn't be the postman. He never comes this early.
3 I'll answer the phone if you like. It can be for me.
4 We can to meet on Wednesday or Thursday. I don't mind.
5 Take an umbrella, just in case. It must rain later.
6 When I finish college, I might to go and work in another country.

5 Find and correct the mistakes with -ing forms and infinitives.
1 If you ask me, to buy a new computer is a waste of money.
2 She apologised for arrive late.
3 I'm better at watch tennis than I am at play it.
4 Would you mind to pass the salt?
5 We're looking forward to hear about your holiday in Greece.
6 We've arranged meeting outside the cinema at 5.30.

COMMON ERRORS: B1 PRELIMINARY

6 Find and correct the mistakes with modals of obligation.

1. You must not to walk on the grass.
2. I has to go. See you later.
3. Have we to buy a book or is the teacher going to give us photocopies?
4. If you want to lose weight, you don't have to eat so many cakes and sweets.
5. Do I should wear a hat to the wedding?
6. Sue won't be here today. She must go to the dentist.

7 Find and correct the mistakes with the present perfect, past simple and *used to*.

Simon: (1) Did you ever go to Paris?
Clare: (2) Yes, several times. In fact, I have gone last November.
Simon: (3) A friend of mine has been last year. He says it's very expensive.
Clare: (4) Well, it used to be but this time I have found it quite cheap.
Simon: (5) Where have you stayed?
Clare: (6) In a little hotel near the Sorbonne. It was there for ages. My great-grandfather has stayed there every time he has gone to Paris.

8 Find and correct the mistakes with comparatives and superlatives.

1. I'm not good at salsa dancing as Tina.
2. Tina has a good sense of rhythm than me.
3. Carey is worst in the salsa class.
4. Carey is even more bad than Ivan.

9 Find and correct the mistakes with *so*, *such*, *too* and *enough*.

1. We had a so good time at the party.
2. Susan is such nice person.
3. This tiramisu is such delicious! Can I have some more?
4. You're not enough old to stay out after midnight.
5. Snowboarding is so fun. I love it.
6. I'm afraid the exam was too much difficult for me. I don't think I'll pass.

10 Find and correct the mistakes with the past simple.

1. Where does your father live when he was a child?
2. Who winned the Eurovision song contest last year?
3. We all feeled ill after the meal.
4. I fell in love with Fernando the first time I seed him.
5. We buyed Mum some perfume for her birthday.
6. I catched a terrible cold while I was in London.

11 Find and correct the mistakes with the past simple and past continuous.

1. Alex listened to some music on his phone while the teacher was telling us what to do for homework.
2. Some of the contestants were rehearsing when the stage was collapsing.
3. I was phoning my friend on her mobile when I was seeing her standing on the corner.
4. You were sitting there watching the match while I cooked the dinner!
5. I had a shower when the telephone rang.
6. Tim slept soundly while the burglars were stealing his new flat-screen TV.

12 Find and correct the mistakes with the past perfect.

1. As soon as I had got to school, I remembered that the teacher had told us there was going to be an exam that day.
2. I felt really nervous because I missed lots of lectures.
3. By the time I got to the classroom, the teacher already started the exam.
4. I had hardly looked at the questions when I had seen that the boy sitting next to me had written almost a whole page.
5. When the teacher had told us to stop writing, I had only answered two of the three questions.
6. I was sure I failed but, in fact, in the end I got quite a good mark.

13 Find and correct the mistakes with countable and uncountable nouns.

1. She was wearing a trousers and a jacket.
2. Are we having a chicken for dinner again?
3. She's got a lovely dark curly hair.
4. How many money do you spend on food and entertainment each week?
5. There are too many furnitures in this room.

14 Find and correct the mistakes with articles.

1. I love living here because sun shines almost every day.
2. There's volcano here that is almost 4,000 metres high.
3. I prefer living on coast to living in countryside though.
4. It's wonderful to be able to swim in sea every day.
5. There's also lake near here which has very clear water.
6. I sometimes go there at night and swim in the light of moon.

15 Find and correct the mistakes with reported speech.

1. She said me that she would be a little bit late.
2. I told to the neighbours that I was going to be away for a few days.
3. Tim told that he would be home on Saturday night.
4. Tanya said that she can't ride a bicycle.
5. Paulo told me he is coming on Monday.
6. Gustave said he will be here by midday but he still hasn't arrived.

16 Find and correct the mistakes with reported questions.

1. She asked me how was I feeling.
2. She asked us did we enjoy our English course.
3. She asked me have I any special plans for the future.
4. She asked me what are you going to do when you finish university.
5. She asked me is there anything special I want to do in the future.
6. She asked me what kinds of things did I like doing in my spare time.

17 Find and correct the mistakes with modals of ability.

1. I can understand the news on the radio now but I can't even understand my teacher a few months ago.
2. I could read short books in English now but I couldn't even read a newspaper at the beginning of the course.
3. I was able to write stories, reports and articles in English now but I can't even write an informal letter when we started using this book.
4. I can express my opinion in English now but I can't even talk about a photo properly last September.
5. I could pronounce most words quite well now but I can't even understand the pronunciation symbols in the dictionary at the beginning of the course.

18 Find and correct the mistakes with relative clauses.

1. Tina, that came to your party, is living in Paris now.
2. Thor Heyerdahl that died in 2000 discovered some pyramids on the island of Tenerife.
3. She's the girl I told you about her.
4. Tim's the boy who's father is a politician.
5. Is Fabio the boy which is going to France next year?

19 Find and correct the mistakes with the passive voice.

1. The original museum were built in 1765.
2. The exam was took by most of the students in the class.
3. The anniversary of the opening of the museum celebrated every year in November.
4. Visitors is attracted to the town by the annual music festival.
5. The sculpture was create by a very young artist.
6. My neighbour's jewellery stolen by a burglar last night.

20 Find and correct the mistakes with get/have something done.

1. I usually have my hair cutted every six weeks.
2. I often getting my friends to create playlists for me – my taste in music is terrible!
3. I prefer to has my groceries delivered – I hate going to the supermarket!
4. I never try to fix my car if there is a problem with it – I always it fixed by a mechanic.
5. I'm have my house painted right now – the painter is making quite a mess!
6. I have my smart dress dry-cleaned yesterday – it looks fantastic now.

21 Find and correct the mistakes with future forms.

1. Oh no! I think I'm being sick.
2. I have to go now. I phone you back later.
3. What do you do next year when you finish school?
4. What time your plane leave?
5. Look at those dark clouds! It rains later.
6. I've already decided. I'll buy Ella a CD for her birthday.

22 Find and correct the mistakes with conditionals.

1. How would you feel if you don't get enough sleep?
2. What would you say if you meet someone famous?
3. Who do you usually talk to when you were worried about something?
4. How do you feel if Australia won the World Cup?
5. What do you do this summer if you can't afford to go on holiday?
6. What would you buy if you would have £100,000?
7. I always forget to take my umbrella when it rained!
8. What would you do if you have the afternoon off work?

COMMON ERRORS: B1 PRELIMINARY

23 Look at these extracts from students' answers and the teacher's comments. Find and correct the mistakes with vocabulary and spelling.

1

My boyfriend is quite well-build. He's medium-hieght (about 1.80) and a little bit overwieght but I still think he's very hansome. The thing I like most about him though is that he is always very honnest.

Watch your spelling.

2

You'll love our house in the mountains. In the winter, when it's been snowing outside, we all sit around the chimney and talk after dinner. It's so cosy. It can be quite hot in summer but, luckily, we have air-conditioned so we keep nice and cool. I hope you can come next year.

You've used the wrong word in one sentence and the wrong word form in another.

3

The person in my family I get through with best is my older sister. We're really good friends. She's about seven years older than me so she looked for me and my younger brother a lot when we were little.

Check your phrasal verbs.

4

I couldn't work up the meaning of a word and I decided to look up it in a dictionary. It wasn't there so I looked in it online but I couldn't find it there either. In the end I gave out and decided to ask the teacher.

Check your phrasal verbs.

5

A lot of people criticise it but I get a lot of enjoy from watching television. I even like the advertisings.

Be careful with word forms.

6

I wanted to buy a new top because at the hot weather. There were some nice ones in sale on a shop near here. I tried one out but I wasn't very keen for the way it looked at me. I'm really tired with looking at clothes that fit me. I never find anything!

Check your prepositions.

Exam strategies

In the exam you need to use strategies that will help you to do the exam tasks. Here are some tips for each paper and examples of mistakes students often make.

Reading

General advice
- Read different things in English as there are different types of text in the Reading exam.
- Don't look up every word in a dictionary when you read. Try to work out the meaning of the word first.

General exam tips
- Read all the instructions carefully. They tell you something about what you will read.
- The answers are always there in the texts, even if you don't see them at first.
- Don't worry if you don't understand a word, you may be able to guess its meaning.

Reading Part 1: Multiple choice, short texts

1 Match the advice (1–3) to the explanations (A–C).

1. Think about what the person who reads or sees the message has to do.
2. Be careful if you see the same word in the text and in the option.
3. Think about the purpose or reason for the message.

A. This does not mean it is the answer – you should look for synonyms.
B. This tells you what the message or sign really means, not just the words.
C. The meaning of the message or sign may tell you to do something.

2 In the question below, a student chose option B. Which piece of advice from Activity 1 did the student forget? What is the correct answer?

> Don't turn this computer off – I'm still working on it.
> I'll be back in ten minutes.
> Please go to the computer in the library if you need one immediately.

A. Wait ten minutes before using this computer.
B. The computer must be turned off after ten minutes.
C. There is another computer that can be used.

EXAM STRATEGIES

Reading Part 2: Multiple matching

3 Match 1–3 to A–C to complete the advice.

1 Highlight what each person needs
2 Choose the option that matches everything the person needs
3 Check your answers

A as some may only match some of their needs.
B because it makes it easier for you to see matches.
C so you don't choose an option more than once.

4 In a question about films to rent, a student made the match below, which is wrong. Which piece of advice from Activity 3 did the student forget? How can you tell?

> Sue wants to rent a film to watch. She likes true stories but prefers them to have a happy ending. She doesn't like musicals.
>
> *This film is about a real-life dancer who fights her way to the top in very difficult circumstances. The final scenes are heart-warming and the songs add emotion and fun. An enjoyable film!*

Reading Part 3: Multiple choice, long text

5 Complete the advice with the words and phrases in the box.

> before   opinions and feelings
> writer's purpose

1 Many questions ask about .... so you should also look for these in the text, not just detailed information.
2 Only one option is correct so you should check that the others are wrong .... making your final decision.
3 The last question relates to the whole text. Read the whole text again before answering it. It could ask about the .... so you should think about the meaning of expressions like *points out*, *explains*, *shows* or *gives you information*.

6 Which pieces of advice from Activity 5 do you need to follow for this question?

> What might the writer say about the text?
> A It gives you all the news about this year's top celebrities.
> B It points out that not all celebrities enjoy being the centre of attention.
> C It explains why I have always secretly wanted to be a celebrity.
> D It tells you how to become a celebrity.

Reading Part 4: Gapped text

7 Put these pieces of advice in the right order.

a Read the text again to make sure it makes sense.
b Read the parts of the text before and after each gap.
c Read the text quickly without paying attention to the gaps.
d Find a sentence where tenses, vocabulary, pronouns (e.g. *they*, *them*) and reference words (e.g. *this*, *these*, *it*, *one*) connect with the information before and after the gap.
e Read the sentences below the text.

8 Read the extract from a text and two sentences the student thought could possibly fill the gap. In the end the student chose sentence B. Is sentence B wrong because of vocabulary, pronouns or reference words?

> I had never even been to a wedding before one of my friends asked three of us to be bridesmaids when she got married. Our friend, the bride, wanted her wedding to be quite traditional but she thought it would be a good idea if the bridesmaids chose their own dresses. This was a sensible idea as we are all very different sizes and shapes. I'm very tall and thin but the other two bridesmaids are quite short. **(1)** *B* My dress had a bright floral pattern in blue and yellow.

> What might the writer say about the text?
> A They both chose dresses in a solid colour, one in blue and the other in yellow.
> B Her dress was quite plain with yellow and blue stripes.

Reading Part 5: Multiple choice cloze

9 Complete the statements about Reading Part 5. You are given the first and last letter of each word.

1. The questions test vocabulary and c.................s.
2. Some examples of things tested include p.................l v.................s and fixed phrases.
3. The four options may have similar m.................s but only one is correct in the text.

10 For each question, choose the correct answers. Then match the questions to the statements in Activity 9.

1. I really want to take .... golf – I've never had the chance to try it before.
   A in   B at   C out   D up
2. I really enjoy reading the .... in newspapers – they're often very interesting.
   A adverts   B articles   C chapters   D essays
3. The friends .... a different resort because the first one was so crowded.
   A fixed   B decided   C took   D chose

Reading Part 6: Open cloze

11 Which piece of advice does <u>not</u> apply to Reading Part 6?

1. Read the title and the whole text to make sure you understand it.
2. Look at the words both sides of each gap.
3. Decide what word is missing.
4. Choose the alternative that correctly fits the gap.
5. Think about things like parts of verbs, prepositions, determiners (*this*, *those*, etc.), connectors (*however*, *but*, *as*, *like*, etc.).
6. Read the whole text again to make sure it makes sense with the words you have written in the gaps.

12 Read the extract from a text and the words a student wrote in the gaps. One of the student's answers is wrong. Which one? What advice didn't the student follow?

> The tour will stop for an afternoon in the small medieval town, **(2)** *where* you will wander round the market, spend time in the museum and then climb the hill above the town to admire the view. Alternatively, you can relax by sitting **(3)** *on* the beautiful gardens and enjoying the flowers.

Writing

General advice

- Make a list of things you should always check when you have finished (e.g. spelling, punctuation and grammar).
- Always check that your writing is relevant to the task and that you have included everything you need to.
- Practise writing things using different words as this will help make your writing more interesting.

General exam tips

- Try to use a range of vocabulary and expressions, as well as different grammatical structures.
- Leave yourself enough time to check you have included everything required in the task and to check your writing for mistakes in spelling, punctuation and grammar.
- In Part 2, read both the questions before choosing which one to answer. Make sure you have enough to say.

… **EXAM STRATEGIES**

Writing Part 1: Email

1 Find and correct the mistakes in the advice about Writing Part 1. Tick (✔) the advice which is correct.

1 You write about 50 words.
2 Write your email using full sentences.
3 You don't have to include all the information asked for in the notes.
4 Check what you have written, especially spelling, punctuation and grammar.

2 Look at the exam task and the answer a student has written.
Which two pieces of advice from Activity 1 has the student forgotten?

Read this email from your English-speaking friend Alex and the notes you have made.

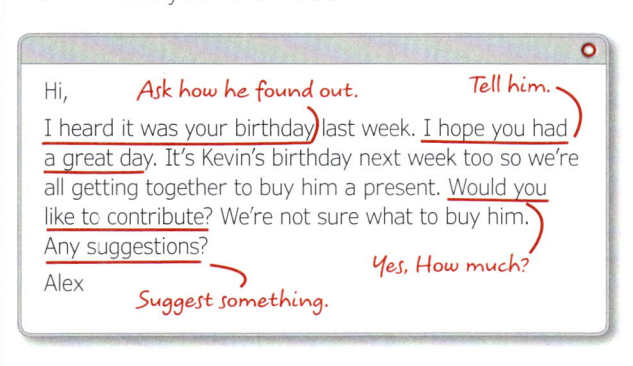

> Hi,
> I heard it was your birthday last week. I hope you had a great day. It's Kevin's birthday next week too so we're all getting together to buy him a present. Would you like to contribute? We're not sure what to buy him. Any suggestions?
> Alex

Ask how he found out.
Tell him.
Yes, How much?
Suggest something.

Write your **email** to Alex using **all the notes**.

Hi Alex,

How did you know it was my birthday? I had an amazing day out with some friends at a really great theme park. Maybe that would be a good idea for Kevin's present. I mean we could all pay for him to go to a theme park.

See you soon.

Jesse

Writing Part 2: Article or story

3 Look at the advice below and decide if each piece of advice is for the article (A), the story (S) or both (B).

In Part 2, you should check that
1 you have started with the given sentence.
2 you have not made any spelling or grammar mistakes.
3 you have used a range of vocabulary and grammar.
4 you have written the right number of words.
5 you have divided your work into paragraphs.
6 you have made your writing as interesting as you can.
7 you have answered all the questions you were asked in the task and included all the necessary information.

4 Look at the exam task and the answer a student has written. Which three pieces of advice from Activity 3 has the student forgotten?

Your English teacher has asked you to write a story.
Your story must begin with this sentence.
I didn't think it was going to be a very good weekend.
Write your **story** in about **100 words**.

I didn't think it was going to be a very good weekend. I wanted to go shopping but there was nobody for me to go with because all my friends were very busy. I was sitting at home feeling quite sad when suddenly the phone rang. It was a girl from my old school who had moved to another town. She wanted to meet me to talk. We met in the local café and talked about everything we were doing now and what we wanted to do in the future. It was nice to talk to her and we decided to go to the cinema together the next day. In the end, I had a really good weekend after all because of my old friend.

5 Look at the exam task and the answer a student has written. Which three pieces of advice from Activity 3 has the student forgotten?

> You see this advertisement on an English-language magazine.
>
> > **Articles wanted!**
> > **How do you spend your free time?**
> > Is it better to spend your free time with your family or your friends?
> > What do you enjoy doing most in your free time?
> > What's the best way to relax?
> > Write an article answering these questions and we will put it on our website.
>
> Write your **article** in about **100 words**.

> I love having free time because I can do whatever I want. I like to spend time with both my freinds and my family because both are important to me. I have two brothers and a sister.
>
> My main hoby is sport, and I realy enjoy watching and playing football with my friends. I usuly do that every weekend.
>
> I often go to my room and listen to music, because then I can play the kind of music I like best. I like diferent kinds of music, including rock and classical.

Listening

General advice

- Listen to as many things in English as you can – use the radio and the internet.
- Don't worry if you don't hear or understand a word – relax and listen for the general meaning.

General exam tips

- Use the time you have to read through all the questions or look at the pictures.
- Read the instructions as you listen to them.
- Don't worry if you haven't chosen all the answers after the first listening.
- Use the second listening to get the answers you missed and to check your answers.
- Check that you have written your answers correctly on the answer sheet.

Listening Part 1: Multiple choice, pictures

1 Match the advice (1–3) to the explanations (A–C).

1 Listen for key words related to the question and for words related to times, days or dates.
2 Listen for words like *best* or *most*.
3 Don't think about the previous text when you go on to the next.

A You may have to listen for something that someone likes best or most.
B You may hear conversations or monologues (one person speaking) but they are not related to each other.
C You may hear vocabulary from all the pictures but only one picture will answer the question.

2 In the question below, a student chose option B. Look at the audio script. Which piece of advice from Activity 1 did the student forget? What is the correct answer?

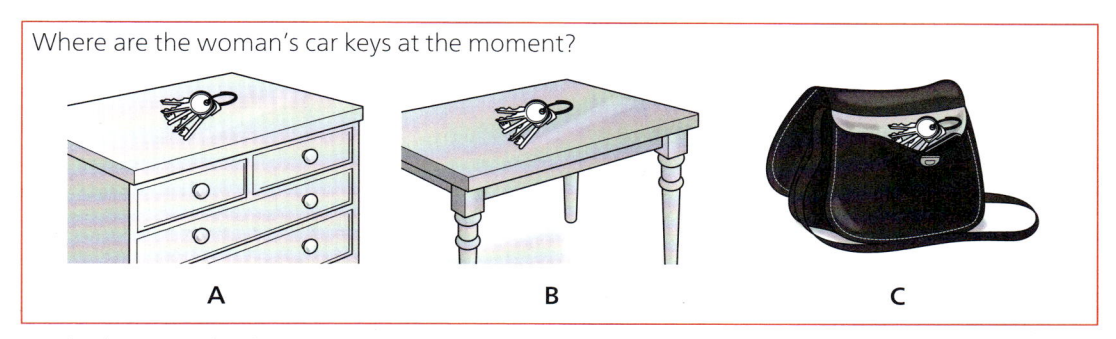

Where are the woman's car keys at the moment?

A   B   C

M: You look annoyed! What's wrong?
F: I've lost my keys – I've looked everywhere.
M: They were in your room last night. I remember seeing them on the chest of drawers. Maybe they're still there.
F: I've looked there already. And I checked the kitchen table this morning – I often put them there, but no luck. I've just looked in the car too.
M: Then they must be in your bag right now – they've probably slipped down to the bottom.
F: You're right – I must have missed them when I looked there before!

Listening Part 2: Multiple choice, short texts

3 Match 1–3 to A–C to complete the advice.

1 Read the question and all the options carefully
2 Listen to the whole of each dialogue before choosing an option
3 Listen to each speaker carefully and think about what they both say
A because you may be asked what they agree about.
B to check that the answer you choose really answers the question.
C because the information giving the correct answer may come anywhere in the conversation.

4 In the question below, a student chose option B. Look at the audio script. Which piece of advice from Activity 3 did the student forget? What is the correct answer?

> You will hear two friends talking about a hockey match. What do they both think about it?
> A The pitch was poor.
> B The referee performed well.
> C The team has improved.

M: That was a great game to watch!

F: It was, though the playing conditions were tough – all that water in the middle of the pitch.

M: I didn't think it was that bad –the players didn't seem to have any problems with it. It was good to see the change from last week when they lost so badly.

F: They were totally different – I haven't seen such a good team effort for ages. I thought the referee was good too, didn't you?

M: I thought he made lots of mistakes.

F: Well, at least it went our way in the end!

Listening Part 3: Gap-fill

5 Read the advice. Which explanation is not correct?

Before you listen, you should read the notes or sentences carefully because

1. that helps you to think about the kind of information to write in each gap.
2. you should check your spelling.
3. you may hear numbers or times, and you should be prepared for this.
4. you shouldn't write words that are already in the question.

6 In the question below, a student wrote the answer 'breakfast'. Look at the audio script. Which piece of advice from Activity 1 did the student forget? What is the correct answer?

> Your information packs will be ready after ....

Remember to be on time for meals. The information about this is outside the canteen. Breakfast starts at 8 every morning and finishes at 10.30 but the canteen is always busy around 9, so that's not a good time to eat. Information packs about the day's activities will be made up for you, but they won't be available until 10 every day in the common room. Dinner starts at 6 p.m. and you should arrive on time for that.

Listening Part 4: Multiple choice, long text

7 Write one word in each gap to complete the advice. You are given the first letter of each word.

1. Most of the questions focus on what the speakers think or feel. Look for and identify words in the question connected with the speakers' o....................... or a....................... .

2. What the speakers say is in the same order as the questions. Don't listen for information in d....................... parts of the conversation.

8 In the question below, a student chose option A. Look at the audio script. What is the correct answer? What mistake has the student made?

A The student has not read the question correctly.
B The student has not listened to the end of Clare's answer.

> What does Clare enjoy most about her job?
> A having contact with students
> B discovering new writers
> C reading travel books

I: What do you enjoy most about your job, Clare?

C: It's great having contact with students. I love talking to them about the different countries they come from. Travelling is one of my hobbies, and I have a list of places I want to visit. But I became a librarian because I've always enjoyed reading. Though I can't do that much when I'm working, the best thing is I do get to find out about writers I didn't know about before.

EXAM STRATEGIES

Speaking

General advice
- Practise your English with friends whenever you can.
- Listen to English on the radio or the internet – it will help you to feel more confident with speaking.
- Practise your pronunciation of new words with friends and/or record yourself reading aloud. You can also check the pronunciation using digital dictionaries.

General exam tips
- Listen carefully to the examiner's instructions. Ask the examiner to repeat them if you are not sure what to do.
- Speak clearly so that both the examiners can hear you.
- Don't worry if you make mistakes and try not to feel nervous.

Speaking Part 1: General questions

The examiner will ask you questions about yourself. Read the advice.

1. Give interesting answers to the examiner's questions.
2. Don't prepare long speeches in advance.
3. Speak naturally and don't hesitate too much.
4. Don't worry about making mistakes.

1 Look at the examiner's question and a student's answer below. Which two pieces of advice has the student forgotten?

> Q: What did you do last Saturday?
> A: Last Saturday? Do you mean … er … that's a very good question. Er … I go … no, I went, yes, went to the cinema. Or did I went … er … go … to shopping? Er … I think …

Speaking Part 2: Individual long turn

You will speak on your own and describe a photograph. Read the advice.

1. Try to describe everything you can see in your photograph.
2. Don't worry if you don't know a word – just move on. You will not lose marks if you don't know a word.
3. Don't worry if the examiner stops you after about a minute.

2 Look at this extract from a long turn. Which piece of advice has the student forgotten?

> In the top corner I can see a … a … I don't know. It's a … maybe it's a … something like a box or perhaps it's a … no, it's not … I'm not sure.

Speaking Part 3: Collaborative task

You will discuss a task with your partner. Read the advice.

1. You don't have to discuss all the pictures.
2. Say what you think and give reasons for your ideas.
3. Always ask your partner for their opinions and ideas.
4. Don't worry if you disagree with your partner.

3 Look at this extract from a conversation between two students. Which piece of advice have they forgotten?

> A: Let's start with this. I think it's a good idea to buy flowers because everyone likes flowers. And I don't think it's a good idea to buy a book. People don't like reading these days.
> B: I think it's a good idea to buy a pen so she can write notes for her course.
> A: I like the camera but it's expensive

Speaking Part 4: Discussion

The examiner will ask you both questions that extend the topic of Part 3. Read the advice.

1. You should listen carefully to the question. Remember that there is no right answer to any question, but what you say should be relevant.
2. Try to give interesting details about your ideas and reasons for your opinions.
3. Remember that you may be asked what you think about your partner's question and answer, so listen to what they say.

4 Look at this extract from Part 4 of a speaking test. Which two pieces of advice have the students forgotten?

> E: What's the best thing to do in your free time if you want to relax?
> A: I like watching TV. I like sport.
> E: What about you?
> B: I don't like sport. I like playing computer games.

Practice test

Reading

Part 1

Questions 1–5

For each question, choose the correct answer.

1. **All books borrowed from the library must be returned before the end of July.**

   A You cannot borrow books until 31 July.

   B If you have borrowed a book from the library, you have to take it back by 31 July.

   C You can keep a book you have borrowed if you tell the library by 31 July.

2. **NEXT WEEK'S COACH TRIP**
   There aren't any seats left on the coach. Anyone who asked to come on the trip and hasn't given me the money should do so before tomorrow.

   A You have to pay for a reserved seat on the coach today.

   B You can reserve a seat on the coach if you pay today.

   C If you haven't paid for the trip yet, your seat on the coach will be given to someone else.

3. **THESE TABLES ARE ONLY FOR CUSTOMERS EATING CAFÉ MEALS. PLEASE EAT YOUR OWN FOOD AT THE PICNIC TABLES OUTSIDE.**

   A You cannot eat food bought in the café at the picnic tables.

   B If you want to eat at the tables, you have to bring your own food.

   C You can eat at the café tables if you bought your food there.

PRACTICE TEST

4

From: Paloma
To: Erik

I think I left a book in your office. It was a present for Andrew and it's his birthday tomorrow!

What does Paloma want Erik to do?

A   buy a present for Andrew

B   give Andrew a book

C   look for a book she bought

5

After opening keep refrigerated and use within 3–4 days.

A   You can use this product four days after opening it.

B   There is enough of this product for three to four days.

C   You should not use this product after three to four days.

Part 2

Questions 6–10

For each question, choose the correct answer.
The people below are all looking for a fitness course.
On the opposite page there are eight advertisements.
Decide which course would be the most suitable for the people below.

6 Yolanda would like to do gentle exercise in the open air in the evenings. She likes to do things with groups of older people.

7 Bashir likes meeting people, team sports and competition. He wants to improve his sporting skills and get stronger and fitter. He is free two afternoons a week.

8 Vikash doesn't have much free time. He wants to be able to exercise for an hour a day in the evenings or early morning. He prefers to do things on his own.

9 Laurent wants something he can do with his wife and teenage children. They all enjoy being outdoors, especially at the seaside. He only has weekends free.

10 Tomoko is very interested in other cultures. She would like to learn to do something that is good exercise but not too tiring. She finishes work at 4.30 p.m.

Fitness courses

A **Sarasvati Yoga School**
In our large mixed ability classes, you can work at your own relaxed speed and learn about yoga in ancient India. From 7 to 9 a.m. and 6 to 8 p.m., on Mondays and Fridays.

B **Running training**
Join us for running training every Tuesday and Thursday in Anderson Park. The complete run starts at 5 p.m. and takes an hour. Fit adults only.

C **Fitness Fans' Gym**
We're open every day from 7 a.m. to midnight. Personal fitness trainers will study your individual needs and design an exercise programme just for you.

D **Sports Club**
Do you want to make new friends, train with others, get professional coaching and play in matches? Get fit and develop your abilities! Join the Sports Club!

E **Water aerobics**
Have fun and get fit in the Wilson indoor pool. Much easier than normal aerobics and great for teenagers. Classes every afternoon from four to five.

F **Beach volleyball**
Join us every Sunday morning at Sunnysands Beach. Kids and adults are welcome to take part. We're not professionals. We just play for fun and exercise!

G **Tara's T'ai Chi**
Most of our members are people in their forties, fifties and sixties who enjoy the gentle movements of T'ai Chi. All our classes are held in Anderson Park. Week nights from 6 to 8 p.m.

H **Ballroom dancing**
Dance your way to fitness in our ballroom dancing class. Perfect for couples. You'll sleep well after two hours of movement! Evenings from 9.30.

Part 3

Questions 11–15

For each question, choose the correct answer.

My Homeshare experience

I looked for a flat when I first came to London but it was really very difficult. I didn't like the idea of sharing with other students. I've seen a lot of student flats and they are sometimes dirty and often untidy. Living on my own wasn't possible because it was just too expensive.

That's when I discovered the Homeshare service. Elderly people who need help around the house offer to share their home with a younger person who needs accommodation. Instead of paying rent, the younger person agrees to help with jobs around the house. These are usually light cleaning and cooking but the most important thing you do is talk to the elderly person for a while. They're often very lonely.

Marjorie was. She's 74 and her husband died 20 years ago. She's a fantastic storyteller and a very clever person. I like to cook and we eat together at least four times a week. That gives us a chance to be together and talk. Marjorie asks me to do quite a lot of cleaning but that's not a problem for me. Homeshare has been great for both of us. It's given me somewhere to stay and both of us a new friend.

PRACTICE TEST

11   What would a reader learn about the writer from reading the text?
   A   She likes her home to be clean and tidy.
   B   She prefers to live alone.
   C   She knew about Homeshare before she came to London.
   D   She can afford to live by herself.

12   The writer thinks she helps Marjorie most by
   A   spending time with her.
   B   doing the cleaning.
   C   cooking her meals.
   D   paying for her accommodation.

13   How does the writer feel about Marjorie?
   A   She feels sorry for her.
   B   She admires her.
   C   She thinks she is too demanding.
   D   She is worried about her.

14   Which of the following best describes the writer?
   A   a young person who couldn't find any other young people to share a flat with
   B   a young person who enjoys sharing her home with an older person
   C   a young person who has to work in another person's house
   D   a young person who would prefer to live alone

15   What might the writer say about this article?
   A   I describe my everyday life.
   B   I explain a service I think is very good.
   C   I talk about a flat I have lived in.
   D   I say why it was difficult to find a flat.

103

Part 4

Questions 16–20

Five sentences have been removed from the text below.
For each question, choose the correct answer.
There are three extra sentences which you do not need to use.

A gift for languages

Although I'm not usually an envious person, I've always envied my friend Carlos. That's not because he's intelligent, handsome and successful, though he is all those things and more. **16** ☐

Carlos's mother is from Finland and his father is Argentinian. **17** ☐ After they had both finished studying, they did some travelling and then got married. After a couple of years in Finland they went to live in France. That's where Carlos was born and where he lived until we both started university in London.

By that time, Carlos spoke three languages fluently: Finnish, Spanish and French. His English wasn't bad, so getting it up to a very high level didn't take him very long either. **18** ☐ Sadly, nobody ever had any trouble guessing that I was French.

After graduation, we both went to Hong Kong and got jobs there. I worked for a bank and Carlos was a research assistant at a university. Although we mainly spoke English there too, we both enrolled in an intensive Cantonese language course that was offered by the university where Carlos worked. **19** ☐ Before long, he was having lively conversations with people at parties, ordering food in restaurants and arguing over the price of things in the local market.

Now he says he'd like to learn Japanese and Korean as well. **20** ☐ As I say, he has a gift for languages, a gift his parents gave him. I only wish I had had the same good fortune.

A In fact, people often thought he was a native speaker.
B They met when they were students in London.
C Our employer had encouraged us to do it.
D The reason is because he has an incredible gift for languages.
E I think that would be an incredibly difficult language to learn too.
F I'm sure he will and that it will only take him a few months.
G No wonder he's so popular.
H I found it really difficult and dropped out after a couple of weeks but Carlos kept going

PRACTICE TEST

Part 5

Questions 21–26

For each question, choose the correct answer.

Helping wild birds

The cold winter months can be very uncomfortable for wild birds. If there is **(21)** .... snow this can also cause the **(22)** .... to fall below freezing and if the ground becomes frozen, it's impossible for the birds to dig for insects to eat. **(23)** .... , the birds can't find any wild berries on the trees.

Many people feed wild birds regularly. They buy nuts and seeds to put in their gardens. However, you don't have to **(24)** .... a lot of money to help birds – you could make **(25)** .... of uneaten bits of food. Mix a few seeds and one or two old biscuits into some fat left over from cooking. Then put this into empty yoghurt **(26)** .... and leave it in the fridge to get cold. Finally, hang the balls of food on a nearby tree. It's great to watch the birds enjoying a feast!

21	A	big	B	heavy	C	large	D	hard
22	A	temperature	B	weather	C	climate	D	air
23	A	Although	B	However	C	Also	D	But
24	A	give	B	take	C	put	D	spend
25	A	use	B	work	C	job	D	advantage
26	A	bottles	B	boxes	C	pots	D	parcels

Part 6

Questions 27–32

For each question, write the correct answer.
Write one word for each gap.

A more colourful school

The head of a school decided to run some art classes in the evenings. These were not only for school students but also for people from the town, and they were very successful. The classes on **(27)** .... to draw and paint animals were **(28)** .... popular that they were completely full.

Unfortunately, the school buildings themselves had **(29)** .... built a long time ago and were quite ugly. The art students wanted to make **(30)** .... more attractive, and to create something special as a 'thank you' to the school for their classes. They decided to paint a huge picture on the school wall, showing **(31)** .... colourful jungle scene with animals hiding among the trees.

Everyone had a good time working on the project, **(32)** .... took ten weeks to finish. The school students were thrilled with their colourful school and the art students were very proud of their work!

Writing

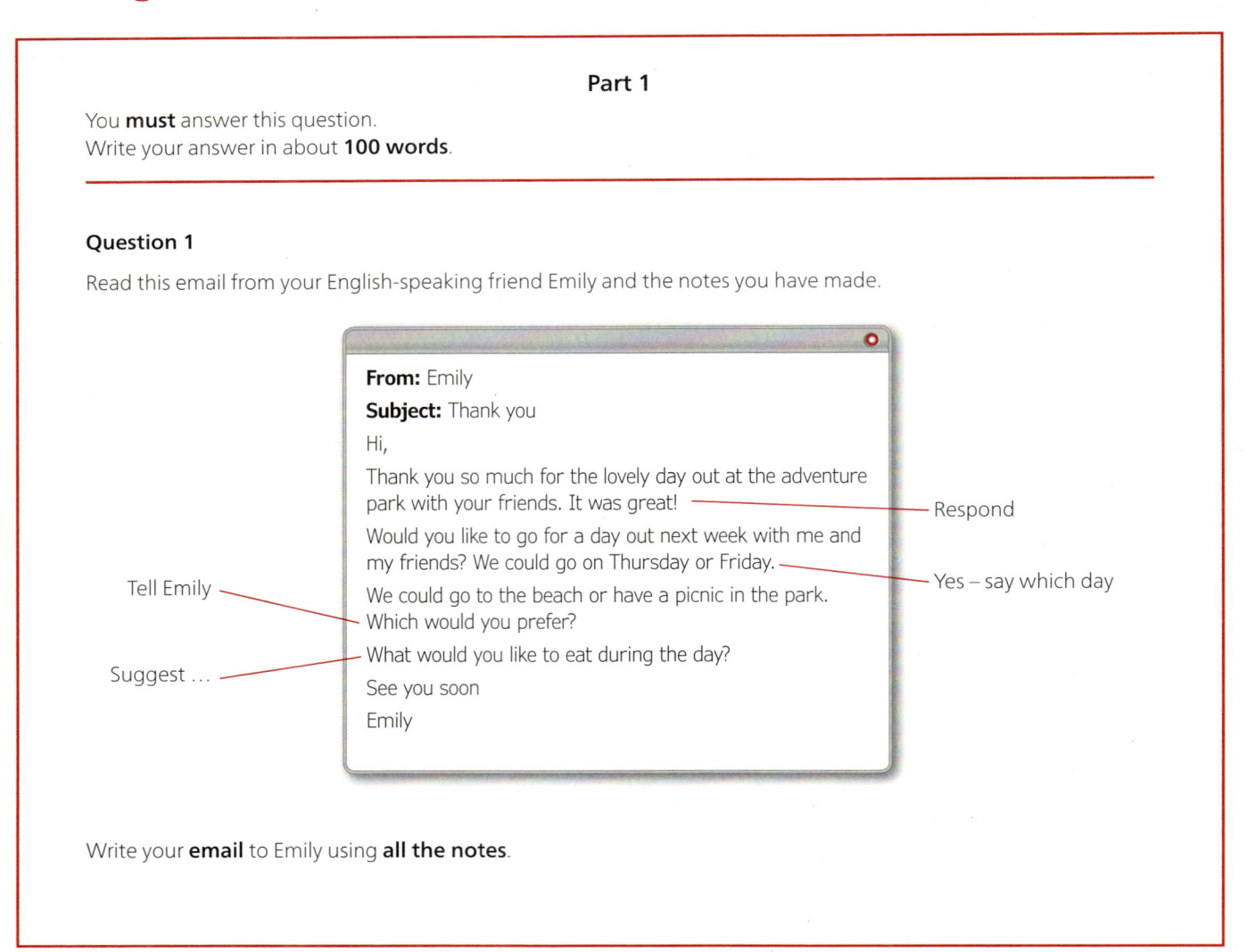

Part 1

You **must** answer this question.
Write your answer in about **100 words**.

Question 1

Read this email from your English-speaking friend Emily and the notes you have made.

> **From:** Emily
> **Subject:** Thank you
> Hi,
> Thank you so much for the lovely day out at the adventure park with your friends. It was great! — *Respond*
> Would you like to go for a day out next week with me and my friends? We could go on Thursday or Friday. — *Yes – say which day*
> We could go to the beach or have a picnic in the park. Which would you prefer? — *Tell Emily*
> What would you like to eat during the day? — *Suggest …*
> See you soon
> Emily

Write your **email** to Emily using **all the notes**.

PRACTICE TEST

Part 2

Choose **one** of these questions.
Write your answer in about **100 words**.

Question 2

You see this notice on an English-language website.

> **Articles wanted!**
>
> **Free time!**
> Where do people go if they want to relax in their free time in your country?
> What do they do?
> How important is it to spend our free time with family or friends?
>
> **Write an article answering these questions and we will put it on our website.**

Write your **article**.

Question 3

Your English teacher has asked you to write a story.
Your story must begin with this sentence.

It was the most enjoyable day of my life.

Write your **story**.

Listening

Part 1 ▶ 41

Questions 1–7

For each question, choose the correct answer.

1   What time does the film start?

   A   B   C

2   What is the man waiting for?

   A   B   C

3   What is the date of the anniversary dinner?

   A   B   C

PRACTICE TEST

4   What is the man going to do on holiday?

   A   B   C

5   What is the woman having problems with at the moment?

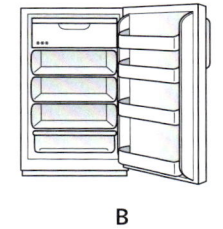

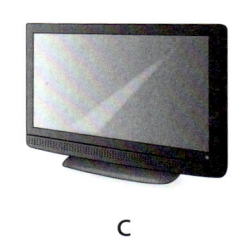

   A   B   C

6   What does the woman decide to buy?

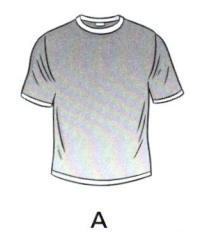

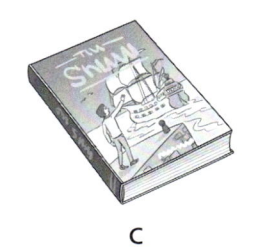

   A   B   C

7   What does the woman want to do?

   A   B   C

109

Part 2 ▶ 42

Questions 8–13

For each question, choose the correct answer.

8 You will hear two friends talking about a concert they went to.
   What do they agree about the concert?
   A The music was too loud.
   B The tickets were too expensive.
   C There were too many people there.

9 You will hear a man telling a friend about a table tennis competition.
   What did he dislike about it?
   A the way it was organised
   B the people taking part
   C the location

10 You will hear two friends talking about a television programme.
   What does the woman think about it?
   A It was too long.
   B It was not very interesting.
   C It was hard to understand.

11 You will hear a woman telling a friend about her new car.
   She is satisfied with
   A the design of the car.
   B the price of the car.
   C the colour of the car.

12 You will hear two friends talking about a football game they watched together.
   What do they agree about it?
   A The team played well.
   B The referee was good.
   C The conditions were excellent.

13 You will hear a man telling a friend about some training he does regularly.
   What does he say about it?
   A The cost of the training sessions is quite cheap.
   B The exercises in the training sessions are easy to do.
   C The people who run the training sessions are helpful.

PRACTICE TEST

Part 3 ▶ 43

Questions 14–19

For each question, write the correct answer in the gap. Write **one** or **two words** or a **number** or a **date** or a **time**.

You will hear a holiday representative talking to some holidaymakers about sailing.

Great Sailing Holidays

Holiday representative

The holiday rep's office is by the **(14)** _____ in the hotel.

Jonas works every evening except **(15)** _____ .

Meals

Breakfast is served from 7 to 10 a.m.

You can collect food for lunch from the kitchen at **(16)** _____ .

Dinner is self-service from 7.30 p.m.

General advice about sailing

Please read the leaflet about **(17)** _____ first.

Make sure you have a lifejacket.

Check the **(18)** _____ before leaving.

Take some **(19)** _____ on the boat as well as a hat and some water.

Part 4 ▶ 44

Questions 20–25

For each question, choose the correct answer.

You will hear an interview with a woman called Angela Morris, who plays country music professionally.

20 Angela says that she became interested in music
    A because her family were musicians.
    B when she had piano lessons at school.
    C after she discovered she had a good voice.

21 What made Angela decide to make music her career?
    A She wanted to please other people.
    B She knew it was right for her.
    C She hoped to become rich.

22 Angela chose to write country songs because
    A she found them easy to think of.
    B she enjoyed the style of music.
    C she wanted to tell stories about people.

23 What was the best advice Angela had when she was starting out?
    A to practise as often as possible
    B to finish her education first
    C to meet other musicians

24 Angela says that her career actually started after she
    A put videos online.
    B advertised her concerts.
    C entered different competitions.

25 Angela says that any young musicians should
    A be careful who they listen to.
    B be prepared to take on other work.
    C be sure they will earn enough money.

PRACTICE TEST

Speaking

Part 1 ▶ 45

The examiner will ask you and your partner some questions about yourselves.

Listen to the recording and answer the questions.

Pause the recording after each bleep and give your answer.

Part 2 ▶ 46

The examiner will ask you and your partner to talk on your own about a photograph.

Look at the photographs below and listen to the examiner's instructions.

A

B

Part 3 ▶ 47

The examiner will ask you and your partner to talk together about a situation.
Look at the pictures below and listen to the examiner's instructions.

Activities the friends could do together on the first day

Part 4 ▶ 48

The examiner will ask you some questions about the topic of your discussion in Part 3.
Listen to the recording and answer the questions.
Pause the recording after each bleep and give your answer.

Answer key

UNIT 1
Grammar

1
1. What is your name?
2. Do you like your name?
3. How did you get your name?
4. What are your interests?
5. What kind of personality do you have?
6. What is your ideal job?

5 1 it – B 2 Do – A 3 What – D 4 How – E 5 What – C

6
Steve: Hi, I'm Steve.
Bailey: I'm Bailey. Nice to meet you.
Steve: Sorry, I didn't catch that – ~~what~~ **what's/what is** your name?
Bailey: ~~Are~~ **Do** you think it's an unusual name?
Steve: Yes! Where ~~it~~ **does it** come from?
Bailey: I think it's popular in Australia.
Steve: ~~Did~~ **Have** you been there?
Bailey: No, I haven't – it's a long way away!
Steve: So who ~~did~~ gave you that name?
Bailey: Actually, it was my dad – he just liked it. So ~~am~~ **do** I!
Steve: ~~Are~~ **Do** you ever have any problems with the name?
Bailey: Well, it can be a name for both boys and girls.
Steve: ~~Have~~ **Do** people find that confusing?
Bailey: Definitely! Before they meet me, they often think I'm a boy!

8
1. Where **did** you go on holiday last year?
2. What **is** your favourite animal?
3. What **do** you enjoy doing at the weekends?
4. What **is** your best friend like?
5. Did you **do** anything special last week?
6. What **do** you think you are going to do this evening?
7. How do you get **to** school every morning?
8. When **was** your last birthday?

Reading
1 1 D 2 H 3 F 4 B 5 G

Vocabulary
1 1 give up 2 influence 3 keep up 4 switch on 5 take up 6 get fit 7 realise 8 carry on with

2 1 take up 2 keep up 3 switch on 4 influence 5 get fit 6 realise 7 carry on with 8 give up

Listening
1 1 B 2 C 3 B 4 C 5 C 6 B 7 A

Vocabulary
1 Across
1 shy 4 cheerful 6 punctual 8 generous 10 nervous
Down
2 honest 3 reliable 5 curious 7 ambitious 9 sensitive 11 organised

2 1 B 2 C 3 A

3
1. middle-aged; curly; overweight
2. good-looking; bald; thin
3. young; smartly-dressed; beard

Grammar
1
1. I **normally** watch a film on television in the evening.
2. I'm **always** happy to go to the cinema with friends.
3. I don't **often** watch films on my tablet because the screen is too small.
4. I'm **frequently** surprised when people say they don't enjoy sport.
5. I don't **usually** go out to restaurants with friends during the week.
6. I go for a run **once a day**.

2
1. correct
2. How do you **normally** meet new people?
3. correct
4. It's **always** nice to make new friends.
5. I chat to my friends **all the time**.
6. correct

Speaking
1
1. What is your name?
2. Where do you live?
3. Do you work or are you a student?
4. What do you do?
5. How do you travel to work or college every day?
6. Do you like the town you live in?
7. Who do you live with?
8. Tell us about your family.
9. What do you like doing at weekends?
10. What is your favourite time of day?

2 A 7 B 6 C 5 D 10

5 1 Where 2 there 3 whether 4 here

Writing
1 The correct order is B, A, D, C.

UNIT 2
Vocabulary
1 1 fried 2 takeaway 3 vegetarian 4 fizzy 5 sweet 6 mild 7 chips 8 raw

115

Grammar

1
1 ~~I'm not really enjoying~~ – I don't really enjoy
2 ~~I cook~~ – I'm cooking
3 correct
4 ~~is weighing~~ – weighs
5 ~~I try~~ – I'm trying
6 ~~I'm not knowing~~ – I don't know

2 False

3
1 am enjoying 2 get up 3 spend 4 don't have
5 cooks 6 Do you know 7 fry 8 make 9 are trying
10 are only having 11 promise 12 know

Speaking

1 Photograph A: bottle of water, bowl, bread, cardigan, fruit, grass, lake, picnic, salad, table, tablecloth
Photograph B: apron, basket, bowl, bread, cakes, curtain, eggs, kitchen, milk, table
Table, bread and bowl are in both photographs.
Knife and bag are not in either photograph.

2
~~curtain~~ – tablecloth
~~sea~~ – lake
~~cakes~~ – salad

3
~~fruit~~ – eggs
~~cups~~ – bowls
~~bag~~ – basket

Reading

1 1 C 2 B 3 A 4 D 5 A

2 1 ancestors 2 emphasis 3 diet 4 ingredients 5 nutritious
6 Processed

3 1 D 2 A 3 B 4 C

Vocabulary

1 1 washable 2 advertisements 3 careless 4 enjoyable
5 spoonful 6 hopeful 7 careful 8 hopeless

2
1 ~~washful~~ – washable
2 ~~careless~~ – careful
3 ~~bagless~~ – bagful
4 ~~enjoyable~~ – enjoyment
5 ~~enjoyment~~ – enjoyable

Grammar

1 1 can't be; must be 2 might rain 3 must be 4 can't be
5 might eat 6 must have

2
1 ~~must be~~ – can't be
2 ~~can't be~~ – must be
3 ~~might be~~ – must be
4 ~~must have~~ – might have; ~~must have~~ – might have
5 ~~must not be~~ – might not be
6 ~~might not be~~ – can't be

Listening

1 1 A 2 B 3 B 4 C 5 A 6 C

2 1 C 2 D 3 A 4 E 5 B

3 1 shopping online, deliver 2 scans the products 3 find special deals 4 check the quality (of food)

Writing

1 The correct order is D, G, A, E, C, F, B.

2 1 Just then 2 suddenly 3 A few moments earlier 4 Eventually

3 The correct order is B, F, D, I, E, C, A, G, H.

4 **Sample answer**
It was one of the worst experiences I have ever had in a restaurant.
I had invited my friend to dinner for her birthday. I wanted her to have a good time, so I told her to choose anything she wanted. She ordered the most expensive things on the menu.
When the waiter brought the bill, it was £50!! Then I realised I didn't have my wallet and I had only got five pounds in my pocket so I didn't have enough money to pay the bill.
My friend had to pay. When I got home I found my wallet on the bed. I felt terrible!

UNIT 3

Vocabulary

1 1 bored 2 nervous 3 tired 4 excited 5 embarrassed
6 satisfied 7 confident 8 surprised 9 amused 10 annoyed

Listening

1 1 B 2 A 3 C 4 A 5 C 6 C

Grammar

1 **verb + -ing form:** can't stand, involve, mind, practise
verb + infinitive: arrange, can't wait, expect, learn

2 1 asking 2 to show 3 spending 4 to tell 5 making
6 to stay 7 trying 8 hurting

3 According to research, ~~to have~~ **having** quality relationships …
If it's difficult ~~seeing~~ **to see** your friends every day or if you can't wait ~~meeting~~ **to meet** them, you can always arrange ~~keeping~~ **to keep** in touch online.
Friends choose ~~loving~~ **to love** you for who you are … To keep a friendship going, you have to decide ~~doing~~ **to do** as much as you can for them too …

Speaking

1
1 false – she is in a baker's
2 false – the customer is wearing a coat but the shop assistant is wearing a T-shirt
3 true
4 false – It is an old-fashioned shop
5 false – she looks happy
6 true

2 1 baker's 2 happy 3 bread 4 apron 5 change 6 coat
7 old-fashioned 8 coffee machine

4 1 bored 2 outdoor 3 mobile phone 4 newspaper 5 tired
6 standing up 7 cardigan 8 bag

ANSWER KEY

Vocabulary
1 1 look it up 2 turn their music up 3 get along well 4 give up 5 looking after 6 keep on 7 hurry up 8 cleaning up 9 hand it in 10 hanging out

Grammar
1 1 must 2 have to 3 have to 4 have to 5 have to 6 Do you have to 7 should 8 have to 9 should 10 do you have to 11 should 12 have to 13 mustn't

Reading
1 1 on 2 down/off 3 his 4 as 5 for 6 why
2 1 who 2 their 3 how 4 of 5 than 6 to
3 1 Belongings 2 second nature 3 post 4 Rather than 5 explain yourself 6 Methods

Vocabulary
1 1 G 2 A 3 E 4 C 5 B 6 D 7 H 8 F

Writing
1 1 true 2 false 3 true 4 true 5 false 6 true 7 false
2 Kristian, because she asks questions and is interested in what Jaden thinks. Stefan just gives information.
3 Stefan
saturday – Saturday
vegitarian – vegetarian
shoping – shopping
Kristian
lunch it would be more easy easier for me
What do you think?
4 Sample answer
Hi Pamela,
Thanks for your email. It would be really great to meet up in person and thank you for inviting me to your conversation evening. I'd love to come. Would you like me to bring something to eat or drink? I'm very good at making cakes!
I will bring Lucy if that's okay, as she wants to meet some new people. I think we might be a bit late because I have to go to the supermarket first, but I will be there before 8 o'clock. I hope that's all right.
See you on Saturday,
Pat

UNIT 4

Speaking
1 They don't reach a decision. The examiner stops them because they have been speaking for long enough.
2 1 think 2 about 3 could 4 What 5 Maybe 6 which

Listening
1 1 C 2 B 3 B 4 C 5 B 6 A 7 A

Grammar
1 1 used to live 2 used to have 3 used to see 4 used to go 5 used to tell 6 used to make
2 1 Didn't you use to go skiing in winter?
2 Yes. We always used to go to Switzerland for two weeks.
3 Did you always use to go in January?
4 Yes. We always used to see the same people there.
5 What did you use to enjoy most?
6 Everything! Falling over was the only thing I didn't use to enjoy. OR Everything! The only thing I didn't use to enjoy was falling over.
3 1 used to get/catch 2 used to wear 3 didn't use to wear 4 used to have 5 used to watch

Reading
1 Possible answers
Photograph A: jeans, leather jacket, T-shirt
Photograph B: collar, fashion parade, make-up, sleeveless top
3 1 A 2 B 3 A 4 B 5 B 6 D
4 1 A 2 D 3 C 4 D 5 C 6 B
5 1 endlessly 2 inspire 3 reproduce 4 wardrobe

Vocabulary
1 1 Although 2 as well as 3 although 4 also 5 in spite of 6 Despite 7 though 8 too
2 1 in spite of/despite 2 as well as 3 Despite/In spite of 4 although/though 5 However 6 though 7 also

Vocabulary
1 1 climate 2 local 3 growth 4 friendly 5 facilities 6 neighbour 7 entertainment 8 lively
2 1 mild 2 transport 3 facilities 4 fresh 5 spaces 6 playgrounds 7 growth 8 friendly 9 lively 10 local
3 1 fresh 2 work 3 public 4 public 5 work 6 fresh

Grammar
1 1 for 2 for 3 since 4 since 5 for 6 since
2 1 How long have you known your closest friend?
2 How long have you been a student here?
3 How long have you had your mobile phone?
4 How long has your friend had the same hairstyle?
5 How long have you liked your favourite singer?
6 How long have you lived in your house?
3 A came out B haven't made C has decided D saw E bought; moved F have done
4 1 F 2 B 3 A 4 C 5 D 6 E

Writing
1 1 true 2 true 3 false 4 true
2 A photograph and something very valuable are not mentioned.
3 1 F 2 E 3 A 4 D 5 B 6 C
4 1 dirty 2 soft 3 exciting 4 used 5 fantastic 6 old

117

5 **Possible answers**

A photograph

I don't normally keep photographs in frames – I prefer to have them on my computer – but I like to look at this one every day because of the people in it. It's a photo of my class from my last year at school.

Something very valuable

I haven't got much jewellery of my own, and most of what I do have is inexpensive. However, I have a diamond ring that has been in my family for many years that my mother gave me when I was eighteen.

6 B, because it has interesting details and adjectives.

7 **Sample answer**

I don't usually keep things, and in fact I often recycle objects, but there is one thing that I love and will never throw away. It's an old necklace.

It isn't very beautiful and it certainly isn't valuable, but it belonged to my grandmother. She wore it all the time, and she gave it to me on my fifteenth birthday. It is important to me because it was important to her, and whenever I look at it I think of her.

I could never throw it away, because it is an important part of my family's history.

UNIT 5
Vocabulary
1 1 sharing 2 hire 3 lend 4 exchange 5 sell 6 rent out
7 swap 8 hire

Vocabulary
1 1 shirt; blouse 2 tie; scarf 3 overcoat; jacket 4 hat; cap
5 shoes; boots 6 jeans; trousers

2 1 C 2 A 3 B

3 1 old-fashioned 2 up-to-date 3 second-hand

4 1 true 2 true 3 false 4 false 5 true 6 true

5 1 try on 2 go with 3 fit 4 iron 5 put on 6 wear out
7 suit 8 take off

6 A

7 1 a beautiful blue silk dress
2 my short cotton skirt
3 a horrible red woollen sweater
4 a cheap blue cotton dress
5 a trendy red velvet jacket
6 a smart black leather jacket

Listening
1 1 false 2 true

2 1 an age
2 a noun / a type of animal
3 a period of time
4 a way of making a booking, e.g. online
5 a noun
6 an amount / a number

3 1 21 2 dogs 3 weekend 4 in person 5 (large) park 6 £50

Grammar
1 1 smaller than
2 more independent than
3 noisier than
4 easier; than
5 more affectionate than
6 softer; than

2 Dogs make **the** best pets, in my opinion. They're much more fun **than** cats, rabbits or tortoises. Tortoises have to be the **most** boring pets in the world. My friend has a tortoise and he says they're **more** interesting than I think. They're also a lot **less** expensive to feed than other animals. They're not nearly **as** friendly and affectionate though. Some people who don't have time to look after a pet themselves share other people's pets, or dog-walk them, which seems **the** best idea to me.

Reading
1 **Possible answers**
2 Piotr plays the drums. He would like to live with other students with similar interests. He loves animals and would like to have a pet.
3 Lakshmi is studying nursing. She wants to specialise in looking after old people. She loves classical music. She can have her meals at the hospital where she will be working.
4 Anneline needs to be near the university so she can study at weekends. She wants to make new friends while she is in the UK, especially people from other parts of the world.
5 Nourridine is studying to be a chef. He would like to be able to cook his own meals. He plans to bring his car to the UK. He would like to live with an English person.

2 **Possible answers**
A We are a young couple with a baby, a cat and a lovely spare room in our flat. The room has wonderful views of many famous places in London, like Saint Paul's Cathedral. We offer a lower rent to someone who can prepare meals and help look after the baby at weekends.
B My husband and I live with our 14-year-old son, Simon, in a beautiful country house. Our other son is studying abroad and we would like to have a student to stay in his room, join us for family meals and also help Simon with his school work.
C There are still shared flats available in our International Student Lodge. You will have access to the library and car park at the university, which is across the road. Students from all over Europe, Asia, Africa and America have made Student Lodge their home. Why not join them?
D I'm a nurse with a flat near the hospital. I'm looking for an older person, possibly a quiet student, to share with me. I often work at night so you'll be on your own a lot of the time. I eat my meals at the hospital so my kitchen is not very well-equipped.
E I am offering free accommodation in exchange for help with my mother, who is now almost 90. You will have your own room but I'm afraid I cannot provide meals or let you use the kitchen. I have a season ticket for the opera, which you are welcome to borrow from time to time.
F I'm looking for someone to share my flat with me. I'm a 22-year-old boy from Manchester. You will have your own room, use of the garage and access to the kitchen and laundry. No pets or smokers, I'm afraid.

ANSWER KEY

G We have a spare room in our house in a village near Cambridge. We're a family with three teenage children who live at home, a fourth who is studying abroad and two very friendly cats. My wife's father also lives with us and does most of the cooking.

H We have a room to rent in our house. There are three of us sharing. I'm from Sweden, Julio's from Argentina and Eddie, the dog, is from England! We are keen guitarists and we play together most evenings. I mean, Julio and I play; Eddie sometimes sings!

3 1 A 2 H 3 E 4 C 5 F

Vocabulary

1 1 blinds 2 curtains 3 carpet 4 garage 5 air conditioning 6 duvet

2 1 antique 2 balcony 3 a garden 4 air conditioning 5 blinds 6 pillows

Speaking

1 Photo A

2 1 floor 2 T-shirt 3 size 4 behind 5 jeans 6 sandals

Grammar

1
1 Nicolas always wears **such** smart clothes.
2 Most performance cars are **too** expensive for someone like me.
3 I didn't know it was **such** a small country.
4 I'm not hungry **enough** to eat a whole pizza!
5 We were **so** tired that we went straight to bed.
6 There are not **enough** open spaces for children to play in my town.

2 1 so 2 so 3 such 4 so

Writing

1 The student has not told Chris about the colours and styles they prefer.

2 Possible answer
I love modern clothes and my favourite colours are blue and green. I really don't like anything in orange.

3 1 true 2 false 3 true 4 true

4 Sample answer
Hi Carla,
Thanks for your email – it's great that we can help each other. Thank you for saying I look nice!
I have always loved cats and I have always wanted to have one of my own but my flat is very small. I would love to look after your cat for five days
When are you going to France? I need to know the exact dates please. I'd also like to know what Smokey likes to eat and whether he has any favourite toys.
Thursday would be a good day to speak. How about 7 in the evening?
Speak to you then.
Best wishes
Sal

UNIT 6

Speaking

1 The examiner asks the students about topics 1, 3, 4 and 5.

2 Xin gave better answers. He answered the questions and gave interesting details. Sophia answered the questions but only gave basic information.

3 1 Actually 2 really; after that 3 First of all 4 by bus

4 1 A 2 B 3 B

5 1 because 2 Also 3 disagree 4 usually 5 so 6 agree 7 same 8 perhaps

Reading

1 1 C 2 B 3 B 4 A 5 C

2 1 oversleep 2 charge 3 period 4 valid 5 demand 6 hand in

3 1 hand in 2 charge 3 demand 4 valid 5 period 6 oversleeps

Vocabulary

1 1 in charge 2 in fact 3 at all 4 in case 5 at all 6 up-to-date 7 up-to-date 8 at least 9 on sale

Grammar

1 1 C 2 A 3 B

2
1 practised – was practising
2 studied – was studying
3 was moving – moved
4 spoke – was speaking
5 was passing – passed
6 was calling – called
7 was laughing – laughed
8 learnt – was learning
9 walked – was walking
10 wasn't understanding – didn't understand

3 1 went 2 arrived 3 were 4 met 5 was talking 6 discovered 7 didn't know 8 cycled 9 bought 10 was raining 11 joined

Vocabulary

1 1 teacher 2 homework 3 course; research 4 report 5 curriculum 6 lecture

2 1 originally 2 Previously 3 Unfortunately 4 basically 5 probably 6 generally 7 hard 8 obviously

Listening

1 1 A 2 B 3 A 4 C 5 A 6 C

Grammar

1 1 got 2 had told 3 felt 4 had missed 5 didn't know 6 got 7 had already given out 8 hadn't had 9 didn't feel 10 seemed 11 had barely looked 12 saw 13 had written 14 said 15 had only answered 16 was 17 had failed 18 came out 19 saw 20 had got

119

2
1 By the time I woke up, I had missed my doctor's appointment.
2 As soon as Adam had collected his luggage, he went to look for a taxi.
3 When Heather had finished doing her homework, she went out.
4 After we had done the shopping, we came home and cleaned the house.
5 By the time Christine got to the beach, it had started to rain.
6 As soon as he had blown out the candles on the birthday cake, he started opening his presents.
7 By the time Stephen finished his breakfast, his sister had left for school.
8 When the teacher arrived, the students had already stopped talking.

Writing

1 and **2**
It was my first day and I was nervous. My mother **had** hung my new school uniform in the wardrobe the night before. She **had** put my new school shoes next to the chest of drawers.

I got up, and after I ~~had~~ **had** my shower, I started to get dressed. Suddenly, I realised that my school shoes ~~hadn't been~~ **weren't** there. Then I ~~had~~ remembered that I had left my bedroom door open the night before.

I ran downstairs and out into the back garden. There was our new puppy, Eddie, with one of my new school shoes in his mouth! He **had** already destroyed the other shoe.

3 Possible answers
Story A
1 It was my first day at university.
2 I was feeling a little bit anxious but also curious about the other students, the lecturers and the course.
3 In fact, something rather strange had happened a few days before.
4 I had been looking at clothes in a shop I really like when I saw a boy I know trying to steal a leather jacket.
5 I decided to call out his name and he was so embarrassed that he put the jacket back.
6 I was still thinking about what had happened when I realised that the lecturer was asking me a question.
7 I tried to remember the last thing I had heard her say but my mind was a complete blank.
8 Finally, I decided to admit that I hadn't been listening.
9 We finished the lecture and she smiled at me as she went out of the room.

Story B
1 It was my first day in a completely new job.
2 I was feeling nervous because I'd never had a proper job before.
3 In fact, something rather strange had happened the night before.
4 I had been in bed for about an hour when I heard someone outside the house calling out my name.
5 I decided to ignore it and soon after I fell asleep.
6 I was still thinking about what had happened when I saw the boss standing in front of my desk.
7 I tried to pretend I had been thinking about the latest sales figures but I don't think he believed me.
8 Finally, I asked him a question about the company and he seemed to be pleased about that.

9 We went on talking about company policy for the next 20 minutes or so.

Story C
1 It was my first day on holiday with my friends.
2 I was feeling really great because I knew we were going to have a really fantastic time.
3 In fact, something rather strange had happened exactly a year before.
4 I had been on my way to the airport when I realised I had left my passport at home.
5 I decided not to go and get it because I knew I could travel on my national ID.
6 I was still thinking about what had happened when I realised that I had left my small backpack at home with all my favourite clothes in it.
7 I tried to phone my mother but I didn't have enough credit on my phone to make an international call.
8 Finally, I managed to send her a text message and she promised to post it to me the next day.
9 We went to the post office every day for a week but the backpack never arrived.

4 Possible answers
Story A: I think she admired me for being so honest.
Story B: I'm sure my boss had no idea I had been day-dreaming.
Story C: I didn't mind. It gave me a perfect excuse to buy lots of new clothes!

UNIT 7
Vocabulary

1 Across
1 snow 7 thunderstorm 8 shower 10 ice 11 gales
Down
2 wind 3 wet 4 sunshine 5 breeze 6 freezing 9 fog

2 1 fog 2 thunderstorm 3 breeze 4 sunshine 5 gales 6 wet

3 1 dry – all the others are connected with wind
2 temperature – all the others are connected with water
3 heat – all the others are connected with storms
4 snowfall – all the others are connected with temperature

Listening

1 1 C 2 D 3 F 4 E 5 A 6 B
2 1 C 2 B 3 B 4 B 5 A 6 C

Grammar

1 1 Many 2 a lot of 3 much 4 Few 5 a lot of 6 much
2 1 noises 2 glass 3 glasses 4 bread 5 paintings 6 noise

Reading

1 The order the items appear in the text is H, C, D, A, G, E, B, F.
2 1 G 2 C 3 E 4 A 5 D
3 1 B 2 A 3 A 4 5 B 6 A

Vocabulary

1 1 C 2 A 3 I 4 E 5 G 6 B 7 D 8 F 9 J 10 H

ANSWER KEY

2
1 correct
2 ~~anxious in~~ – anxious about
3 ~~keen about~~ – keen on
4 ~~disappointed for~~ – disappointed by
5 correct
6 ~~useful by~~ – useful for
7 ~~familiar on~~ – familiar with
8 ~~involved about~~ – involved in/with
9 correct
10 ~~fond with~~ – fond of

Grammar

1 1 advice 2 a thunderstorm; the noise 3 Glass 4 smoke; fire 5 bread 6 The coffee 7 water; the tap 8 cheese; milk

2 1 – 2 – 3 the 4 The 5 – 6 – 7 a 8 an 9 The 10 the 11 a 12 – 13 The 14 – 15 the 16 the

3 We had **a wonderful time** in **Egypt**. As you know, we took **a cruise** down **the Nile**. We started in **Cairo**. **The boat** was really luxurious and **the itinerary** was amazing. We saw all **the most famous** archaeological sites like **the Pyramids of Giza** and **the Valley of the Kings**. **The guides** were great and t**he other people** on **the boat** were good fun. I tried to learn **a bit** of **Arabic** but everyone spoke good English. On **the last night** there was **a special party** with **fantastic food** and **wonderful music**. By **the time** we got to **bed**, **the sun** had already come up

Speaking

1 1 false 2 true

2 1 Both 2 Martin 3 Ana

3 1 agree 2 Why 3 think 4 How about 5 What 6 right

4 1 A 2 F 3 E 4 D 5 B 6 C

5 1 C 2 F 3 E 4 B

Writing

1 Statements 3 and 4 do not refer to a cruise.

2 1 B 2 A 3 C 4 C 5 D 6 E 7 A 8 A 9 F

3 Hi Sara,
How are you? We've just got back from a (1) ~~cruze~~ **cruise**. It was great!
(2) We sailed from Barcelona around the Canary Islands. I loved seeing all (3) the different places. On one island there was (4) a fantastic market. I (5) ~~buy~~ **bought** some lovely earrings. There (6) ~~was~~ **were** really nice people on board the ship and we made lots of friends.
(7) If you want to relax a cruise is perfect, and I can recommend ours although you may get bored with the days (8) at sea.
Well, write soon and (9) ~~say~~ **tell** me if you book a trip!
Love,
Analise

4 Sample answer
Hi Jordan,
It would be great to see you next weekend. The best place to meet is the café near the cinema. We could meet at around 10, then we can have a coffee together and plan what to do.
There's a music festival on Saturday evening so we could go to that. The best place to eat is the Bistro, because there's a new chef, the menu is really tasty and it's not expensive.
I don't think we'll have time to go swimming because it takes an hour to get to the beach. We can do that next time you come!
Looking forward to seeing you,
Sam

UNIT 8
Listening

1 1 false 2 false 3 true

2 1 21/twenty-one 2 smile 3 clothes 4 Spanish 5 photograph 6 24/24th/twenty-fourth

Vocabulary

1 ballet dancer; chat show; designer clothes; film studio; magazine cover; radio broadcast; rock star; show business; soap opera; stadium concert; stage actor; talent show; television commercial

2 1 chat show 2 ballet dancer 3 rock star 4 stadium concert 5 stage actor 6 soap operas 7 television commercials 8 magazine covers 9 designer clothes 10 talent show

Grammar

1
1 (that) he had seen Miley Cyrus in an airport once
2 (that) he had met Emma Watson in a café in March
3 (that) she didn't believe him though
4 (that) he had never met anyone famous
5 (that) he was always saying that he had seen someone famous somewhere or other
6 (that) she had been to the Academy Awards ceremony a couple of times
7 (that) it had been amazing
8 (that) she couldn't go this/that year because there was something really important she had to do that day
9 (that) she would tell me if she was going (the) next/following year
10 (that) I could join her

2
1 correct
2 ~~She said me~~ **She told me (that) / She said (that)** she didn't like having her photo taken.
3 ~~She told she~~ **She told me (that) / She said (that)** she would be at home on Saturday night.
4 correct
5 correct
6 ~~Carla said us~~ **Carla told us (that) / Carla said (that)** she had tried to get a part in a movie.
7 correct
8 ~~Luke said me~~ **Luke told me (that) / Luke said (that)** he would be late for the interview.
9 ~~She told to me~~ **She told me / She said** that she was going home.
10 correct

121

3 1 'I can speak Japanese.'
2 'I don't like having my photo taken.'
3 'I'll be at home on Saturday night.'
4 'You have to practise more.'
5 'I don't want to be on a TV show.'
6 'I tried to get a part in a movie.'
7 'You can borrow my camera.'
8 'I'll be late for the interview.'
9 'I'm going home.'
10 'I was late for school yesterday.'

4 1 had grown up 2 had always surfed 3 had surfed
4 knew 5 had always loved 6 had (only) started
7 had never (really) shown 8 wanted

Speaking

1 1 B 2 A 3 B 4 B

2 1 uniform 2 tournament 3 autographs 4 sports bag
5 spectators 6 remote control 7 shelves 8 actors 9 tidy
10 rug

3 1 In 2 In 3 On 4 in 5 On 6 In

4 1 On the right of 2 They're 3 I can see 4 Underneath
5 there is 6 Above

Grammar

1 1 He asked me if/whether I found Brad Pit attractive.
2 He asked me what I liked most about him.
3 He asked me if/whether I thought he was more attractive than Johnny Depp.
4 He asked me what I had thought of his latest film.
5 He asked me if/whether Angelina Jolie was/had been in it too.
6 He asked me who else was/had been in it.
7 He asked me if/whether I had seen any of her films.
8 He asked me if/whether I was going to the cinema that weekend.
9 He asked me if/whether he could come with me.
10 He asked me how much the tickets would cost.

2 1 She asked me where ~~did I live~~ **I lived**.
2 She asked me ~~have you always lived~~ **if/whether I had always lived** there.
3 correct
4 She also asked me what ~~I am studying~~ **I was studying** at the moment.
5 correct
6 correct
7 She asked if ~~I have got~~ **I had got** any special plans for the future.
8 She wanted to know what ~~was I going~~ **I was going** to do when I finished studying.
9 correct
10 She wanted to know ~~do I enjoy~~ **if/whether I enjoyed** watching television or listening to music.

Reading

1 A

2 1 B 2 A 3 D 4 C 5 A 6 C

3 1 harmful 2 past 3 fascination 4 grief 5 upset 6 curiosity
7 last 8 successful

Vocabulary

1 1 -ed 2 -ing

2 1 depressing 2 fascinated 3 surprising 4 frightened
5 interesting 6 encouraging 7 amazed 8 worrying

3 1 depressed 2 fascinating 3 encouraged 4 interested
5 amazing 6 frightening 7 surprised 8 worried

Writing

1 You should follow tips 1, 3, 4 and 5.

2 1 actually 2 In my opinion 3 In fact 4 so that 5 because
6 although

UNIT 9
Grammar

1 1 can; can't 2 Can 3 managed to 4 couldn't 5 managed to
6 Will you be able to

2 1 They were ~~be~~ able to see an island in the distance.
2 Did you ~~could~~ manage to finish that painting?
3 Could you ~~to~~ tell me where I can buy art materials?
4 Will you be able to ~~manage~~ come to the meeting?
5 My cousin is able to ~~can~~ design web pages.
6 We won't be ~~not~~ able to send you the tickets until next week.

3 1 able 2 can 3 can 4 could 5 could 6 can't 7 able
8 couldn't

Reading

1 1 A 2 C 3 G 4 H 5 F

2 1 outfit 2 stuck 3 studio 4 techniques 5 trouble
6 materials

Vocabulary

1 1 tried 2 plans 3 good (at) 4 needed 5 shown 6 finish

2 1 Sonia is not a very good sculptor but she's very good at painting. / Sonia is not a very good sculptor but she's a very good painter.
2 She has shown her work all over Europe and Asia.
3 She needed a visa for some of the countries she visited.
4 I tried to enrol in a course at the art college but my application arrived too late.
5 I hope to finish my studies early next year.
6 I planned to study painting and drawing.

3 1 would like; let us know 2 departs 3 further 4 completed
5 request 6 provides

ANSWER KEY

Listening
1 1 E 2 D 3 B 4 C 5 F 6 A
2 1 C 2 C 3 C 4 B 5 A 6 A

Grammar
1 1 who 2 who 3 who 4 that 5 who 6 that 7 which 8 which

2
1 Joseph Conrad, who is one of the world's greatest writers in English, was not a native speaker of that language.
2 His father, who had translated Shakespeare's plays into Polish, died when Joseph was only 11.
3 Joseph then lived with his uncle, who was a very careful man.
4 However he let Joseph, who was only 16 at the time, go away to sea.
5 His experiences on board ships, which sailed to countries like India, Africa and Australia, inspired many of his novels.

Vocabulary
1 1 firefighter 2 scientist 3 teacher
2 1 teamwork 2 problem solving 3 communication skills
3 1 not 2 not 3 again 4 not 5 not 6 about yourself
4 1 unhappy 2 disagree 3 unwell 4 irregular 5 unemployment 6 dislike 7 unexciting 8 impossible 9 impatient 10 disadvantage
5 1 impatient 2 dislike 3 unwell 4 self-employed 5 retrain 6 impossible 7 irregular 8 unhappy

Speaking
1 1 suppose 2 Personally 3 not sure 4 Speaking 5 opinion 6 seems
2 A
3 1 false 2 true 3 false 4 true 5 true
4 Maria: I don't think that

Carlos: In my opinion; I suppose; I'm not sure; Speaking for myself,

Maria: I guess

Carlos: Personally,

Maria: It seems to me that

Writing
1 Student A follows tips 1, 2 and 5.
Student B follows tips 1, 2, 3, 4 and 6.

2 Possible answers

Student A
I had always wanted to be famous until one day in March. A few weeks earlier I had been chosen to read one of my short stories on a radio programme.
As soon as I arrived an unfriendly woman came up to me and said 'Come straight into the studio. You're on in five minutes. Watch the red light.' 'But what about the sound check?' I asked anxiously. 'There's no time for that!' she said, and rushed off.
I suddenly realised that I'd left my glasses at home. I saw the red light come on but I couldn't see what I had written. Luckily I could remember my story but I knew then that I didn't want to be famous.

Student B
I had always wanted to be famous until one day in March. I had sent a short story I had written about a horrible murder on a train in to a competition. The prize was €100 and the chance to read the story aloud on the radio.
When the competition results came out I was really disappointed. I hadn't won! My friend said kindly 'Don't worry. You'll win next time!'
Then that night we were watching an exciting movie on TV about a murder on a train. 'That's really strange! It's exactly the same as my story.' I told her. I felt really embarrassed and relieved that I hadn't won the competition.

UNIT 10
Grammar
1 1 B 2 B
2 1 true 2 true 3 false 4 true 5 false 6 true
3 has it never been used; is shaped; is tempted; have been placed; are protected; can be stored; can be brought back; can be plugged into; is equipped; can't be carried around; was made
4
1 Many people see advertisements before they buy a product.
2 Designers present their spring and summer fashions in Fashion Weeks in London, Paris and Milan.
3 Hair stylists and make-up artists help models with their hair and make-up.
4 The person who stole the jewels put them on sale last week.
5 A famous Italian model designed the spring collection.
6 Somebody else has already worn this jacket.

5 1 are often advertised 2 is bought 3 is checked 4 have been sold 5 are often found 6 was sold 7 have been pulled down 8 were given 9 are sometimes made 10 was being advertised

Reading
1 1 out 2 whose 3 had 4 amount 5 been 6 why
2 1 intended 2 concealed 3 estimated 4 regretted 5 items 6 cash

Vocabulary
1 1 from 2 on 3 for 4 to 5 for 6 of 7 in
2
1 borrow books ~~for~~ – borrow books **from**
2 listen ~~at~~ – listen **to**
3 insists ~~about~~ – insists **on**
4 make an appointment ~~to~~ – make an appointment **for**
5 provides activities ~~with~~ – provides activities **for**
6 lent my book ~~for~~ – lent my book **to**
7 compared ~~by~~ – compared **to**
8 gave a book ~~for~~ – gave a book **to**

3 1 to 2 for 3 for 4 in 5 on 6 to 7 of 8 from 9 to

Vocabulary

1 1 G 2 B 3 A 4 D 5 H 6 E 7 F 8 C

2 1 boutiques 2 computer store 3 baker/baker's/bakery 4 newsagent('s) 5 supermarket 6 department stores

3 1 baker/baker's/bakery 2 florist('s) 3 sports shop 4 supermarket 5 computer store 6 furniture store 7 butcher('s) 8 jeweller's

4 1 C 2 H 3 E 4 A 5 F 6 B 7 D 8 G

Grammar

1
1 correct
2 We are ~~have~~ **having** our house repainted next week.
3 Julio will ~~getting~~ **get** his jeans cleaned very soon – they're so dirty!
4 correct
5 It's so great that you can get everything ~~deliver~~ **delivered** directly to your door!
6 correct
7 My friend always ~~having~~ **has** her shoes made by hand in Italy.
8 I'd love to have all my food ~~cook~~ **cooked** for me by a chef!

2
1 Where do you get your hair cut?
2 How often do you get your car serviced?
3 Why did you get a tattoo done?
4 How old were you when you got your ears pierced?
5 When did you get your teeth whitened?
6 Where did you get that shirt made?
7 How often do you get your eyes tested?
8 When did she have her portrait painted?

3 1 G 2 E 3 C 4 D 5 A 6 B 7 F 8 H

Listening

1 1 identity 2 golden 3 pounds 4 laptops 5 newspaper 6 convenient 7 viewing 8 discounts 9 bargain 10 Saturday

2 1 Golden 2 2 3 Laptops 4 9 5 identity 6 newspaper

Speaking

1 B

2 1 false 2 false 3 false 4 true 5 true 6 true 7 true 8 false – they don't talk about the sunglasses

3 1 true 2 agree 3 a good point 4 guess 5 absolutely right 6 sure that's true

4 1 C, J 2 D, G 3 E, H 4 A, I 5 B, F

Writing

1 1 A 2 B

2 Student A
Maybe your friend ~~have~~ **has** mentioned
my friends all ~~get~~ **got** together
I'd ~~said them~~ **told them / said** I wanted
Student B
~~neccesary~~ – ne**c**essary
~~imaggination~~ – ima**g**ination
~~delisious~~ – deli**c**ious

3 **Possible answers**
Student A
Add this sentence at the end:
That's why it's more important to think about the present itself and not about how much it costs.
Student B
Change the first sentence to this question.
Is it really necessary to spend a lot of money on a gift for a friend?

4 **Sample answer**
Is it possible to receive the perfect gift? I am not a person who wants lots of things, but there is something I would really like to receive as a gift and that is a book about birds.
It may seem strange, but actually I have wanted one for a long time. I always take every opportunity to watch birds in my garden and I would love to learn more about them. It would make me very happy if I could have a book with beautiful pictures and detailed information in it.
It's something I have just got to have!

UNIT 11

Vocabulary

1 1 go 2 share 3 make 4 souvenirs 5 guidebooks 6 trip

2 1 D 2 C 3 A 4 B

3 1 setting off 2 ended up 3 look for 4 get rid of 5 set up 6 turned into

Reading

1 False

2 1 C 2 B 3 B 4 A 5 D

3 1 confused 2 embarrassed 3 irritating 4 likely 5 greeted

Vocabulary

1 1 C 2 F 3 H 4 A 5 B 6 G 7 D 8 E

2 1 hand-painted, hand-sewn
2 self-assured, self-confident
3 well-/badly-paid, well-/badly-written

3 1 self-service 2 one-way 3 hand-painted 4 well-paid

Grammar

1
1 will get on; will like
2 are you meeting; are meeting; (are) having
3 will have to; is going to get
4 am going to study; am going to take; am going to visit

2
1 are you going to do
2 does your plane leave
3 is going to rain
4 I have; I'll probably study
5 Are you having; I'm just going to have
6 starts
7 are you going to do
8 I'm having; are meeting
9 does the lesson start
10 you'll have

124

ANSWER KEY

Speaking

1 Maria, B

2 1 classroom 2 pictures 3 sweater 4 T-shirt 5 hair 6 maps 7 happy 8 pencils 9 bridge 10 river 11 buildings 12 jeans 13 T-shirt 14 bag 15 casual 16 clear

4 1 False – they both do
2 True
3 False – they both do
4 True

Listening

1 1 A 2 C 3 B 4 B 5 C 6 C 7 A

Grammar

1 1 will 2 am/'m going to 3 will 4 will 5 are going to 6 will 7 are you going to 8 am/'m not going to 9 am/'m going to 10 will

2 1 I'm going to help you – I'll help you
2 correct
3 she will not get – she isn't going to get
4 He'll wear them – He's going to wear them
5 correct
6 correct
7 He'll have his hair cut. – He's going to have his hair cut.
8 correct

Writing

1 B

2 1 It's great to hear 2 I can 3 but 4 too 5 Let me know 6 All the best

UNIT 12

Listening

1 1 B 2 A 3 C 4 B 5 A 6 A

Grammar

1 1 C 2 E 3 A 4 B 5 F 6 D

2 1 If I don't have anything to do on Saturday mornings, I have breakfast in a café.
2 If I have a match, I have something quick to eat at home.
3 I walk to the park if it's a nice day.
4 If it's raining, my friend drives me to work.
5 The coach tells us off for playing badly if we lose.
6 If we win, he takes us all out for a pizza.

3 1 You'll never swim fast if you practise **unless you practise / if you don't practise** a lot.
2 I tell **I'll tell** you if I decide to take that climbing course.
3 If we'll miss **we miss** the last train, we'll have to walk home.
4 Unless you will work **work** hard, you won't be successful.
5 You feel **You'll feel** very proud if you get to the top of the mountain.
6 If you ask me to do something, I do **I'll do** it for you.

4 1 get 2 look 3 speak 4 will roll 5 gets 6 treat 7 respond/will respond 8 stop 9 will change

Vocabulary

1 1 C 2 G 3 F 4 D 5 B 6 H 7 A 8 E

2 1 athletics 2 surfing 3 tennis 4 hiking

3 1 join in – enter; prize ✔
2 instructor ✔; enter – join in
3 compete – train; safety – fitness
4 experienced ✔; fitness – safety
5 practice ✔; train – compete

4 1 played 2 goes 3 play 4 do 5 playing 6 go 7 go 8 doing 9 doing

Grammar

1 1 If I were bitten by a poisonous spider, I will **would** go straight to the hospital.
2 If I see **saw** a big vicious dog coming towards me, I would run away.
3 correct
4 correct
5 If I saw a shark while I was swimming, I will **would** try to swim away.
6 If a bear comes **came** up to me while I was hiking in the woods, I would try to frighten it away.

2 A would walk B would lie C would tell D would stand E would hit F would put

3 1 F 2 D 3 A 4 C 5 E 6 B

4 A 6 B 1 C 2 D 5 E 4 F 3

5 1 would/might 2 could 3 would 4 was/were 5 would 6 would

Speaking

1 1 false 2 false 3 true 4 true

2 1 yes 2 yes 3 yes 4 yes 5 yes

3 1 think 2 don't 3 right; point 4 disagree 5 already 6 opinion 7 guess 8 understand 9 let's 10 agree

4 1 D 2 A 3 B 4 C

Reading

1 1 A 2 A 3 B 4 A 5 B

2 1 B 2 A 3 A 4 B 5 B

3 1 welcome 2 delayed 3 approaching 4 recommended 5 Unfortunately 6 dangerous

Vocabulary

1 1 remember 2 take 3 trips 4 bring 5 reminding 6 come 7 go 8 travel

2 1 work 2 lend 3 miss 4 stay 5 losing 6 live 7 job 8 learn 9 borrow 10 teach

Writing

1 Student A has followed tips 1, 2, 3 and 5.
Student B has followed tips 2 and 4.

2 Possible answer

Student A
I didn't believe I could do it. When my friend suggested joining an indoor rock climbing gym, my immediate reaction was 'No way!' But one afternoon I went to watch him. Reaching the top of the wall obviously made my friend feel fantastic so I decided to give it a try.
As I got further and further above the ground my arms and legs began to shake. I was terrified. I was just about to give up when a voice inside me said, 'Not this time!' Somehow I got to the top of the wall. My friend was really impressed!

Student B
I didn't believe I could do it. I had to take part in a class debate, and although everyone hates speaking in public, I'm really scared of it.
So when my teacher told me about the debate I panicked. 'I'm sure you can do it well,' my teacher said.
I spent weeks planning what I could say. I practised hundreds of times in front of the mirror and even recorded myself. It helped, but I was still worried.
The big day came. When I got up to speak I couldn't believe how good I was! I will never be afraid of public speaking again.

VOCABULARY BANK
Using a dictionary

1 A 6 B 2 C 7 D 4 E 1 F 5 G 3 H 8

2 1 important 2 choice 3 little 4 except 5 record (n)

3 1 include 2 verb 3 yes 4 2 5 exclude 6 in 7 long
8 second 9 yes
10 no; the verb is transitive – it needs an object.

Collocations

1 1 on 2 in 3 at 4 out of 5 by 6 for

2 1 pieces 2 stock; stock 3 time 4 private 5 least
6 the same time 7 hand 8 order 9 foot 10 board
11 a long time 12 a reason

3 1 of 2 about 3 at 4 for 5 to 6 with

4 1 brilliant/good at 2 jealous of 3 bored with 4 suitable for
5 proud of 6 polite to 7 responsible for 8 late for
9 angry with 10 terrible/bad at 11 grateful for
12 worried about

5 1 for 2 from 3 on 4 to 5 of 6 at

6 1 take care of 2 borrow; from 3 recover from
4 depends on 5 approve of 6 concentrate on 7 remind; of
8 replied to 9 waiting for 10 belongs to 11 stay at
12 arrive at

7 1 take 2 make 3 have 4 do

8 1 had 2 saving 3 make 4 perform 5 keeping 6 run
7 break 8 print 9 gain 10 pay 11 doing 12 give

Word formation

1 1 im- 2 ir- 3 un- 4 dis-

2 1 B 2 D 3 A 4 C

3 1 disrespectful 2 self-control 3 re-do 4 immature
5 mini-break 6 non-fiction 7 retrain 8 unreliable

5 1 -y 2 -ly 3 -able 4 -less 5 -ful 6 -ment

6 actor; artist; builder; designer; director; farmer; instructor; journalist; photographer; reporter; sailor; scientist

7 1 acceptable 2 foggy 3 designer 4 actor 5 loudly
6 disagreement 7 pleasurable 8 careless 9 patiently
10 disappointment

9 1 B 2 F 3 A 4 D 5 H 6 C 7 E 8 G

10 1 show business 2 signpost 3 music festival
4 hard disk 5 railway line 6 exchange visit 7 information pack
8 snowstorm

11 1 F 2 A 3 B 4 H 5 G 6 E 7 D 8 C

12 1 never-ending 2 broken-hearted 3 two-hour
4 one-way 5 long-distance 6 world-famous
7 energy-efficient 8 homemade

Phrasal verbs

1 1 E 2 B 3 H 4 G 5 D 6 A 7 F 8 C

2 1 look up 2 give up 3 bring up 4 hang up

3 1 G 2 B 3 A 4 E 5 H 6 F 7 C 8 D

4 1 get on 2 get on with 3 keeps on 4 carried on

5 1 F 2 G 3 C 4 A 5 D 6 B 7 H 8 E

6 1 went off 2 worn off 3 set off 4 put; off

7 1 C 2 F 3 D 4 A 5 H 6 E 7 G 8 B

8 1 going out 2 set out 3 handed out 4 run out of

9 1 B 2 H 3 F 4 A 5 C 6 D 7 E 8 G

10 1 look after 2 looking forward to 3 call in on 4 thrown; away

Different meanings of get

1 1 buy 2 receive 3 improve 4 arrive 5 move 6 find
7 become 8 prepare

Easily confused words

1 1 packet 2 sensible 3 foreigners 4 advice 5 told 6 opinion
7 scenery 8 remind 9 lend 10 bring

Same sound, different spelling

1 1 except 2 there 3 hear 4 weather 5 see 6 Where

COMMON ERRORS: B1 PRELIMINARY

1 1 ~~What~~ **What's** your name?
2 Where **are** you from?
3 What **do** you do?
4 Where **are** you going?
5 How many times **have** you been outside your country?
6 What **did** you enjoy most about the experience?

2 1 I **regularly** watch ~~regularly~~ films with my friends.
2 I'm **normally** good at getting things ~~normally~~ done but this week I've felt very tired.
3 I'm **always** working ~~always~~ when my friends come round to chat.
4 I **generally** love going ~~generally~~ shopping but not when the shops are crowded.

ANSWER KEY

5 I don't **often** watch ~~often~~ television but sometimes I do at the weekend.
6 I try to do ~~every day~~ some exercise **every day**.

3
1 People who ~~lives~~ **live** in glass houses shouldn't throw stones.
2 My sister ~~ride~~ **rides** her bicycle to college every day.
3 When ~~do~~ **are** you coming to visit us again?
4 ~~I going~~ **I am / I'm going** away for the weekend so I'll be a bit late on Monday.
5 My brother ~~don't~~ **doesn't** like hip hop music.
6 You ~~takes~~ **take** the tram to La Laguna. It ~~stop~~ **stops** opposite the university.

4
1 He ~~must to be~~ **must be** exhausted. The match has been going on for over five hours.
2 It ~~mustn't~~ **can't** be the postman. He never comes this early.
3 I'll answer the phone if you like. It **may/might/could** be for me.
4 We ~~can to meet~~ **can meet** on Wednesday or Thursday. I don't mind.
5 Take an umbrella, just in case. It ~~can~~ **may/might/could** rain later.
6 When I finish college, I ~~might to go~~ **might go** and work in another country.

5
1 If you ask me, ~~to buy~~ **buying** a new computer is a waste of money.
2 She apologised for ~~arrive~~ **arriving** late.
3 I'm better at ~~watch~~ **watching** tennis than I am at ~~play~~ **playing** it.
4 Would you mind ~~to pass~~ **passing** the salt?
5 We're looking forward to ~~hear~~ **hearing** about your holiday in Greece.
6 We've arranged ~~meeting~~ **to meet** outside the cinema at 5.30.

6
1 You ~~must not to walk~~ **must not walk** on the grass.
2 I ~~has~~ **have** to go. See you later.
3 ~~Have we~~ **Do we have** to buy a book or is the teacher going to give us photocopies?
4 If you want to lose weight, you ~~don't have to~~ **shouldn't** eat so many cakes and sweets.
5 ~~Do I should wear~~ **Should I wear** a hat to the wedding?
6 Sue won't be here today. She ~~must~~ **had to** go to the dentist.

7
1 ~~Did you ever go~~ **Have you ever been** to Paris?
2 Yes, several times. In fact, ~~I have gone~~ **went** last November.
3 A friend of mine ~~have gone~~ **went** last year. He says it's very expensive.
4 Well, it used to be but this time I ~~have found~~ **found** it quite cheap.
5 Where ~~have you stayed~~ **did you stay**?
6 In a little hotel near the Sorbonne. ~~It was~~ **It's been** there for ages. My great-grandfather ~~has stayed~~ **used to stay/stayed** there every time he ~~has gone~~ **went** to Paris.

8
1 I'm not ~~good at~~ **as/so good at** salsa dancing as Tina.
2 Tina has a ~~good~~ **better** sense of rhythm than me.
3 Carey is **the** worst in the salsa class.
4 Carey is even ~~more bad~~ **worse** than Ivan.

9
1 We had ~~a so~~ **such a** good time at the party.
2 Susan is such **a** nice person.
3 This tiramisu is ~~such~~ **so** delicious! Can I have some more?
4 You're not ~~enough old~~ **old enough** to stay out after midnight.
5 Snowboarding is ~~so fun~~ **such fun / so much fun**. I love it.
6 I'm afraid the exam was ~~too much difficult~~ **much too difficult / too difficult** for me. I don't think I'll pass.

10
1 Where ~~does~~ **did** your father live when he was a child?
2 Who ~~winned~~ **won** the Eurovision song contest last year?
3 We all ~~feeled~~ **felt** ill after the meal.
4 I fell in love with Fernando the first time I ~~seed~~ **saw** him.
5 We ~~buyed~~ **bought** Mum some perfume for her birthday.
6 I ~~catched~~ **caught** a terrible cold while I was in London.

11
1 Alex ~~listened~~ **was listening** to some music on his phone while the teacher was telling us what to do for homework.
2 Some of the contestants were rehearsing when the stage ~~was collapsing~~ **collapsed**.
3 I was phoning my friend on her mobile when I ~~was seeing~~ **saw** her standing on the corner.
4 You were sitting there watching the match while I ~~cooked~~ **was cooking** the dinner!
5 I ~~had~~ **was having** a shower when the telephone rang.
6 Tim ~~slept~~ **was sleeping** soundly while the burglars were stealing his new flat-screen TV.

12
1 As soon as I ~~had got~~ **got** to school, I remembered that the teacher had told us there was going to be an exam that day.
2 I felt really nervous because I ~~missed~~ **had missed** lots of lectures.
3 By the time I got to the classroom, the teacher ~~already started~~ **had already started** the exam.
4 I had hardly looked at the questions when I ~~had seen~~ **saw** that the boy sitting next to me had written almost a whole page.
5 When the teacher ~~had told~~ **told** us to stop writing, I had only answered two of the three questions.
6 I was sure I ~~failed~~ **had failed** but, in fact, in the end I got quite a good mark.

13
1 She was wearing ~~a~~ trousers and a jacket.
2 Are we having **a** chicken for dinner again?
3 She's got ~~a~~ lovely dark curly hair.
4 How ~~many~~ **much** money do you spend on food and entertainment each week?
5 There ~~are too many furnitures~~ **is too much furniture** in this room.

14
1 I love living here because **the** sun shines almost every day.
2 There's **a** volcano here that is almost 4,000 metres high.
3 I prefer living on **the** coast to living in **the** countryside though.
4 It's wonderful to be able to swim in **the** sea every day.
5 There's also **a** lake near here which has very clear water.
6 I sometimes go there at night and swim in the light of **the** moon.

15
1 ~~She said me~~ **She told me / She said** that she would be a little bit late.
2 I told ~~to~~ the neighbours that I was going to be away for a few days.
3 Tim ~~told~~ **said** that he would be home on Saturday night.
4 Tanya said that she ~~can't~~ **couldn't** ride a bicycle.
5 Paulo told me he ~~is~~ **was** coming on Monday.
6 Gustave said he ~~will~~ **would** be here by midday but he still hasn't arrived.

16
1 She asked me how ~~I feeling~~ **I was feeling**.
2 She asked us ~~did we enjoy~~ **if/whether we enjoyed** our English course.
3 She asked me ~~have I~~ **if/whether I had** any special plans for the future.
4 She asked me what ~~are you going~~ **I was going** to do when I finished university.

127

5 She asked me ~~is there~~ **if/whether there was** anything special I ~~want~~ **wanted** to do in the future.

6 She asked me what kinds of things ~~did I like~~ **I liked** doing in my spare time.

17
1 I can understand the news on the radio now but I ~~can't~~ **couldn't** even understand my teacher a few months ago.

2 I ~~could~~ **can** read short books in English now but I couldn't even read a newspaper at the beginning of the course.

3 I ~~was able to~~ **am able to / can** write stories, reports and articles in English now but I ~~can't even~~ **couldn't even / wasn't even able to** write an informal letter when we started using this book.

4 I can express my opinion in English now but I ~~can't~~ **couldn't** even talk about a photo properly last September.

5 I ~~could~~ **can** pronounce most words quite well now but I ~~can't~~ **couldn't** even understand the pronunciation symbols in the dictionary at the beginning of the course.

18
1 Tina, ~~that~~ **who** came to your party, is living in Paris now.

2 Thor Heyerdahl, ~~that~~ **who** died in 2000, discovered some pyramids on the island of Tenerife.

3 She's the girl I told you about ~~her~~.

4 Tim's the boy ~~who's~~ **whose** father is a politician.

5 Is Fabio the boy ~~which~~ **who/that** is going to France next year?

19
1 The original museum ~~were~~ **was** built in 1765.

2 The exam was ~~took~~ **taken** by most of the students in the class.

3 The anniversary of the opening of the museum **is** celebrated every year in November.

4 Visitors ~~is~~ **are** attracted to the town by the annual music festival.

5 The sculpture was ~~create~~ **created** by a very young artist.

6 My neighbour's jewellery **was** stolen by a burglar last night.

20
1 I usually have my hair ~~cutted~~ **cut** every six weeks.

2 I often ~~getting~~ **get** my friends to create playlists for me – my taste in music is terrible!

3 I prefer to ~~has~~ **have** my groceries delivered – I hate going to the supermarket!

4 I never try to fix my car if there is a problem with it – I always **get/have** it fixed by a mechanic.

5 I'm ~~have~~ **having** my house painted right now – the painter is making quite a mess!

6 I ~~have~~ **had** my smart dress dry-cleaned yesterday – it looks fantastic now.

21
1 Oh no! I think I'm ~~being~~ **going to be** sick.

2 I have to go now. ~~I phone~~ **I'll phone** you back later.

3 What ~~do you do~~ **are you going to do** next year when you finish school?

4 What time **does** your plane leave?

5 Look at those dark clouds. It ~~rains~~ **is going to rain** later.

6 I've already decided. ~~I'll buy~~ **I'm going to buy** Ella a CD for her birthday.

22
1 How ~~would~~ **do** you feel if you don't get enough sleep? / How would you feel if you ~~don't~~ **didn't** get enough sleep?

2 What would you say if you ~~meet~~ **met** someone famous?

3 Who do you usually talk to when you ~~were~~ **are** worried about something?

4 How ~~do~~ **would** you feel if Australia won the World Cup?

5 What ~~do~~ **will** you do this summer if you can't afford to go on holiday?

6 What would you buy if you ~~would have~~ **had** £100,000?

7 I always forget to take my umbrella when it ~~rained~~ **rains**!

8 What would you do if you ~~have~~ **had** the afternoon off work?

23
1 My boyfriend is quite ~~well-build~~ **well-built**. He's ~~medium-hieght~~ **medium-height** (about 1.80) and a little bit ~~overwieght~~ **overweight** but I still think he's very ~~hansome~~ **handsome**. The thing I like most about him though is that he is always very ~~honnest~~ **honest**.

2 You'll love our house in the mountains. In the winter, when it's been snowing outside, we all sit around the ~~chimney~~ **fire** and talk after dinner. It's so cosy. It can be quite hot in summer but, luckily, we have ~~air-conditioned~~ **air-conditioning** so we keep nice and cool. I hope you can come next year.

3 The person in my family I get ~~through~~ **on** with best is my older sister. We're really good friends. She's about seven years older than me so she looked ~~for~~ **after** me and my younger brother a lot when we were little.

4 I couldn't work ~~up~~ **out** the meaning of a word and I decided to ~~look up it~~ **look it up** in a dictionary. It wasn't there so I looked ~~in~~ **for** it online but I couldn't find it there either. In the end I gave ~~out~~ **up** and decided to ask the teacher.

5 A lot of people criticise it but I get a lot of ~~enjoy~~ **enjoyment** from watching television. I even like the ~~advertisings~~ **advertisements**.

6 I wanted to buy a new top because ~~at~~ **of** the hot weather. There were some nice ones ~~in~~ **on** sale ~~on~~ **in** a shop near here. I tried one ~~out~~ **on** but I wasn't very keen ~~for~~ **on** the way it looked ~~at~~ **on** me. I'm really tired ~~with~~ **of** looking ~~at~~ **for** clothes that fit me. I never find anything!

EXAM STRATEGIES

Reading

1 **1** C **2** A **3** B

2 The student forgot advice 2. The correct answer is C.

3 **1** B **2** A **3** C

4 The student forgot advice 2. The film is only partly a match for Sue. It is a true story and has a happy ending, which match Sue's needs, but it is a musical, which she doesn't want.

5 **1** opinions and feelings **2** before **3** writer's purpose

6 You need to follow advice 3 and also advice 2.

7 The correct order is c, e, b, d, a.

8 It is wrong because of reference words – *They* in sentence A refers to the two friends.

9 **1** collocations **2** phrasal verbs **3** meanings

10 **1** D, Statement 2 **2** B, Statement 1 **3** D, Statement 3

11 Statement 4

12 The answer to question 3 is wrong. The student didn't follow advice 5.

Writing

1 **1** You should write about ~~50~~ **100** words.
2 correct
3 You ~~don't have to~~ **must** include all the information asked for in the notes.
4 correct

2 The student has forgotten advice 1 and 3. They have only written about 50 words and have not included the information asked for in the notes.

ANSWER KEY

3 1 S 2 B 3 B 4 B 5 B 6 B 7 A

4 The student has forgotten advice 3, 4 and 5. There is not a range of language, the story is too long and there are no paragraphs.

5 The student has forgotten advice 2, 6 and 7. There are spelling mistakes, the article is not interesting to read and the writer has not included all the necessary information as they have not explained what they do to relax.

Listening

1 1 C 2 A 3 B

2 The correct answer is C. The student has forgotten advice 1. The places in all the options are mentioned but they are at different times or have been discounted. Only C is where the keys are *at the moment*.

3 1 B 2 C 3 A

4 The correct answer is C. The student has forgotten Advice 3. All the options are mentioned by one or other of the speakers (the poor condition of the pitch and the good referee), but only C is what they both think about the match.

5 Explanation 2

6 The correct answer is 10. The student has forgotten Advice 1. It's important to think about the kind of information that may be needed in the space, and check that your answer is both correct and makes sense. 'Breakfast' is not the right answer because it goes on until 10.30, and the information packs are available from 10. There are several times mentioned here, but only one fits the space and follows *after*.

7 1 opinion(s), attitude(s) 2 different

8 The correct answer is B. The student has made mistake B. They have chosen the first thing they heard and have not listened to the end of Clare's answer, where she says *the best thing is …* . She does say that she loves talking to students but this is not what she enjoys most.

Speaking

1 Advice 3 and 4. The student is hesitating too much because they are worried about making grammar mistakes.

2 Advice 2. The student is worried because they don't know a word, but it doesn't matter if this happens. It is better to move on and keep talking about other things in the photograph.

3 Advice 3. It is important for students to ask each other for their opinion as this makes a good discussion. They will get better marks for interacting with each other.

4 Advice 1 and 2. Both students give irrelevant information, and they don't answer the question about 'the best thing to do'. Neither student gives interesting details about their ideas or reasons for their opinions. Student B did listen to what Student A said, as they say 'I don't like sport'.

PRACTICE TEST
Reading

Part 1
1 B 2 A 3 C 4 C 5 C

Part 2
6 G 7 D 8 C 9 F 10 A

Part 3
11 A 12 A 13 B 14 B 15 C

Part 4
16 D 17 B 18 A 19 H 20 F

Part 5
21 B 22 A 23 C 24 D 25 A 26 C

Part 6
27 how 28 so 29 been 30 them 31 a 32 which

Writing

Question 1
Sample answer

Hi Emily,

I'm so glad you enjoyed the day at the adventure park – I did too!

Yes, I would love to go out for the day with you and your family next week – Friday would be the best day for me. It would be great to go to the beach, because I enjoy swimming, and I think the weather will be fine next week.

I enjoy eating cheese sandwiches when I'm out, so they would be great. I like chocolate cake too!

Thank you for asking me, and I'm looking forward to seeing you next week!

Question 2
Sample answer

Relaxing in your free time

Is it easy to relax in your free time? In my country people often go to a park or to the beach, because they can have a quiet time there and do whatever they want. They usually sunbathe, play games or have a picnic with their friends, relaxing together.

It's very important for everyone to relax and spend their free time with family and friends. This is because everyday life is usually very busy and it's good to get away from work and studies, and not worry about anything.

I think it's very healthy to do this, although it's not always easy!

Question 3
Sample answer

It was the most enjoyable day of my life. I woke up early with a feeling that something was going to happen, but I did not know what it was. I went downstairs, checked my email, and jumped for joy. My best friend, who had moved to another city a year ago, was coming to visit me and was arriving at 10 o'clock!

I got dressed quickly and rushed to the station. There she was, waiting for me! We talked and talked, and had a wonderful time.

I was very sad when she went back home, but we will meet again soon.

Listening

Part 1
1 C 2 C 3 B 4 B 5 C 6 A 7 C

Part 2
8 C 9 B 10 C 11 A 12 A 13 C

Part 3
14 reception desk 15 Wednesday 16 9 (a.m.) 17 safety
18 weather 19 sun cream

Part 4
20 C 21 B 22 C 23 A 24 C 25 A

129

Audio scripts

UNIT 1
▶ 01

S = Steve   B = Bailey
S: Hi, I'm Steve.
B: I'm Bailey. Nice to meet you.
S: Sorry, I didn't catch that – what's your name?
B: Bailey. Do you think it's an unusual name?
S: Yes! Where does it come from?
B: I think it's popular in Australia.
S: Have you been there?
B: No, I haven't – it's a long way away!
S: So who gave you that name?
B: Actually, it was my dad – he just liked it. So do I!
S: you ever have any problems with the name?
B: Well, it can be a name for both boys and girls.
S: Do people find that confusing?
B: Definitely! Before they meet me, they often think I'm a boy!

▶ 02

F = Female   M = Male

1 Which picture shows the woman's brother?
F: Have you seen the pictures of my brother I uploaded to my photo page?
M: I don't know what he looks like – does he have fair hair like you?
F: Not at all – he's got dark curly hair and he's quite thin – he used to be fatter but he lost a lot of weight when he started playing tennis every week. He wears glasses for reading but not every day – and he's not wearing them on the Facebook photo.

2 How did the man find out about the football result?
F: Did you find out about the football result? I couldn't see it in today's newspaper.
M: No, it was an evening game and it went into extra time so it finished too late for the morning papers. I had hoped to listen to the whole commentary on my laptop but the WiFi was bad, so I couldn't even get the live feed. Luckily, there was a report on the late night news on television so I was able to see the goals then.

3 What will the weather be like at the weekend?
The weather has been unsettled lately, with temperatures lower than normal for the time of year. Even so, some places have had plenty of sunshine today, though the sun hasn't really warmed the air much. However, that's all set to change. Tonight, rain will move in to the north, where there might even be some light snow showers as temperatures drop, although the snow will melt quickly. The rain will be heavy in all areas and looks set to continue until Saturday – probably Sunday as well. So wear warm clothes and don't forget an umbrella!

4 Where will the man go first?
F: Why are you going now? Your haircut isn't until 11.30.
M: I know, but I have to go to the bank to pay a bill. And while I'm in town, I can take those library books back – then we won't have to pay a fine because they're late! But I must get some petrol before anything else, otherwise we'll run out and I won't go anywhere!
F: Could you stop at the post office and get some stamps? I must write some letters.
M: Okay. I'll have to do that after my haircut though.

5 What did the woman buy for Julia's birthday?
M: Did you get something for Julia's birthday? I've got her a new pen.
F: I looked everywhere and couldn't make up my mind. I almost bought her a necklace but it was very expensive – especially as there were matching earrings too. Then I remembered that she needs gloves, and there was this good deal in one shop with a scarf too – so I got them both. Next year I'll have to get her something different though. Maybe just a good book – she likes reading.

6 Which television programme does the man want to watch?
F: What do you want to watch on television tonight? There's a great concert – that new female singer's going to be on.
M: I'm not in the right mood for that – I want something more exciting. I'd quite like to give that new science fiction series a try – you know, the one we recorded last week. I suppose we could watch that documentary about formula one racing after that – though it doesn't start until ten and I'm quite tired.

7 What will the woman wear to the theatre?
F: I need advice! I'm going to the theatre tomorrow night and I can't decide what to wear. I've got that smart suit with the short skirt and jacket but it's rather like a work outfit.
M: How about that long skirt? You've got the new white cardigan to go with it.
F: It's a bit summery. It's still cold so I'd have to wear a jacket with it. I think it'll have to be the suit. I like wearing trousers but I don't think they're suitable for the theatre.
M: Whatever you feel comfortable in!

AUDIO SCRIPTS

UNIT 2
▶ 07

I = Interviewer   C = Chris Jones

I: Today we're talking to Chris Jones, a successful young chef who has just begun a career in television. Chris, tell us why you became a chef.

C: I've always loved cooking. When I was young, I spent ages in the kitchen watching my mother prepare meals – she helped me a lot. When I was at school, my friends laughed at me. They were into things like sport and thought cooking was for girls! Although my teachers said it was a crazy idea, I was determined.

I: Why did you decide to open your own restaurant?

C: I studied nutrition at college, then went to work in a restaurant in France. I wanted to get as much experience as possible, and I learned a lot there. The chef taught me to cook his special dishes, which gave me ideas for recipes. I wanted other people to see and eat my new meals and that was what made me start my own restaurant. I didn't really care about the money but it's quite nice to work for myself.

I: What's your favourite food?

C: When I was a child, I loved typical home-cooked food like cakes and sausages. But I got interested in unusual combinations of tastes and now I love creating different healthy salads. Top of my list though is fish. There are so many different things you can do with it and it's easy to create new recipes.

I: Then you started working in television. Tell us about that.

C: It was strange! By chance, a TV producer came into my restaurant. He liked my food, we started talking and he said that he was looking for a chef to do a new series of cooking programmes. I went to the studio for an audition. There were other chefs there, so I was amazed when they offered me the job.

I: How did you feel before the first programme?

C: We did loads of practice and it was very exciting. There was a lot for me to remember though, and I was nervous in case the food wasn't good. You see, I was cooking it during the programme, which was live, not recorded, and if anything had gone wrong, I would have been very embarrassed.

I: So how do you see the future?

C: There are so many things I want to do! There may be a new television series but I'll definitely write a book – that's a good way to get people to try my recipes so it's top of my list. I'll keep my restaurant, and I might open some more, though that's not a priority. It would be great to travel too, so I can try food from all over the world.

UNIT 3
▶ 08

1 You will hear two friends talking about a visit to a restaurant.

F: I really enjoyed that meal.

M: I thought the menu was very good. There were lots of different choices – it was difficult to decide what to have. It was all well-cooked and very tasty.

F: I thought the waiter was lovely – really kind and friendly.

M: Yes, but we waited a long time for the first course – and I was really hungry! The rest of the meal took ages too.

F: I suppose so. It was a nice place, though, and the music was just right.

M: It was better than I'd expected, to be honest.

2 You will hear a woman telling a friend about a visit to the theatre.

M: How was the theatre last night?

F: Oh, the play was quite exciting in spite of a rather poor story, and I had a great view, but the rest of the evening wasn't so good.

M: Why – what happened?

F Oh, the man in front of me was talking to his friend the whole time – it was difficult to concentrate. I thought he was rude, actually.

M: Didn't you tell him to be quiet?

F: I asked the manager to speak to him, and he did, but it didn't make any difference.

M: You should have asked to move somewhere else.

F: I will next time!

3 You will hear two friends talking about a class they both attended.

M: What did you think of the class?

F: I like the teacher – she's lively and makes it interesting. She can be a bit disorganised, though, and she doesn't do enough preparation.

M: I wasn't sure what her focus was. I tried to ask her afterwards, but she didn't want to stop and talk to me – a bit rude, I thought.

F: That's a shame, but to be honest you missed the class last week and this one was linked to it. That's probably why it seemed a bit unclear.

M: I don't think she thinks about it properly before the lesson, though.

4 You will hear two friends talking about a party they both went to.

M: That was a fun party last Saturday.

F: Did you think so? I was a bit bored.

M: Okay. I enjoyed the food, although they were the wrong snacks for the occasion. Who eats sandwiches at a party? The music was okay too, though it wasn't my usual style.

F: Not my favourite, I'm afraid – and it was very loud. I couldn't talk to anyone properly because I couldn't hear them.

M: You have to admit it was nice to catch up with old friends. That made it for me.

F: It would have been great without the music!

5 You will hear a woman telling a friend about a tennis match she played in.

F: I played so badly! I need to do something to improve.

M: You weren't so bad – you just need to have more confidence in yourself.

F: I don't have a regular partner – it would be much easier if I did. I need to improve my strength and stamina first, though, and my coach is going to do something about that.

M: I come to the courts and just hit balls as often as I can.

F: That's what I need – I'd love to join you regularly instead of just now and again. Then if I work out in the gym as well I should get better.

6 You will hear two friends talking about a new cinema.

M: Did you like the new cinema?

F: It was better value than I'd expected but that's because there are special offers at the moment. That must be just for the first few weeks.

M: I'm sure prices will go up once people start going regularly – I actually thought it cost quite a lot.

F: Oh, and the seats weren't great – the leg-room was terrible.

M: My back hurt after an hour or so.

F: And they didn't clear up after the film – there were sweet papers lying around.

M: I didn't notice. People shouldn't drop litter anyway. It's very bad manners.

UNIT 4

12

E = Examiner

E: Some students want to make a time capsule so that people who live a hundred years from now can learn about life today.

Here are some things they can put in the capsule.

Talk together about the different things the students could put in the time capsule and say which would be most interesting.

M: Well, the capsule doesn't look very big so, do you think we should choose small things?

F: Maybe. But the clothes would be a really good way of showing what people wear today. Don't you agree?

M: Definitely, but I think the fashion magazine would show what we look like now anyway. I mean, not just the clothes we wear but also hairstyles, jewellery and make-up.

F: Actually, I think you're probably right. And the magazine will take up less space in the capsule.

M: How about the mobile phone? We could put different kinds of music on it, and photos and videos as well.

F: Yeah, maybe. But the technology will be very different a hundred years from now. They might not be able to use it.

M: Hmm … you could be right. And the battery will have run out, of course! What do you think about the money?

F: I'd definitely put that in. After all, it doesn't take up much space and it will be interesting for people to see the images and writing on the coins and notes. How about the newspaper?

M: It's a bit big. Maybe we could just use the front page. They'd know what the main news stories were that day on the internet.

F: Good idea. Then we could fit the recipe in as well. That would tell them about the kind of food we eat.

M: What about the photo of the city? Cities probably will have changed a lot by 2119!

F: That's true. So which would be most interesting for people in the future? It's difficult!

E: Thank you.

13

1 Where is the art gallery?

F: Excuse me, can you tell me where the art gallery is, please?

M: Of course. Just keep going along this road until you get to the traffic lights at the crossroads. There's a big department store on the left on this side of the lights, and a museum just past the lights on the same side of the road. The art gallery is opposite the museum, on the right.

F: Thanks very much.

2 What did the woman like best in the museum?

M: It's a great museum. I thought those old bowls were fascinating! They had beautiful shapes painted on them – it must have taken ages to do that!

F: That's true but I quite liked the costumes from 200 years ago. It's interesting that people were shorter then, and the dresses were lovely.

M: Yes, I agree about that.

F: But for me it was the jewellery section that was most interesting – I could have stayed there all day!

3 When is the best day for students to visit the museum?

The museum is open from nine to five every day except Sundays, when it is closed. There is a 20 percent discount for anyone over 65 on Tuesdays, and anyone at school or college can get in for free on Wednesday if they show their identity card. On all other days they have to pay full price. Family tickets are available on Saturdays, when children under 12 are free if they come with two adults.

4 What did the man buy in the museum shop?

F: So what did you buy?

M: Well, I wanted to get a mug – you know, one of those with a picture of something from the museum on it, like a vase, but they only had black ones left and I didn't like them. I decided that a key-ring with a picture of the museum on it was the best thing to get, although I nearly bought a pen because there was this beautiful silver one in an old style. But it was a bit expensive and I didn't want to spend too much.

5 What does the woman say is most useful to her?

M: What are you doing?

F: I'm planning my English homework. I've got to write about the thing that is most useful in my life. I'm not sure what to say. I use my laptop for work and also chatting to friends but I don't take it everywhere with me. It's too big!

M: What about a book?

F: I think I'll say a dictionary. I suppose most people will write about their mobile phones. Or I could say a tablet – but I'll stick with my choice.

6 What has the man kept the longest?

F: I've been tidying up my room. It's great to throw things away sometimes.

M: Yes, but isn't it difficult to throw away things that have happy memories? I've got lots of things that I want to keep. Like, I have a ticket from my first visit to the theatre last year and a teddy bear that belonged to my mother – that must be the oldest thing I have. I keep a photograph of my grandmother on my wall but that was only taken a couple of years ago so it's not very old. But I wouldn't want to lose any of them!

7 Where does the woman want to go at the weekend?

M: What shall we do on Saturday?

F: Good question! We went to the art gallery last weekend, which was great – I really enjoyed that. What about the museum? I hear it's got some new exhibits that would be interesting. And it's free too! Or there's that new film at the cinema. Though it didn't get very good reviews so let's not go and see that.

UNIT 5

▶ 14

H = Helen   J = Joe

H: Hi, Joe! I didn't expect to find you in the shopping centre. I thought you hated buying clothes!

J: Hi, Helen. Oh, I do! It's a complete waste of time as far as I'm concerned! But my sister's getting married next month and I have to get some formal clothes to wear. I'm not doing very well though. I tried to borrow some from a friend but they didn't fit me.

H: Shall I help? I've got a few minutes to spare and I'm always happy to talk about clothes! I want to work in fashion if I can so I may have some ideas for you.

J: That would be great! I know that I have to get a suit. That's not too bad – I can do that – but choosing a shirt and tie is a nightmare! I have loads of jeans and T-shirts but I never wear smart clothes like that so I don't know where to start.

H: Colour's the important thing – they have to go together. What's your favourite colour?

J: I have no idea. Blue, I suppose.

H: Great! That's easy – that goes with most other colours. A good thing you didn't say orange or purple – that would be much more difficult! What about a dark blue suit, a white shirt and a light blue striped tie?

J: Is that boring? It sounds rather old-fashioned to me and I don't want anyone to think I'm not up-to-date in what I wear.

H: Well, it's not exactly trendy! But as it's for a wedding, I think it would be a safe choice and you would look nice.

J: Well, thanks. Would you like to come to the shop with me and help me choose?

H: Sorry, I haven't got time right now. But if you haven't managed to find anything by next Saturday, I'll come with you then. I'm going shopping with my friend anyway so helping you won't take long. There's a great second-hand shop that sells really good stuff. You might get something cheap there. And if you don't wear formal clothes very often, that might be a good idea.

J: Sounds great!

▶ 15

Do you love animals but have no time to look after one full-time? Do you spend all your time earning money, which is still not enough for you to keep a pet? Here's the answer: join our Pet Share Club and rent a pet! You must be over 21 to join but the perfect age is over 25. We even have members up to 75! You will need to prove your age by showing your identity card when you register with the club.

We have all sorts of pets to rent: rabbits, cats and so on – but dogs are the favourites.

Once you have joined, we give you a card, which you must show every time you rent a pet. You can take a pet home for a day, a week or even a month – it's up to you, but the majority of our members find a weekend is best. Every time you want to rent a pet, you need to make a booking. You can do this on the website, by phone, in a text or in person, which is the best and fastest way.

We try to match new members with a pet we think suits their personality but we also encourage them to choose an animal that is a good size for their home. It's not a good idea to choose a large animal if you live in a small flat, no matter how sweet it is! And it's important that you are able to give the animal enough exercise so although you don't need a big garden, you need to have a large park close to your home.

So how much does it cost? There's a monthly payment of £25 on top of the annual membership fee of £50. There's also a charge for every time you rent a pet; that's £20 at weekends or £12 on weekdays.

Why not give us a try? You'll love it! And you can rent a pet as often as you like. It could change your life!

▶ 16

I can see two people who are both wearing casual clothes. They are both smiling so they are enjoying themselves. They are trying on shoes. The woman on the left is trying on a pair of high-heeled sandals, and she is wearing jeans, a T-shirt and a cardigan. The other woman has longer hair, and she is also wearing jeans and a cardigan. Both the women are sitting on comfortable chairs and there are a lot of shoes on the floor around them. There is a bag on the floor next to the woman on the right, and there are four boxes next to the woman on the left.

UNIT 6

▶ 18

E = Examiner   S = Sofia   X = Xin

- **E:** Sofia, what do you enjoy doing with your friends at the weekends?
- **S:** I like shopping or going to a friend's house for a meal.
- **E:** Xin, what did you do yesterday evening?
- **X:** Actually, I went to the cinema with my friends. We saw a really good film, which was very exciting, and after that we went to a pizza restaurant for a meal.
- **E:** Sofia, what do you want to do after you leave college?
- **S:** I am going to be a teacher.
- **E:** Xin, what do you do every morning?
- **X:** First of all, I eat a big breakfast – I like to eat lots of toast and jam. Then I go to college by bus.

▶ 19

E = Examiner   C = Carlos   M = Maria

- **E:** Carlos, do you prefer winter holidays, or summer holidays?
- **C:** I love winter holidays because I really like skiing. Also, I think the mountains are beautiful. The air is very fresh and it is very healthy.
- **E:** What do you think, Maria?
- **M:** I disagree with Carlos. I prefer summer holidays. I usually go to the beach in summer. I love hot weather, and I don't like being cold, so summer is better for me.
- **E:** Do you think people have enough holidays, Maria?
- **M:** I think people work too hard and so they need to relax. They should have lots of holidays!
- **E:** Do you agree Carlos?
- **C:** Yes, I think the same as Maria. I think people should spend more time with their family and have fun. So perhaps we should have more holidays!

▶ 20

1 **You will hear two friends talking about a history lesson.**

- **F:** Well, that was better than I'd expected – I never thought that history could be so interesting.
- **M:** For me some of it wasn't very interesting, and I found myself thinking about other things. I guess I did find it a bit hard to follow, too – all those dates!
- **F:** Oh, but they're fascinating! It's not hard if you concentrate and try to imagine what life was like then. It's so important to know what happened before we were born.
- **M:** We can learn from what went on before, certainly, and that's useful. I just don't enjoy it very much!

2 **You will hear a woman telling a friend about her music lessons.**

- **M:** Are you enjoying your music lessons?
- **F:** Well, the teacher's very patient and he explains everything several times but I don't always get what he means, so I can't do what he wants.
- **M:** But you practise a lot, don't you?
- **F:** That's not the problem – I actually enjoy that. I just don't think I'm very good at it!
- **M:** It must be nice to be able to play whatever you like, though.
- **F:** Oh, I can't do that yet! Though I like what we're working on and often sing along with it.
- **M:** Well, I'm sure you'll improve with time.

3 **You will hear two students talking about a lecture they went to.**

- **M:** Well, that was an interesting lecture! It was good that the speaker made a lot of jokes, too – I enjoyed that.

AUDIO SCRIPTS

F: I prefer speakers who are serious – I think it's easier to concentrate then. I thought it wasn't always easy to understand what he was saying, or what he meant.

M: I think he said things more than once, which did mean I wasn't sure exactly what he was talking about. It was a useful subject, though – I think it will help me with my project work this weekend.

F: I'm not sure – I think my reference book will be more useful.

4 You will hear a woman telling a friend about learning to drive.

M: Are you enjoying learning to drive?

F: It's not too bad, thanks – I've got my test next week, and I feel ready for it.

M: I hope it goes well!

F: Thanks. I've spent a lot of money over the weeks, though I guess everyone does – I knew learning to drive was expensive, but it's been too much really. On the other hand, I was lucky because my instructor was great, and we got on well.

M: You'll have to give me her name – I'm going to start driving lessons soon and it's good to have a recommendation.

5 You will hear a man telling a friend about a college course he is going to do.

F: So you've definitely decided to go to college, then?

M: Yes. I thought about it carefully, because it isn't cheap, but that wasn't the biggest problem. I wanted to do it because it was interesting, and not just because it would get me a job – I know it won't do that.

F: I understand that.

M: I was also worried that I might not be good enough – it does seem to be very challenging – but then I thought I should try it anyway.

F: So when do you start?

M: September – I can't wait!

6 You will hear two friends talking about playing tennis.

M: I enjoyed that game – but I'm really tired now.

F: You should come to the gym more often – that would help.

M: I don't think that's my problem – though I'm not as fit as you are! I know I need to think more about what I eat – like not so much chocolate!

F: That's very unhealthy! I'm not surprised you get tired.

M: I think I just need to have more games. If you could just practise with me regularly that would be great.

F: I don't mind doing that.

UNIT 7

▶ 21

I = Interviewer   N = Nadia Winters

I: Today we're talking to Nadia Winters, who is the youngest weather presenter on television. Nadia, what subjects did you enjoy at school?

N: Well, I was always fascinated by the weather and I loved geography as well, but science subjects, like biology, weren't my favourites. I had to do science, though, because I wanted to have a job connected with the weather. On the other hand, I was also keen on drama though I didn't do much of it.

I: Did you always hope to work in television?

N: According to my parents, I used to watch the news on television in the evenings with them. I'd turn the sound off, turn the subtitles on and read the weather forecast from them. So I not only wanted to appear on television, I actually wanted to be a weather presenter. I was never worried about performing in front of other people.

I: Was it easy to get your first job on television?

N: Although I studied media at college, I knew it wouldn't be easy to get a job. I started out working very long hours behind the cameras but I was lucky when one weather presenter went to work for another television channel and I got the chance to take over. It was a challenge but I knew it was the right thing for me and I did my best. Luckily, I was good at it!

I: What's the best thing about your job?

N: There are lots of things I love: I get to travel a lot, which is great, and I meet so many people – I guess that's the biggest thrill for me. Of course, it's fun to be famous but that can be difficult too – I can't go shopping without people speaking to me.

I: Do you need special skills to be a television weather presenter?

N: The bit of drama I did at school definitely influenced me at first. Everyone starts trying to act while they're presenting. But then I realised I couldn't think about acting at the same time as I was giving detailed information. The key is confidence, which comes from just being yourself. People watch me to find out what the weather's going to be like. I don't get too technical because people generally just want to know what clothes to wear that day!

I: Is it easy to give correct details in your forecasts?

N: The further forward we go, the less accurate it's possible to be. Everyone says, 'summers used to be so much better,' but last year wasn't actually bad and the rain we had in June was much needed because April and most of March were completely dry. Personally, I love windy weather – it's so dramatic!

I: Nadia, thank you!

22

M = Martin   A = Ana

M: I think surfing is the best.
A: Well, I think all these things would be good for a day out at the beach – they could all be fun.
M: I don't think sitting on the beach doing nothing is much fun. They want to do some exciting activities together. Do you agree?
A: You may be right, but they don't want to spend a lot of money. Going to a café would be cheaper. It's friendly too.
M: That's okay, but it's a bit boring. We should choose surfing – that's really thrilling, and they could have a really good time. Do you think the same as me?
A: Maybe some of them won't like it. And it could be expensive to rent a board. We need to think about other things before we decide. I think walking is best, and they could find new places to visit. I like that idea.
M: They could go walking, I suppose, but surfing is still my favourite. We must choose that.
A: It's too expensive. I think fishing's a good idea.

23

1   I think that a beach holiday is the best – I love the water and I like going out in a boat.
2   I think that people work very hard, and they need to spend more time relaxing. It's important to have a break from work.
3   I love visiting places I haven't been to before, and I always try to go to the famous places. I think it's important to do that.
4   I love buying ice creams when I'm at the beach – they always seem to taste better there! I don't usually spend much money on anything else.

UNIT 8

24

We're looking for people to appear on our reality TV show. It's completely new – no one will be put in a house and watched, do any strange tasks or live in the jungle. In fact, you'll interview celebrities to find out about their lives, although they won't know you're coming! That's the fun part!

We don't want anyone who is nervous or shy, instead we want outgoing people with good communication skills. The minimum age is 18 and the maximum 24, although we will consider others outside these limits if they are suitable. Ideally, people will be around 21.

We don't expect anyone to have any television experience as the point of the programme is ordinary people asking questions that celebrities will not expect. We give training on presenting techniques, like not staring into the cameras and how to speak and smile naturally. We also help with things like hairstyles and make-up, and we provide clothes for the presenter – we want to bring out their personality because that makes the programme lively and interesting.

One thing that's absolutely necessary is the ability to speak other languages because many celebrities come from other countries – Italian and French are useful, although Spanish is the top priority.

Send an email with your phone number and one photograph. Please don't send any videos. The address is on the programme's website, although you can't apply directly there. Don't send any more information at this stage. We will call you back and invite you for an audition. You must apply by 15 April as we will be interviewing from 23 to 24 April, and will choose successful applicants by 25 April. Training starts on 30 April and filming begins on 1 June. It's a very exciting project and we hope lots of people will apply!

UNIT 9

26

I = Interviewer   B = Brian Wentworth

I: Brian, why did you become a computer games designer?
B: I grew up playing games, though my family weren't keen – I played with friends. I studied computer graphics and animation at college. That course taught me so much about how to make things look realistic, which fascinated me and confirmed what I wanted to do. But I couldn't start working in game design immediately. I had to work in an office for a while first.
I: What's most difficult about your job?
B: It can be hard to get a new idea, especially on your own. Some people think it's easier to work in a team, sharing ideas, but that has its own problems: trying to explain your thoughts to other people, for example. For me though, it's keeping going when things go wrong – sometimes I feel like giving up.
I: What do you enjoy most about designing games?
B: Creating something new that people want to play is satisfying. I love the process, from coming up with an idea to seeing it happen. And if the game also looks good, that's great. The best thing though is when I watch people enjoying games I've worked on – that makes me feel good.
I: You worked on Village Games, didn't you? What did you think about that?
B: That was the most complicated game so far. I wanted players to create their own story while they were playing. Those kinds of games are very popular but they're difficult to design. With Village Games it was hard to make it challenging but not impossible. I didn't want players to feel so frustrated that they stop playing, but they have to feel they have achieved something.
I: Do you think children should be encouraged to play computer games?

B: I believe they're really useful because they encourage children to think creatively. In future that might help to find answers to world problems like global warming and over-eating. Some parents think they're a waste of time though! I have to say that not all children like them – there are plenty who prefer sport because it's more physical.

I: What makes a good games designer?

B: It's not so vital to be a player although most designers are. It's good to have an idea of people's personalities so that you can create realistic characters in your games. In my opinion though, the best developers are patient and understand how long it really takes to produce a great game.

I: Thank you for talking to us, Brian.

▶ 27

1 I have to work well with my colleagues – what we do is dangerous, and so we depend on each other. Trusting the team is the most important thing and it's that aspect of the job that I like best. We also have to pay great attention to detail, as if things go wrong – like the water not coming through or the hose not working properly – then we can't do our job.

2 I love doing the research and coming up with new ideas that can change things for the future – especially in medicine. I work in a laboratory most of the time and although there's a team of us working on the same project, I do tend to do experiments on my own. That means I don't need leadership skills but I do need to be good at problem solving, which I really like.

3 I have to manage so many different things in a day – it's not easy dealing with a lot of children all at the same time! It's vital to have good communication skills because if they understand why you want to do something, they are more likely to enjoy it. I get such a feeling of satisfaction when the class understands what they are learning!

UNIT 10

▶ 28

1 Could I have a large loaf, please?
2 A bunch of roses, please.
3 I need a new tennis racket please, but not a very expensive one.
4 There's a long queue at the checkout – I think we should come back another day.
5 I need a bigger hard drive for my laptop.
6 I'm looking for a sofa to fit my new living room.
7 Half a kilo of sausages, please.
8 I'd like my ring re-sized, please – it's too small.

▶ 32

Okay, now here's some information about the special sale taking place in the town next Saturday evening. Unfortunately, there's been a change of venue: it was originally planned to be in the Cross Keys Hotel but it's been moved to the Golden Hotel in the town centre as this is a more convenient location for everyone. There is parking at the hotel for £5 and a few spaces in the multi-storey car park in the town centre for £8, although anyone who doesn't mind a short walk can save money and park for £2 near the leisure centre.

There are lots of exciting and interesting things for sale, all at amazing discounts. Some examples of items for sale include televisions, stereos and, best of all, laptops at 50 percent off! They will be sold very quickly so don't miss out! Everything will be available for viewing on Friday evening from seven to eight, but make sure you get here early on Saturday as it's a case of first come, first served! The doors open at nine and the sale finishes at four.

There are extra discounts for people over 65 so remember to bring your identity cards with you – and everyone must bring their credit card for purchases!

We will all benefit from this sale as ten percent of all profits will be given to the local wildlife sanctuary. So come along and support the sale. You can help the town and get a bargain for yourself! If you want to know more, then look on our website, or the website of the hotel – but there's much more detailed information in the local newspaper this week. I'll be there and hope to see you all! Now on to other news …

▶ 33

L = Lena   J = Jakub

L: So let's think about this carefully. If I wanted to advertise my shop, I definitely wouldn't spend a lot of money on the gift I gave my customers. That would mean I was losing money!

J: That's true – so we need to choose something cheap. Giving tickets is not a good idea – they're expensive. The last time I went to a football match, it cost a fortune!

L: Yes, I agree, and also they don't really advertise the shop, do they?

J: That's a good point – I hadn't thought of that. What about the bag? It has the shop's logo on it, and so other people will see it if you carry it around the town. I suppose that would be good for the shop.

L: Yes, but not everyone wants to carry a bag like that – it's quite big, so if you fill it up it would be heavy. Personally, I like the idea of a scarf.

J: I'm not sure that's the best choice, although I guess customers might like it – it looks quite trendy. It doesn't have the shop's logo on it, though, so it's not going to advertise the shop, is it?

L: You're absolutely right! I hadn't noticed that. Okay then, what about the tennis balls – everyone needs those, and they're not expensive for the shop to give away.

J: I agree with you, but they won't advertise it either. The same goes for the book – actually, I don't know why a book would be a good idea. Not everyone enjoys reading about tennis, and it certainly isn't good advertising for the shop because no-one else would see it.

L: Okay, then I think that the baseball cap is the best gift – it definitely has the logo on it and everyone loves wearing them.

J: I'm not sure that's true – my sister hates them! But they would be a good thing for advertising, and lots of people do wear them when they do sport.

L: Then let's go for that.

▶ 34

E = Examiner   J = Jakub   L = Lena

1

E: Would you like to have a free gift from a shop?

J: Yes, it would be great! I love getting something for nothing.

E: Do you agree, Lena?

L: Actually I think it's better to pay for something you really want instead of just being given something you might not use.

2

E: Do you think giving a free gift is a good way to advertise a shop?

L: I don't think it's a very good idea really. I think it would be better to have big advertisements in the town centre so that lots of people see them.

E: How about you, Jakub?

J: I agree with Lena. I don't think that people will notice the logo on any free gift, and also the gift might just get thrown away.

3

E: Do you often buy things you see advertisements for?

L: Absolutely not! I only buy things I choose for myself, not things I see in advertisements.

E: What do you think, Jakub?

J: I agree – I don't like advertisements at all, especially on television so I try not to watch them.

4

E: Do you like to buy the same things as your friends?

J: I like to go shopping with my friends, and we do buy the same things quite often.

E: How about you, Lena?

L: No, it's not the same for me – even if I go shopping with my friends, we often buy different things.

5

E: Do you think it's better to watch sport in a stadium or on television?

L: That's easy – it's much better to watch it on television because its more comfortable and it's not so noisy.

E: What do you think, Jakub?

J: I don't agree – it's much more fun to be with lots of people watching a live game! You don't get any excitement on television.

UNIT 11

▶ 35

E = Examiner   M = Maria   J = Juan

E: Maria, what did you do last weekend?

M: I went to the cinema with some friends from the course I'm doing. It was a very good film and we all enjoyed it.

E: Juan, do you think you will use English in your future work?

J: No, not really.

E: Maria, how do you usually get to college?

M: Well, I try different things because the traffic is often very bad. Sometimes I cycle, sometimes I walk but usually I get the bus.

E: Juan, what are you going to do tomorrow?

J: I'm going to go to college.

▶ 37

1 Which activity does the woman decide to do?

M: So what are you going to do today?

F: There's so much to choose from! I loved the tennis lesson last week but my arm is a bit sore today. The aerobics class is always very good. When I do that I always feel fantastic afterwards, so that's a really good option. Though it's so hot today I'm not sure whether I'd really enjoy it. I'm going on holiday next month so it would be a good idea to improve my scuba diving skills before then – so I guess I'll do that.

M: I think I'll join you!

2 Which photograph are they talking about?

F: That's a great photo! When was it taken?

M: Last year, on holiday, when we visited this brilliant castle. It was meant to be a day out with the whole family, including Mum and Dad though Gran decided not to come as it was very hot.

F: I can't see your sister.

M: That's because she was taking the photo! And Dad had just gone round the corner to buy tickets for us all to get in to the castle – he's in photos we took later, though.

3 When will the new leisure centre open officially?

F: Tell us about the new leisure centre – is it open yet?

M: We're all thrilled that it's finally finished! Building work started a year ago and although it seems a long time, the facilities we're providing are excellent, including a state-of-the-art pool. We're holding a special preview day for families to come and see all the activities on offer for free on 15 July, although the official opening day is not until 20 July. People can register for membership of the centre from 16 July. There will be special discounts for anyone who signs on for a two-year membership, and for people over 65.

4 How will the family travel to their holiday destination this year?

M: Are you looking forward to the holiday?

F: I really am! We try to do something different every year, not like some people who always go back to the same place and do the same things. Two years ago we went camping and cycled to the camp site. It took us two days to get there but it was really great. This time we'd planned to go to the beach by bus because it's better for the environment, but Gran is coming with us so it'll have to be the car after all.

M: Oh well, next year you can do something different!

5 What does the man decide to eat for lunch?

F: So what would you like?

M: I quite like the look of the steak, though I did have it yesterday. What kind of pasta is it?

F: Pasta with tomatoes and salad – and cheese, of course.

M: Hmm … I'm not so keen on tomatoes, though I do like salad. And it's good for me! I'd really like the burger, though I don't want the chips. I'm trying to lose weight. Maybe I'd better stick to my first choice.

F: How would you like it cooked?

6 What did the woman like best about being on holiday?

M: So what was the best thing about your holiday?

F: Everything was fantastic! I bought loads of things. There were so many souvenirs that were handmade and great for presents. I got a beautiful vase for my gran. It was a lovely resort too, though I didn't spend much time taking photographs – it was actually too hot! When I'm at home, I don't get much time just to walk in the countryside, so that was what really made the holiday for me. I can't wait to go back!

7 When will the plane take off?

We apologise for the delay in the departure of flight 502 to New York, scheduled for 16.40. This is due to the late arrival of the incoming flight, which will now land at 17.00. Passengers should wait in the departure lounge until called to the boarding gate, which is estimated to be in two hours' time. This means that the new departure time will be 19.30. Once again, we apologise for any inconvenience.

UNIT 12
▶ 38

1 You will hear two friends talking about a website.

M: It's a great website – it's got so much useful stuff on it. I often go to it if I want to find out what's going on in the world.

F: I know lots of people say that, but I've never found it particularly helpful. It looks very strange to me. I guess you'll think I'm strange but I prefer newspapers!

M: But it's such a user-friendly site – plus it's much more up-to-date than newspapers can ever be. I don't know anyone who doesn't like it.

F: So I'm unusual, then.

M: Perhaps you should try it again.

2 You will hear a woman talking to a friend about sky diving.

M: So is your sky diving going well?

F: Oh yes, I love it! I do it as often as I can.

M: What's so good about it?

F: Well, we get to sky dive in so many unusual locations. I never imagined I'd see so much beautiful scenery. That's great, though I guess it's the people I do it with that's the best thing – I have to rely on them, and I've made so many good friends. And of course it's thrilling but you'd expect that – it goes without saying.

M: Hmm – I'm not sure I'd want to do it!

3 You will hear a man talking to a friend about the travelling he does.

F: How was your latest trip?

M: Oh, it was fantastic! Everyone I met was so helpful and keen to talk to me – though I did know that the country had a reputation for being friendly. The scenery was lovely too.

F: How did you get around?

M: Buses and trains, mostly. I upgraded my seat on buses so that long journeys were more comfortable. That meant I paid more than I needed, though it was worth it. I'd thought I might have difficulty getting to some remote areas but there were so many options for getting around there that I never had any problems.

F: Sounds great!

4 You will hear two friends talking about a television documentary they both saw.

M: There was a good documentary on last night called 'Special Talents'. Did you see it?

F: Yes, I did, although it was on rather late! It could have been really interesting. The presenter explained how some people have a natural talent for something, but then didn't explain why sometimes they choose not to develop it. I wanted to know more but he didn't give any reasons. I think that should have been the main part of the documentary. After all, we wouldn't have beautiful music if composers like Mozart had chosen to ignore their talent.

M: I guess you're right.

5 You will hear two friends talking about a cycling race they took part in.

F: That was tough – just a pity I didn't win!

M: I know what you mean! But I had a really good time, even though I was rather nervous at the start.

F: I'd been afraid I wouldn't know where to go, but actually the whole thing ran beautifully – the route was clearly marked.

M: I guess they'd worked really hard to get everything right, especially as the race was such a huge distance for non-professional riders – I'd never done such a difficult race before.

F: I actually finished more quickly than I'd expected! I'll train more for the next one, though.

M: Me too.

6 You will hear two friends talking about an adventure holiday they have heard about.

M: I'm keen to go on that adventure holiday, though I'm not sure whether I'll be able to keep up with all the activities. I don't enjoy exercise and I don't train hard like you.

F: That shouldn't be a problem – you can probably choose what activities you take part in so you can do the easy ones.

M: I need to know the details – you've got your phone so how about going online right now and doing some research? It'd be great to know about the cost, in case our mates want to come with us. I think they'd enjoy it.

▶ 39

1 I was racing along the track when I slipped and fell. I twisted my ankle, which was very painful.

2 I was sitting on my board waiting for a big wave but when it came, it was so big that I fell off!

3 I was playing a doubles match with three friends but it started raining and we had to stop because the grass got wet and slippery on the court.

4 I first started walking short distances but I loved it and bought all the right equipment. Now I go for very long treks with friends and it's great exercise.

▶ 40

M: So the man is going hiking with some friends and we must choose what he should take with him.

F: Yes, but his bag can't be heavy. So let's start. What do you think about the camera? It would be nice for him to be able to take photos, but it could be heavy and too big for the bag.

M: I agree, and if he has his mobile phone in his pocket he won't need a camera anyway.

F: Yes, the phone is definitely something he should take because he might need to contact someone if they need any kind of help. The book will be heavy too, don't you think?

M: You're right – that's a good point. And if he's with his friends he won't have time to read anyway – it's only a day trip.

F: We don't know what the weather will be like but if it's sunny then he'll need the sun cream.

M: Possibly, but if he's taking the baseball cap he won't need it.

F: I disagree – the hat won't cover his arms and legs, and he should protect himself from the sun. He can wear the cap so he can take that anyway! It doesn't need to go in his bag.

M: Okay – so we've already said he must take the phone and a cap, and you think he needs sun cream – but in my opinion it's essential to have something to eat if they're out for the day.

F: I agree, but they should each take different food – there are four people who will be hiking together – so the biscuits would be good for him to take. They'll need energy! The bottle of water is heavy, though it's obviously important to take a drink so I guess he mustn't leave that behind.

M: I understand what you're saying, and I think you're right. What do you think about the headphones? He might want to listen to music while he's walking.

F: But on the other hand he's with his friends, so he'll be talking to them, not listening to music. They're quite big, too, so it's probably not a good idea to take them.

M: Fine. So what do we think will be most useful – the phone, the food and drink and what else?

F: I don't think the book will be useful, or the camera. So let's say just the phone and the food and drink – oh, and the sun cream.

M: Okay – I agree with you.

AUDIO SCRIPTS

PRACTICE TEST
Listening

▶ 41

1 What time does the film start?

F: What time do you think we should meet before the film?

M: Well, my bus won't get to the town centre before late afternoon, though we don't have to pick the tickets up from the box office until 7.30. The programme doesn't actually begin until 8.15. Let's meet at 6, then we can have a quick meal and get to the cinema in good time.

F: Fine with me.

2 What is the man waiting for?

M: I wish the postman would come soon.

F: Why? You got that parcel yesterday in the post.

M: I know. That was the new books I ordered online. There should have been a postcard as well from my friend. She's away on holiday but the post is very slow from Australia! Perhaps it will come tomorrow. I'm expecting a letter from my sister today. She's sending me a cheque for my birthday next week. I'm looking forward to spending it!

3 What is the date of the anniversary dinner?

It's my parent's wedding anniversary this weekend. Can you believe that they've been married for 30 years? We cooked a meal at home for their 29th anniversary last year but we're all going out for a big dinner at a restaurant on Saturday. That's the 21st, although the anniversary itself is on Monday the 23rd. Not everyone can come then though because of work.

4 What is the man going to do on holiday?

F: What are you going to do for your holiday this year? I thought you were going to the beach.

M: I did that last year but I found lying around doing nothing very boring, so I'm going walking in the Italian lakes this year. I think other things like cycling are just too much exercise for me when I'm on holiday!

F: I know what you mean – though I like winter holidays myself.

5 What is the woman having problems with at the moment?

M: What's the matter? You look angry!

F: Oh, lots of things. Everything seems to be going wrong and it's very expensive to get them fixed! First it was the fridge. It wasn't keeping things cold enough but it's all right now, luckily. Then the television stopped working last night and I'm waiting for the engineer to come. I expect the computer will be the next thing to have a problem, although it hasn't happened yet!

6 What does the woman decide to buy?

M: So what are you going to spend your birthday money on?

F: Well, I'm not sure. My sister has suggested loads of things but I can't decide. I thought about a DVD but they're cheaper to borrow or download so it's a bit of a waste really. I think I'll just get a new T-shirt – that's always useful!

M: You read a lot of books, don't you? What about a new novel – I read about one that's only just been published that's got great reviews.

F: No, they're so expensive in hardback and I'm reading a great one now anyway.

7 What does the woman want to do?

F: I'm quite tired. Let's not go to the cinema tonight.

M: I was looking forward to the film but, okay, we can go tomorrow.

F: You know what? I'd like to go home and watch a DVD. That would be relaxing.

M: What about going out to a restaurant?

F: I'm not hungry and I certainly don't want to do anything too tiring.

▶ 42

8 You will hear two friends talking about a concert they went to.

F: What did you think of the concert?

M: It was so crowded, and when everyone stood up I couldn't see anything. That was so annoying.

F: It's always like that – the crowd can make it exciting, though there were more than usual there last night which wasn't so good. The music was brilliant, though – the band played really well.

M: They were so noisy – I would have preferred it to be a bit quieter.

F: But it was good value – they played for more than two hours.

M: I know, but it was still a lot to pay for one concert.

9 You will hear a man telling a friend about a table tennis competition.

F: I heard you did well in the table tennis competition!

M: Yes, I came second which was a bit of a surprise for me!

F: How long was the competition?

M: Two days. It took place over the weekend, in a really nice place – it was a leisure centre up in the mountains. The food was delicious, though the other competitors weren't actually that keen to talk to anyone else so I didn't make any new friends, which was a shame. The competition itself was planned very well, so that was a positive.

F: Will you take part again?

M: I'm not sure.

141

10 You will hear two friends talking about a television programme.

M: I loved that programme on deep sea fishing last night – some of the scenes of fishing in the storm were so dramatic!

F: I usually enjoy programmes about nature, and this had some fascinating information – like I didn't know how dangerous it could be – but some of the stuff about the boats was really technical. I couldn't follow everything the fishermen said.

M: But the pictures were beautiful – they must have been hard to film.

F: That's true – I could have watched them for hours! I'll watch the next programme in the series and see what I think.

11 You will hear a woman telling a friend about her new car.

M: That's a lovely car!

F: Thanks – I'm lucky to have it. It's very easy to drive. I guess that's because it's very well thought-out and it's comfortable for long journeys. I'm happy with that.

M: Was it expensive?

F: Well, I hoped to get a good deal, because I couldn't afford much, but in the end it cost more than I wanted to pay.

M: I like the colour.

F: I didn't choose that, and I'm not keen on it, but it was the only car in the showroom I could have without waiting several weeks for a different one.

12 You will hear two friends talking about a football game they watched together.

M: That was a great game!

F: Yes, it was, even though the pitch was rather poor – there was a lot of mud in the middle.

M: I didn't think it was that bad – it didn't seem to give the players any problems. They really were fantastic and it was good to watch.

F: They were much better than last week – in fact, I haven't seen such a good performance from them for ages. The referee did well, too, I thought.

M: He made a few mistakes that could have changed the result.

F: Well, at least everyone went home happy in the end!

13 You will hear a man telling a friend about some training he does regularly.

M: I've started a new training programme – I want to get fit.

F: How's it going?

M: Fine. I can understand the things I have to do, like stretching, but they're quite tiring and hard to get right. It's difficult to keep going sometimes.

F: Is that a problem?

M: Not really – there are plenty of coaches around and they encourage me – they're really kind. Just before I started there was a special offer for new people joining the classes, but I missed it so it costs a lot.

F: Will you keep going?

M: I hope so, though I may get bored eventually.

▶ 43

Hello, everyone! I'm Jonas Watson and I work for Great Sailing Holidays. It's my job to make sure that you have a wonderful time. My office is next to the reception desk, which is at the front of the hotel, and I'm there Monday to Friday morning from 9 to 10, and every evening from 6 to 8 apart from Wednesday.

In your rooms, you'll find information about the hotel. Breakfast starts at 7 every morning and finishes at 10 but it gets busy around 8 to 8.30, so it's better to eat before or after that time. As you'll be out sailing all day, you can pick up sandwiches for lunch at 9 every morning from the kitchen. Dinner starts at 7.30 and is self-service, so you can eat when you like.

Now to the most important part of your holiday: the sailing. Tomorrow we'll all meet at the beach at 10.15 for your first lesson. I know some of you have sailed before but it's a good idea to go over some basic information again before you go out on your own. You'll also find a leaflet in your rooms about safety. You must read that before you do anything else. We want you to enjoy yourselves but we don't want to have any problems! So before you get in a boat, make sure that you have a lifejacket. You can collect one from my office this evening.

Some general rules: find out about the weather before you go out in the boat. Also tell someone where you're going and what time you expect to be back. Don't forget to take sun cream, a hat and a bottle of water with you – it can get hot out on the water. Okay. Does anyone have any questions?

AUDIO SCRIPTS

▶ 44

I = Interviewer   A = Angela Morris

I: I'm talking to Angela Morris, a successful young musician. So, Angela, how did you get interested in music?

A: Even though they weren't musical, my parents wanted me and my brothers to try it so we all had piano lessons at school, which I hated. My brothers loved sport and I enjoyed drama but we were encouraged to continue playing together as we got older. I found out I could sing pretty well, which was the start of everything.

I: Why did you decide to turn your hobby into a career?

A: I was discouraged at first – after all, loads of musicians work for years without becoming famous or making any money out of it. People told me to keep it as a hobby and it was hard not to listen to them. But I guess it was when I realised that it was the only thing that made me happy.

I: Why did you decide to write and sing country music?

A: For me it was writing about what happens in people's lives. When you write a country song you start with that idea and the music follows, although it can be hard to find the best tune. People don't realise that the word 'country' can cover everything from traditional music to pop or even rock.

I: What was the best advice you had when you were starting out?

A: My parents told me to carry on studying in case I didn't make it in the music industry. My singing teacher told me to try to find other people I could write songs with – like on social media – which was quite useful, but the thing I've always remembered is to play and sing whenever I could so I was always improving.

I: So how did your career actually start?

A: Some people advertise whenever they're playing, in case someone important is there. But I decided to go in for loads of talent shows, and that worked. Of course, putting videos on the internet is a popular way for young people to become well-known, though I never tried that.

I: What would you say to any young musicians listening now?

A: You'll always hope you can make money doing what you love, but it's not easy. You must find out if you are good enough. Don't rely on what friends and family say. I contacted music critics and asked for their opinion, because I wanted to hear the truth. And don't be afraid to make new contacts wherever possible.

Speaking

▶ 45

What's your name?

Where do you live?

Do you work or are you a student?

What do you do? What do you study?

Do you watch television very often?

What did you do on your last birthday?

Do you enjoy playing or watching sport?

Where will you go on your summer holiday this year?

▶ 46

Now, I'd like each of you to talk on your own about something. I'm going to give each of you a photograph and I'd like you to talk about it.

Student A, here is your photograph. It shows a family having breakfast.

Student B, you just listen.

Student A, please tell us what you can see in the photograph.

Thank you. Student B, here is your photograph. It shows people cycling in a city.

Student A, you just listen.

Student B, please tell us what you can see in the photograph.

▶ 47

Now, in this part of the test you're going to talk about something together for about two minutes. I'm going to describe a situation to you.

A young man is going to visit some friends in another country. He hasn't seen his friends for a long time. He is thinking about the activities they could do together on the first day.

The pictures show some activities they could do together.

Talk together about the activities they could do together on the first day and decide which would be best.

All right? Now, talk together.

▶ 48

What would you do first if you were visiting a friend you hadn't seen for a long time?

Do you prefer to plan what to do when you visit a friend or decide what to do when you arrive?

Do you think it's better to relax and just talk to a friend or do lots of different activities with them?

Do you usually prefer to do things with a lot of friends or just one friend?

Is there a country you'd really like to visit in the future?

Thank you. That is the end of the test.

Pearson Education Limited
KAO TWO, KAO Park, Hockham Way,
Harlow, Essex, CM17 9SR, England
and Associated Companies throughout the world

www.pearsonELT.com/gold

© Pearson Education Limited 2019

The right of Sally Burgess and Jacky Newbrook to be identified as authors of this Work has been asserted by them in accordance with the Copyright, Designs and Patents Act, 1988.

All rights reserved. No part of this publication may be reproduced, stored in a retrieval system, or transmitted in any form or by any means, electronic, mechanical, photocopying, recording or otherwise without the prior written permission of the copyright holders.

New Edition first published 2019
Second impression 2019

ISBN: 978-1-292-20235-8 (Gold Preliminary New Edition Exam Maximiser)

ISBN: 978-1-292-20236-5 (Gold Preliminary New Edition Exam Maximiser with Key)

Set in Frutiger Neue LT Pro Thin
Printed in Slovakia by Neografia

Acknowledgements
We are grateful to the following for permission to reproduce copyright material:

Photos
The publisher would like to thank the following for their kind permission to reproduce their photographs:

123RF.com: Aleksandr Davydov 33, Alexander Ermolaev 32, Jacques Durocher 100, Shannon Fagan 33, Sylvain Robin 100, 100, Wavebreak Media Ltd 55, Ysbrand Cosijn 26, atic12 33, dglimages 55, moodboard 100, racorn 55; **Alamy Stock Photo**: Alan Burles 51, Andriy Popov 51, Asia Images Group Pte Ltd 34, Chris Harris 69, Design Pics Inc. 43, Ewing Galloway / ClassicStock 26, Hero Images Inc. 113, 13, Ian Shaw 69, Kumar Sriskandan 20, 20, Realimage 113, Tetra Images 34, TongRo Images 13, imageBROKER 17; **Getty Images:** Toby Burrows 18, Victor Virgile / Gamma-Rapho 26; **Pearson Education Ltd**: Jon Barlow 33; **Shutterstock.com**: AJR_photo 100, Monkey Business Images 16, Motortion Films 67, Rido 33, Terence Mendoza 55, absolut 55.

All other images © Pearson Education

Every effort has been made to trace the copyright holders and we apologise in advance for any unintentional omissions. We would be pleased to insert the appropriate acknowledgement in any subsequent edition of this publication.

Illustrated by Oxford Designers and Illustrators